THE NEW TESTAMENT: AN INTRODUCTION
Volume 4
Matthew and The Canon

THE NEW TESTAMENT: AN INTRODUCTION

Volume 4
Matthew and The Canon

Paul Nadim Tarazi

OCABS PRESS
ST PAUL, MINNESOTA 55112
2009

THE NEW TESTAMENT: AN INTRODUCTION

Copyright © 2009 by
Paul Nadim Tarazi

Vol. 1: Paul & Mark
Vol. 2: Luke & Acts
Vol. 3: John & Revelation
Vol 4: Matthew & The Canon

ISBN 1-60191-007-X

To Bassam

Abbreviations

Books of the Old Testament*

Gen	Genesis	Job	Job	Hab	Habakkuk
Ex	Exodus	Ps	Psalms	Zeph	Zephaniah
Lev	Leviticus	Prov	Proverbs	Hag	Haggai
Num	Numbers	Eccl	Ecclesiastes	Zech	Zechariah
Deut	Deuteronomy	Song	Song of Solomon	Mal	Malachi
Josh	Joshua	Is	Isaiah	Tob	Tobit
Judg	Judges	Jer	Jeremiah	Jdt	Judith
Ruth	Ruth	Lam	Lamentations	Wis	Wisdom
1 Sam	1 Samuel	Ezek	Ezekiel	Sir Sirach	(Ecclesiasticus)
2 Sam	2 Samuel	Dan	Daniel	Bar	Baruch
1 Kg	1 Kings	Hos	Hosea	1 Esd	1 Esdras
2 Kg	2 Kings	Joel	Joel	2 Esd	2 Esdras
1 Chr	1 Chronicles	Am	Amos	1 Macc	1 Maccabees
2 Chr	2 Chronicles	Ob	Obadiah	2 Macc	2 Maccabees
Ezra	Ezra	Jon	Jonah	3 Macc	3 Maccabees
Neh	Nehemiah	Mic	Micah	4 Macc	4 Maccabees
Esth	Esther	Nah	Nahum		

Books of the New Testament

Mt	Matthew	Eph	Ephesians	Heb	Hebrews
Mk	Mark	Phil	Philippians	Jas	James
Lk	Luke	Col	Colossians	1 Pet	1 Peter
Jn	John	1 Thess	1 Thessalonians	2 Pet	2 Peter
Acts	Acts	2 Thess	2 Thessalonians	1 Jn	1 John
Rom	Romans	1 Tim	1 Timothy	2 Jn	2 John
1 Cor	1 Corinthians	2 Tim	2 Timothy	3 Jn	3 John
2 Cor	2 Corinthians	Titus	Titus	Jude	Jude
Gal	Galatians	Philem	Philemon	Rev	Revelation

Books by the Author

1 Thess	*I Thessalonians: A Commentary*, St. Vladimir's Seminary Press, Crestwood 1982
Gal	*Galatians: A Commentary*, St. Vladimir's Seminary Press, Crestwood 1994
NTI1-3	*The New Testament: an Introduction*, vols. 1-3, St. Vladimir's Seminary Press, 1999-2004
OTI1-3	*The New Testament: an Introduction*, vols. 1-3, St. Vladimir's Seminary Press, 1991-96

*Following the larger canon known as the Septuagint.

Contents

Introduction   13

Part I - The New Testament Canon

1 The Origins   25
The "Problem" Posed by Galatians · The Gospels · Mark as the Pauline evangelion · Jesus the Teacher · Jesus, the Son of Man · What is a Gospel Book?

2 Toward A Scriptural Canon   41
The Scriptural Paradigm · The Scriptural Story · The Law and the Prophets · The Apostle · The Producers of the New Testament Literature · Mark · Luke · Ephesus, the Pauline Headquarters · The Form of Scripture · Authorship in the Ancient World · The Lukan Production · Romans and the Case for the Lukan Production · Hebrews · The Pastoral Epistles

3 The Formation of the New Testament Canon   85
Was the Old Testament Canon Planned or Haphazard? · How About the New Testament? · Galatians, Mark, Colossians, and 2 Thessalonians · The New Torah · Luke-Acts and the Apocalypse · John · Matthew and the Integration of the non-Pauline Leadership into the Canon

Part II - The Gospel of Matthew

4 Birth and Infancy of the Messiah   109
The Genealogy of Jesus Christ (1:1-17) · The Birth of Jesus Christ (1:18-25) · The Visit of the Magi (2:1-12) · The Flight to Egypt (2:13-15) · The Slaying of the Infants and the Return from Egypt (2:16-23)

5 The Beginnings of the Message of the Messiah   121
The Preaching of John the Baptist (3:1-12) · The Baptism of Jesus (3:13-17) · The Temptation of Jesus (4:1-11) · The Beginning of Jesus' Ministry (4:12-17) · The Calling of the Four Fishermen (4:18-22) · Great Multitude (4:23-25)

6 The First Book of the Law of the Messiah   129
The Beatitudes (5:1-12) · Salt and Light (5:13-16) · The Fulfillment of the Law (5:17-20) · The Antitheses (5:21-48) · Anger (5:21-26) · Adultery and Divorce (5:27-32) · Oaths (5:33-37) · Retaliation (5:38-42) · Love for Enemies (5:43-48) · Pauline Terminology · The Righteousness of the Kingdom (6:1-18) · Treasure in Heaven and

Earthly Cares (6:19-34) · God is the Sole Judge of All (7:1-12) · The Narrow Gate (7:13-14) · The Eschatological Judgment (7:15-23) · The Two Foundations (7:24-29)

7 The Second Book of the Law of the Messiah   151

The First Set of Miracles (8:1-17) · On Following Jesus (8:18-22) · The Second Set of Miracles (8:23-9:8) · Calling of Matthew (9:9-13) · The Question of Fasting (9:14-17) · The Gospel Is Proclaimed to All · A Ruler's Daughter and the Woman with a Hemorrhage (9:18-26) · Healing of Two Blind Men (9:27-31) · Healing of the Dumb Demoniac (9:32-34) · The Harvest is Great (9:35-38) · Prolegomena to the Mission of the Twelve · Mission of the Twelve (10:1-42)

8 The Third Book of the Law of the Messiah   173

The Pauline Gospel (11:1) · Messengers of John the Baptist (11:2-6) · Jesus' Witness Concerning John the Baptist (11:7-19) · Woe to Unrepentent Cities (11:20-24) · God's Fatherhood and Christ's Yoke (11:25-30) · Plucking Grain on the Sabbath (12:1-8) · Healing the Withered Hand (12:9-14) · The Chosen Servant (12:15-21) · Jesus and Beelzebul (12:22-32) · A Tree and its Fruits (12:33-37) · The Demand for a Sign (12:38-42) · The Parable of the Sower and the Purpose of the Parables (13:1-23) · The Parable of the Weeds among the Wheat and its Explanation (13:24-30, 36-43) · Three Matthean Parables (13:44-50)

9 The Fourth Book of the Law of the Messiah   193

The Rejection of Jesus at Nazareth (13:53-58) · The Wandering in the Wilderness of the Nations · The Death of John the Baptist (14:1-12) · Walking on the Water (14:22-36) · The Tradition of the Elders (15:1-20) · The Canaanite Woman (15:21-28) · Healing of Many People (15:29-31) · Feeding of the Four Thousand (15:32-39) · The Teaching of the Pharisees and Sadducees (16:1-4) · Peter's Confession (16:13-20) · Jesus Foretells His Death and Resurrection (16:21-28) · The Transfiguration of Jesus (17:1-13) · Healing of the Demoniac Boy (17:14-21) · The Temple Tax (17:24-27) · Matthew 18 · The Greatest in the Kingdom (18:1-5) · Temptations to Sin (18:6-9) · Parable of the Lost Sheep (18:10-14) · A Brother Who Sins (18:15-20) · The Unforgiving Servant (18:21-35)

10 The Fifth Book of the Law of the Messiah   223

Teaching About Divorce (19:1-12) · Little Children Blessed (19:13-15) · The Rich Young Man (19:16-22) · The Workers in the Vineyard (20:1-16) · The Passion of the Son of Man (20:17-19) · The Request of James and John (20:20-28) · The Healing of the Two Blind Men (20:29-34) · Triumphal Entry into Jerusalem (21:1-9) · The Cleansing of the Temple (21:10-17) · Jerusalem's Refusal and Condemnation (21:18-32) · The Parable of the Vineyard and the Tenants (21:33-46) · The Parable of the Marriage Feast (22:1-14) · Paying Taxes to Caesar (22:15-22) · The Resurrection (22:23-33) · The Great Commandment (22:34-40) · The Messiah as David's Son (22:41-46) · Woe to the Scribes and Pharisees (23:1-36) · Lament over Jerusalem (23:37-39) · The Beginning of Woes

(24:1-14) · The Great Tribulation (24:15-22) · The Coming of the Son of Man (24:29-31) · The Unknown Day and Hour (24:36-44) · The Faithful and the Unfaithful Servant (24:45-51) · The Parable of the Ten Maidens (25:1-13) · The Parable of the Talents (25:14-30) · The Judgment of All the Nations (25:31-46)

11 The False Judgment of the Messiah and His Vindication by God 265

The Plot to Kill Jesus (26:1-5) · The Anointing at Bethany (26:6-13) · Judas Agrees to Betray Jesus (26:14-16) · Preparation for the Passover with the Disciples (26:17-19) · The Lord's Supper (26:20-35) · Gethsemane (26:36-46) · Betrayal and Arrest of Jesus (26:47-56) · Jesus Given over to Pilate (27:1-2) · The Death of Judas (27:3-10) · The Passion, Death, and Burial of Jesus (27:11-61) · The Guard at the Tomb (27:62-66) · The Resurrection of Jesus (Mt 28:1-10) · The Report of the Guard (28:11-15) · The Commissioning of the Disciples (28:16-20)

Index 289

Introduction

This is the last volume of my New Testament Introduction tetralogy. It follows the same line as the preceding ones in trying to show through the methodology of the cumulative argument that the entire literature of the New Testament is a well and tightly devised series of books conveying "in many and various ways" the same message. It is indeed by following the pattern of the Old Testament scripture in which the one God "spoke of old" his one message "in many and various ways to our fathers the prophets" (Heb 1:1), that the New Testament books, relaying the same message spoken "in these last days to us by his Son" (v.2), were both conceived and written *as scripture*.[1] That we are dealing in both scriptures with the same message is made clear by the Apostle in Romans: "Paul, a servant of Jesus Christ, called to be an apostle, set apart for the gospel of God which he promised beforehand through his prophets in the holy scriptures." (1:1-2). The "gospel" then is nothing else but the scriptural God's *torah* heralded to the nations, as is clearly stated in Isaiah concerning the mission of the Lord's servant:

> Behold my servant, whom I uphold, my chosen, in whom my soul delights; I have put my Spirit upon him, he will bring forth justice to the nations. He will not cry or lift up his voice, or make it heard in the street; a bruised reed he will not break, and a dimly burning wick he will not quench; he will faithfully bring forth justice. He will not fail or be discouraged till he has established justice in the earth; and the coastlands wait for his law. Thus says God, the Lord, who created the heavens and stretched them out, who spread forth the earth and what comes from it, who gives breath to

---

[1] See my *New Testament Introduction, Volume 1: Paul and Mark*, (Crestwood, NY: St Vladimir's Press, 1999), 35-36; hereinafter referred to as *NTI₁*.

the people upon it and spirit to those who walk in it: "I am the Lord, I have called you in righteousness, I have taken you by the hand and kept you; I have given you as a covenant to the people, a light to the nations, to open the eyes that are blind, to bring out the prisoners from the dungeon, from the prison those who sit in darkness. I am the Lord, that is my name; my glory I give to no other, nor my praise to graven images." (Is 42:1-8)

"It is too light a thing that you should be my servant to raise up the tribes of Jacob and to restore the preserved of Israel; I will give you as a light to the nations, that my salvation may reach to the end of the earth." Thus says the Lord, the Redeemer of Israel and his Holy One, to one deeply despised, abhorred by the nations, the servant of rulers: "Kings shall see and arise; princes, and they shall prostrate themselves; because of the Lord, who is faithful, the Holy One of Israel, who has chosen you." (Is 49:6-7)

Though the present work is entitled "Matthew and the Canon," I intentionally begin with discussing the "canon" and end with Matthew in order to reflect my conviction that the "canonization" of the New Testament literature was not the outcome of a series of later decisions starting in the second century, but rather a phenomenon inherent to the conception and writing of the books themselves. That is to say, the New Testament canon was imposed rather than chosen. The following generations were bound to either accept the books *as canon* or reject them. The "odyssey" of "book lists" starting with the 2nd century merely reflects the acceptance of, or rather submission to, this canon or, conversely, its rejection.[2] Matthew, in my conviction, is the last writing in this process, and was written intentionally as a "closing" book that seals as well as ends

---

[2] I am in the process of writing an extensive article further substantiating and defending such a position which is summarily presented in this book along the same lines I followed in the previous volumes of this tetralogy.

the New Testament canonical process. Consequently, the reason behind the writing of Matthew is discussed within the part dealing with the "rise" and "closure" of the New Testament "canon." Hence the lack of an extensive introduction to this present volume as was the case with the previous ones. By the same token, the lack of bibliography concerning the first part of this volume has to do with the fact that the classical discussions of "canon" deal with the "book lists" and not the canon as an intra-scriptural phenomenon.

I should like, however, to revisit two issues that are recurring in my reading of the Gospels: John the Baptist and Mary the Magdalene. All along I have taken the position that the Baptist is a stand-in for Saul the Jew before his calling to apostleship. Given the name of the Baptist, John, and the stress in his teaching on repentance, it would be better if one considered him as a stand-in for John Mark. The Gospel of Mark would then represent the appeal by the author to have his readers to follow his example of "repenting" from his initial stand (sticking with Barnabas against Paul: Acts 15:37-39) and rejoining Paul's mission: "Mark the cousin of Barnabas concerning whom you have received instructions—if he comes to you, receive him." (Col 4:10). As for Mary Magdalene, until now I considered her equivalent to Mary, the mother of Jesus, and thus representing the community of Timothy, Paul's faithful son. However, the Magdalene is referred to in Luke as one "from whom seven demons had gone out" (8:2), a comment endorsed in the Markan additional ending: "Now when he rose early on the first day of the week, he appeared first to Mary Magdalene, from whom he had cast out seven demons." (Mk 16:9) Yet, at the same time, "she went and told those who had been with him" (v.10), that is, "the disciples and Peter" (v.7). Consequently, since after having been cured she becomes a reference for Peter, the Magdalene would be better considered as part of the Markan (and thus Petrine) community who, upon repentance, joined the party of Timothy (and, thus, ultimately of Paul). The most suitable way to handle the surname Magdalene is to read it as pertaining to the *migdol* ([watch]tower) whence one keeps watch as to what the Lord is doing with his vineyard (Is 5:1-2). The Markan community, through its leader, kept such watch and at the end realized that the earthly Jerusalem (of James, Peter, and John Mark himself) was not the reference, but rather the heavenly Jerusalem whose emissary was Paul (Gal 4:25-28), and ultimately joined with the Pauline community headed by Timothy. My readers are to remember that my "corrected" readings of the Baptist and the Magdalene do not affect their "function" in the Gospels. They represent a Jewish leader (the like of Saul or John Mark) and his followers, respectively, who started by being reticent to accept the message of Jesus, which was fully inclusive of the Gentiles, and ultimately ended by submitting to it.[3]

I would be remiss if I did not thank Mr. Timothy Clark, my colleague at St Vladimir's Orthodox Theological Seminary. Despite his tight schedule due to work on his doctoral dissertation and his teaching load, he freely gave his time to edit this present volume. My readers should thank him for any and all clarity and fluidity in the present work. Needless to say, he is absolved of any shortcoming or incongruity in the argumentation. This responsibility is totally mine.

---

[3] Jesus healed Mary Magdalene of the seven evil spirits that possessed her (Lk 8:2).

Commentaries

Allison, D. C. *Matthew: A Shorter Commentary.* London /New York: T & T Clark, 2004. A compendium of his lager three-volume commentary he co-authored with W. D. Davies in the International Critical Commentary Series.

Bradley, M. C. *Matthew: Poet, Historian, Dialectician.* Studies in Biblical Literature. New York/Bern: Lang, 2007. The author is a Professor of Philosophy.

France, R. T. *The Gospel of Matthew.* New International Commentary on the New Testament. Grand Rapids/ Cambridge, UK: Eerdmans, 2007.

Garland, D. E. *Reading Matthew: A Literary and Theological Commentary on the First Gospel.* Reading the New Testament Series. New York: Crossroad Publishing, 1993.

Gibbs, J. A. *Matthew 1:1-11:1.* Concordia Commentary. St Louis, MO: Concordia, 2006. Opts for an early date, in the 50's, for the writing of this Gospel.

Gundry, R. H. *Matthew: A Commentary on his Handbook for a Mixed Church under Persecution.* Grand Rapids, MI: Eerdmans, 1994.

Harrington, D. J. *Gospel of Matthew.* Sacra Pagina. Collegeville, MN: Liturgical Press, 1991

Hauerwas, S. *Matthew.* Theological Commentary on the Bible. Grand Rapids: Brazos, 2006. The author takes the position that the Gospel was written with the intention of making a disciple out of its hearer.

Keener, C. S. *A Commentary on the Gospel of Matthew.* Grand Rapids/Cambridge, UK: Eerdmans, 1999. One of its interests is the social-historical-rhetorical contexts of the Matthean traditions.

Luz. U. *Matthew 1-7. A Commentary.* Hermeneia—A Critical
and Historical Commentary on the Bible. Minneapolis, MN:
Fortress, 2007. Detailed and thorough. Requires knowledge of
Greek.

Luz. U. *Matthew 8-20. A Commentary.* Hermeneia—A Critical
ad Historical Commentary on the Bible. Minneapolis, MN:
Fortress, 2005. Detailed and thorough. Requires knowledge of
Greek.

Luz. U. *Matthew 21-28. A Commentary.* Hermeneia—A Critical
ad Historical Commentary on the Bible. Minneapolis, MN:
Fortress, 2001. Detailed and thorough. Requires knowledge of
Greek.

Mounce, R. H. *Matthew.* New International Biblical
Commentary. Peabody, MA: Hendrickson, 1991.

Menninger, R. E. *Israel and the Church in the Gospel of Matthew.*
American University Studies, Series 7: Theology and Religion
162. New York/San Francisco/Bern: Lang, 1994. Concludes
that Matthews' premise is that the Church is the true Israel.

Nolland, John. *Gospel of Matthew: A Commentary on the Greek
Text.* New International Greek Testament Commentary.
Grand Rapids, MI: Eerdmans, 2005. A redaction critical
commentary.

Reid, B. E. *The Gospel According to Matthew.* New Collegeville
Bible Commentary. Collegeville, MN: Liturgical Press: 2005.

Senior, D. *Matthew.* Abingdon New Testament Commentaries.
Nashville, TN: Abingdon Press, 1998

Witherington, B. *Matthew.* Smyth and Helwys Bible
Commentary. Macon, GA: Smyth and Helwys, 2006.
Underscores Jesus as Sage in Matthew and thus reads that
Gospel as a Wisdom book.

Studies

Agourides, S. "Matthew as Theologian of the Church of his time (Tradition and Renewal)." *Deltion Biblikon Meleton* 22 (1993): 5-17.

Allison, Dale C. *New Moses: A Matthean Typology.* Minneapolis, MN: Augsburg Fortress, 1993.

Allison, Dale C. *Studies in Matthew: Interpretation Past and Present.* Grand Rapids, MI: Baker Academic, 2005. A collection of thirteen essays.

Aune, D. E., ed. *Gospel of Matthew in Current Study: Studies in Memory of William G. Thompson, S. J.* Grand Rapids, MI: Eerdmans, 2001.

Barnet, J. *Not the Righteous but Sinners: M. M. Bakhtin's Theory of Aesthetics and the Problem of Reader-Character Interaction in Matthew's Gospel.* Journal for the Study of the New Testament, Supplement Series 246. London/New York: T&T Clark International, 2003.

Carter, W. "Kernels and Narrative Blocks: The Structure of Matthew's Gospel." *Catholic Biblical Quarterly* 54 (1992): 463-481.

Carter, W. *Matthew: Storyteller, Interpreter, Evangelist.* Rev. ed. Peabody, MA: Hendrickson Publishers, 2004.

Carter, W. and J. P. Heil. *Matthew's Parables: Audience-Oriented Perspectives.* Catholic Biblical Quarterly. Monograph series. Washington, DC: Catholic Biblical Association of America, 1998.

Combrink, H. J. B. "The Structure of Matthew as Narrative." *Tyndale Bulletin* 34 (1983): 61-80.

Doyle, B. R. "Matthew's Intention as Discerned by His Structure." *Revue Biblique* 95 (1988): 34-54.

Engelbrecht, J. "The Language of the Gospel of Matthew." *Neotestamentica* 24 (1990): 199-213.

Gench, F. T. *Wisdom in the Christology of Matthew.* Lanham, MD/New York/Oxford: University Press of America, 1997.

Giesen, H. "Galiläa – mehr als eine Landschaft. Bibeltheologisher Stellenwert Galiläas im Matthäusevangelium." *Ephemerides Theologicae Lovanienses* 77 (2001): 23-45.

Hays, R. B. "The Gospel of Matthew: Reconfigured Torah." *HTS Theological Studies* 61 (2005): 165-190

Heil, J. P. "Ezekiel 34 and the Narrative Strategy of the Shepherd and Sheep Metaphor in Matthew." *Catholic Biblical Quarterly* 55 (1993): 698-708.

Hernant, D. *Matthieu: un écrivain? Les cinq discours du premier Evangile, un corpus organizé.* Lyon: PROFAC, 1999. Concludes that the framework of the discourses follows a chiastic pattern ABCB'A'.

Hertig, P. *Matthew's Narrative Use of Galilee in the Multicultural and Missiological Journey of Jesus.* Mellen Biblical Press Series 46. Lewiston, NY/Queenston, Ont/Lampeter, UK: Mellen Press, 1998.

Hill, D. "In Quest of Matthean Christology." *Irish Biblical Studies* 8 (1986): 135-142.

Hill, R. C. *St. John Chrysostom: Spiritual Gems from the Gospel of Matthew.* Brookline, MA: Holy Cross Orthodox Press, 2004.

Howell, D. B. *Matthew's Inclusive Story: A Study in the Narrative Rhetoric of the First Gospel.* Journal for the Study of the New Testament. Supplement Series. Sheffield: JSOT Press, 1990.

Kingsbury, J. D. "The Plot of Matthew's Story." *Interpretation* 46 (1992): 347-356.

Kingsbury, J. D. "The Rhetoric of Comprehension in the Gospel of Matthew." *New Testament Studies* 41 (1995): 358-377.

Knowles, M. *Jeremiah in Matthew's Gospel. The Rejected-Prophet Motif in Matthean Redaction.* Journal for the Study of the New Testament, Supplement Series 68. Sheffield, UK: JSOT Press, 1993.

Kupp, David D. *Matthew's Emmanuel: Divine Presence and God's People in the First Gospel.* Society for New Testament Studies. Cambridge/New York: Cambridge University Press, 1996.

Luz, U. *Theology of the Gospel of Matthew.* Cambridge/New York: Cambridge University Press, 1995.

Luz, U. *Studies in Matthew.* Grand Rapids, MI: Eerdmans, 2005.

Matera, F. J. "The Plot of Matthew's Gospel." *Catholic Biblical Quarterly* 42 (19876): 233-253.

Menken, M. J. J. "The References to Jeremiah in the Gospel according to Matthew (Mt 2,17; 16,14; 27,9)." *Ephemerides Theologicae Lovanienses* 60 (1984): 5-24.

Mohrlang, R. *Matthew and Paul: A Comparison of Ethical Perspectives.* Society for New Testament Studies. Monograph series. New York, NY: Cambridge University Press, 1984.

Müller, M. "The Gospel of Matthew and the Mosaic Law – A Chapter of a Biblical Theology." *Studia Theologica* 46 (1992): 109-120.

McKenna, M. *Matthew. The Book of Mercy.* Hyde Park NY: New City, 2007. Discusses the Gospel from the perspective of one its major tenets: divine mercy.

Neirynck, F. "AΠO TOTE HPΞATO and the Structure of Matthew." *Ephemerides Theologicae Lovanienses* 64 (1988): 21-59.

Pamment, M. "The Son of Man in the First Gospel." *New Testament Studies* 29 (1983): 116-129.

Powell, M. A. "The Plot and Subplots of Matthew's Gospel." *New Testament Studies* 38 (1992): 187-204.

Russell, E. A. "'Antisemitism' in the Gospel of Matthew." *Irish Biblical Studies* 8 (1986): 183-196.

Senior, D. "Between Two Worlds: Gentiles and Jewish Christians in Matthew's Gospel." *Catholic Biblical Quarterly* 61 (1999): 1-23.

Sim D. C. *The Gospel of Matthew and Christian Judaism. The History and Social Setting of The Matthean Community.* Studies n the New Testament and Its World. Edinburgh: T&T Clark, 1998. Locates the Matthean community at Antioch toward the end of the first century.

Smith, C. R. "Literary Evidences of a Fivefold Structure in the Gospel of Matthew." *New Testament Studies* 43 (1997): 540-551.

Smyth, K. "The Structural Principle of Matthew's Gospel." *Irish Biblical Studies* 4 (1982): 207-220.

Stanton, G., ed. *The Interpretation of Matthew, 2nd ed.* Studies in New Testament Interpretation. Edinburgh: T&T Clark, 1995. Collection of articles.

Ulrich, D. W. "The Missional Audience of the Gospel of Matthew." *Catholic Biblical Quarterly* 69 (2007): 64-83. *Catholic Biblical Quarterly* 61 (1999): 1-23.

Weren, W. J. C. "The Macrostructure of Matthew's Gospel: A New Proposal." *Biblica* 87 (2006): 171-200.

Withers, M. F. "Jesus in the Footsteps of Jeremiah." *Catholic Biblical Quarterly* 68 (2006): 229-247.

Part I

The New Testament Canon

1

The Origins

The "Problem" Posed by Galatians

The Gospels are replete of stories woven around the disciples', and especially Peter's, misunderstanding of Jesus' teaching as well as of pericopes dealing with table fellowship scenes. Furthermore, in these pericopes Jesus' opponents are time and again critical of his sharing food with persons considered by them to be unworthy of such fellowship. It is no exaggeration to say that Jesus' teaching, its misunderstanding by the disciples, and the subsequent corrective explanation by Jesus, on the one hand, and Jesus' repeated invitation to the Jewish leaders to share table fellowship with the unworthy and sinful others, on the other hand, are the two foci of the literary fabric of all four Gospels. This being the case, one would expect that, by the time Jesus sends his disciples out on the mission to relay his teaching to the world, those disciples, especially Peter, James, and John, whom he used to single out for extra teaching sessions, would be fully convinced. However, the exact opposite takes place. Paul's letter to the Galatians, especially 1:12-2:14, reflects a situation whereby he practically had to wage anew the battle Jesus supposedly had won over his disciples' stubborn misunderstanding or even outright lack of understanding. Besides, one would have expected Paul or his disciples who wrote in his name to have appealed to "the teacher," Jesus, in order to settle their differences with Peter, James, and John. It is indeed strange that throughout the Pauline literature there is not one single reference to "words of Jesus." It is as though the battle Paul waged against his colleagues took place without reference to

Jesus' teaching. This seems quite odd in light of Paul's fortnight visit with Peter (Gal 1:18). Moreover, in this same epistle, Paul insists that his apostleship is "not from men, nor through man" (1:1) and that "the gospel which was preached by me is not man's gospel. For I did not receive it from man, nor was I taught it, but it came through a revelation of Jesus Christ ... But when he who had set me apart before I was born, and had called me through his grace, was pleased to reveal his Son to me, in order that I might preach him among the Gentiles, I did not confer with flesh and blood, nor did I go up to Jerusalem to those who were apostles before me, but I went away into Arabia; and again I returned to Damascus. Then after three years I went up to Jerusalem to visit Cephas." (1:11-12, 15-18) That is to say, Paul insists that the gospel concerning Jesus Christ was revealed to him directly by God himself. He even insists that his understanding of that gospel is the only valid one and that any other rendering of it is actually a perversion thereof that is liable of nothing less than God's curse:

> I am astonished that you are so quickly deserting him who called you in the grace of Christ and turning to a different gospel--not that there is another gospel, but there are some who trouble you and want to pervert the gospel of Christ. But even if we, or an angel from heaven, should preach to you a gospel contrary to that which we preached to you, let him be accursed. As we have said before, so now I say again, If any one is preaching to you a gospel contrary to that which you received, let him be accursed. (1:6-9)[1]

---

[1] In the Corinthian correspondence we find a similar stand: "According to the grace of God given to me, like a skilled master builder I laid a foundation, and another man is building upon it. Let each man take care how he builds upon it. For no other foundation can any one lay than that which is laid, which is Jesus Christ ... Do you not know that you are God's temple and that God's Spirit dwells in you? If any one destroys God's temple, God will destroy him" (1 Cor 3:10-11, 16-17); "For if some

How is one to explain all these incongruities?

The Gospels

The classical stand in New Testament scholarship, even among the most "liberal" or "critical" scholars, is the non-provable assumption that the Gospels contain to some extent the "actual" teaching of Jesus, whether before or after his resurrection. This seemingly innocuous presupposition actually created the impasse in which the study of the New Testament, and of the Bible in its entirety, lies today. The entire gamut of approaches—from the literalistic, with its highlighting in red of the "words" of Jesus to the theological, which starts with the later formulas of Christian faith and performs an unabashed eisegesis of the scriptural text forcing it into a preordained and yet unpolished expression of one's own belief—do not take into consideration that one has to "explain" how the Pauline teaching, which was laid in writing and was read in the Pauline churches as the official and authoritative "gospel word" of God before the Gospels were circulated, did not validate itself with, at least, some "words" of Jesus as the originator of this teaching. Another series of related questions are the following:

1. Why has not any of "those who were apostles before me [Paul]" (Gal 1:17) thought of writing down a collection of the Lord's "sayings" or "life" before Galatians? Put

---

one comes and preaches another Jesus than the one we preached, or if you receive a different spirit from the one you received, or if you accept a different gospel from the one you accepted, you submit to it readily enough ... For such men are false apostles, deceitful workmen, disguising themselves as apostles of Christ. And no wonder, for even Satan disguises himself as an angel of light. So it is not strange if his servants also disguise themselves as servants of righteousness. Their end will correspond to their deeds." (2 Cor 11:4, 13-15)

otherwise, given that, at least according to Galatians, Paul was preaching a "questionable" gospel for at least three years without reference to the "apostles" and even "brother of the Lord," why has not any of them written an "official" document during this lengthy period to counteract Paul's teaching or, at least, to set the record straight concerning it?

2. Why was nothing written by any of them after Paul's fortnight visit with Peter? According to Paul (Gal 1:18-24) the reason seems to be that they had not found any reason to do so, meaning that Paul was preaching "the truth of the gospel" (1:5, 14; 5:7), i.e., the only true gospel (1:6-7).

3. Why have they not written anything during the following fourteen[2] years when, again according to Galatians, they had serious trouble with that teaching, indeed so serious that it necessitated a meeting at the highest level between them, on the one hand, and Paul and Barnabas, on the other hand (2:1-10)? From what one can gather from the New Testament, the earliest such writings would be the letter of James to the Jewish diaspora and, according to Acts, the synodal letter to the Gentiles (Acts 15:23-29). Furthermore, both were triggered by the Jerusalem meeting. The letter of James was, most probably, a response to Paul's Galatians: Paul wrote to the Gentiles and James reciprocated with a

---

[2] Or eleven, if one chooses to compute into the fourteen years of Gal 2:2 the three years of 1:18.

counter-letter to the diaspora Jews.[3] Notice that these two non-Pauline literary productions do not refer to "words of Jesus."

The earliest New Testament literary production, which does not refer to Paul as its author, is the Gospel of Mark.[4] If one subscribes to the theory of the independent document "Q" that contained only sayings of Jesus and was used by Luke and Matthew, then it is even more striking that Mark imposed itself as a Gospel in its own right, in spite of the fact that it does not give too much attention to the "sayings of the Lord," nor for that matter to Jesus' infancy. Scholars have noticed this oddity that they came up with the hypothesis that the gospels of Luke and Matthew must have used an independent source, an allegedly self-standing document, which they dubbed "Q," from the German "Quelle," meaning "source."[5] Even if such a document existed, one would still have to account for the following: Q has never survived on its own as its counterpart, the Gnostic "Gospel of Thomas," did. It survived as part of the Gospels of Luke and Matthew. This means that Q never acquired the status of Gospel on its own. Contrariwise, not only was Mark considered as Gospel, but it actually created and launched the appellation of "gospel" to speak of a book. Mark dubs itself as "gospel" (*evangelion*; 1:1) in the same way as Luke refers to itself as "word" (*logon*; Acts 1:1),[6] and John and Matthew, as "book" (Jn

---

[3] See later my discussion of this epistle.

[4] Some scholars opt for the gospel of John. However, if the latter is the earliest Gospel it would be difficult to explain why only Luke, of the three "Synoptics," seems to have close connections with it.

[5] Many scholars have justifiably questioned the existence of such a document.

[6] Or "narrative (*diēgēsin*) of the things (*pragmatōn*) which have been accomplished among us, just as they were delivered to us by those who from the beginning were eyewitnesses and ministers of the word (*logou*)" (Lk 1:1-2).

20:30, *bibliō*; Mt 1:1, *biblos*). Consequently, just as Paul defined the "gospel" as being the "authoritative apostolic preaching," Mark defined the literary genre "gospel."

Mark as the Pauline evangelion

Of all four Gospels it is Mark that not only entitles itself as "gospel," but is also the only one in which this term is central to the extent that one can say that the entire book revolves around it. Indeed, although Mark and Matthew are the only ones that use this term,[7] Mark is obviously the original. Indeed, Matthew uses the phrase "the gospel of the kingdom" (4:23; 9.35) which is special to him since it is an integral part of the Matthean formula "And he (Jesus) went about all Galilee (the cities and villages), teaching in their synagogues and preaching the gospel of the kingdom and healing every disease and every infirmity (among the people)." It clearly bears his signature since, on the following occasion, he expands the Markan "the gospel" (Mk 13:10) into "this gospel of the kingdom" (Mt 24:14). In the last occurrence, instead of the Markan "the gospel" (Mk 14:9) Matthew has "this gospel" (Mt 24:14), a shortened version of "this gospel of the kingdom."[8]

In Mark, on the other hand, the noun "gospel" is an integral part of the entire work as is evident from its use in different contexts as well as ways: "The beginning of the gospel of Jesus Christ, the Son of God" (1:1); "Now after John was arrested, Jesus came into Galilee, preaching the gospel of God and saying,

---

[7] The Greek original for "preaching the gospel" in RSV Lk 9:6 and 20:1 is actually the present participle of the verb *evangelizomai* (evangelize) and does not have the noun *evangelion* (gospel).

[8] See below on the value of the demonstrative "this" as Matthew's way of presenting his book as a Gospel.

'The time is fulfilled, and the kingdom of God is at hand; repent, and believe in the gospel'" (1:14-15); "For whoever would save his life will lose it; and whoever loses his life for my sake and the gospel's will save it" (8:35); "Truly, I say to you, there is no one who has left house or brothers or sisters or mother or father or children or lands, for my sake and for the gospel, who will not receive a hundredfold now in this time, houses and brothers and sisters and mothers and children and lands, with persecutions, and in the age to come eternal life" (10:29-30); "And the gospel must first be preached to all nations" (13:10); "And truly, I say to you, wherever the gospel is preached in the whole world, what she has done will be told in memory of her." (14:9) Even its occurrence in Mark's longer ending (16:9-20), which is made up of statements taken up from the other three Gospels, is phrased to fit its other usages in Mark: "Go into all the world and preach the gospel to the whole creation." (16:15) Both the phrase "preach the gospel" (*kēryssein to evangelion*) and the noun "creation" (*ktisis*) are found only in Mark of the four Gospels.[9]

A closer look at these instances will readily show that Mark's expressions and usages, which are either special to him or borrowed by Matthew from him, are closely similar to what is found in the Pauline literature. "The beginning of the gospel" (Mk 1:1) occurs only in Philippians 4:15 in the rest of the New Testament. "Preaching the gospel" (Mk 1:14; 13:10; 14:9; 16:15) is found in Galatians 2:2 and Colossians 1:23.[10]

---

[9] The former in Mk 1:14, and the latter in Mk 10:6 and 13:19.

[10] One may add the instances where the verb *kēryssō* (preach) appears in a context where the reference is expressly to the gospel: Rom 10:13-17; 1 Cor 9:18-27; 15:1-12.

"Believing in the gospel" occurs in Ephesians 1:13.[11] The addition "and for the gospel's sake" (Mk 8:35; 10:29), which is omitted in Luke (9:24) and Matthew (10:39; 16:25), is telling of the centrality of this term for Mark, which is not the case for the other Evangelists. Finally, both the absolute "the gospel" (*to evangelion*) in Mark 8:35 and 10:29 as well as in 1:15; 13:10 and 14:9, and the full phrase "the gospel of God" (*to evangelion tou theou*) in 1:14, both special to Mark among the Gospels, are a trade mark of the Pauline literature.[12] Moreover, Mark's shorter ending, a two sentence addition after 16:8, uses the phrase *to kērygma* as another way to speak of the gospel's message. This betrays the Evangelist's special interest in the notion of "gospel" and, by the same token, his close reliance on Paul.[13]

The absoluteness of the gospel indicates that there is, and can be, only *one* gospel as Paul stressed in Galatians 1:6-7.[14] However, this one gospel is "my [Paul's] gospel" (Rom 2:6; 16:25; 2 Tim 2:8), that is, as Paul teaches "everywhere in every church" (4:15-17).[15] On the other hand, this one gospel found expressly in Paul's teaching and now laid down in writing in his letters (Gal 1:8-9) is also "the gospel of Jesus Christ."[16] How is one to understand this phrase? Galatians makes it clear that it is

---

[11] One may add Rom 1:16 (For I am not ashamed of the gospel: it is the power of God for salvation to every one who *has faith* [*pistevonti*], to the Jew first and also to the Greek.) and 10:16 (But they have not all obeyed the gospel; for Isaiah says, "Lord, who *has believed* what he has heard from us?").

[12] See Rom 1:16; 10:16; 11:28; 1 Cor 4:15; 9:14 (twice), 18, 23; 15:1; 2 Cor 8:18; Gal 1:11; 2:2, 5, 7, 14; Eph 3:6; 6:19; Phil 1:5, 7, 12, 16; 2:22; 4:3, 15; Col 1:5, 23; 1 Thess 2:4.

[13] See Rom 16:25; 1Cor 1:21; 2:4; 15:14; 2 Tim 4:17; Tit 1:3.

[14] See also my comments on Gal 2:7-8 in my *Galatians: A Commentary* (Crestwood, NY: St Vladimir's Press, 1999); hereinafter referred to as *Gal.*

[15] See also Rom 6:17; 1 Cor 7:17; 11:16; 14:33-34; 2 Cor 8:18.

[16] Phil 1:27; 1 Thess 3:2; 2 Thess 1:8.

not the gospel that Jesus reveals, but rather the one that reveals Jesus:

> For I would have you know, brethren, that the gospel which was preached by me is not man's gospel. For I did not receive it from man, nor was I taught it, but it came through a revelation of Jesus Christ... For... when he who had set me apart before I was born, and had called me through his grace, was pleased to reveal his Son to me, in order that I might preach him among the Gentiles, I did not confer with flesh and blood. (1:11-12, 15-16)

The same recurs in 2 Corinthians where God is the revealer and Jesus Christ is the revealed:

> Therefore, having this ministry by the mercy of God, we do not lose heart. We have renounced disgraceful, underhanded ways; we refuse to practice cunning or to tamper with God's word, but by the open statement of the truth we would commend ourselves to every man's conscience in the sight of God. And even if our gospel is veiled, it is veiled only to those who are perishing. In their case the god of this world has blinded the minds of the unbelievers, to keep them from seeing the light of the gospel of the glory of Christ, who is the likeness of God. For what we preach is not ourselves, but Jesus Christ as Lord, with ourselves as your servants for Jesus' sake. (4:1-5)[17]

This understanding is further corroborated in the instances where the gospel is referred to as "word" (*logos*): "For we are not, like so many, peddlers of God's word; but as men of sincerity, as commissioned by God, in the sight of God we speak in Christ" (2 Cor 2:17); "All this is from God, who through Christ reconciled us to himself and gave us the ministry of reconciliation; that is, in Christ God was reconciling the world

---

[17] See also Rom 1:1-4; 1 Thess 3:2; 2 Thess 2:13-14.

to himself, not counting their trespasses against them, and entrusting to us the message (*logon*) of reconciliation" (5:18-19); "Continue steadfastly in prayer, being watchful in it with thanksgiving; and pray for us also, that God may open to us a door for the word, to declare the mystery of Christ, on account of which I am in prison, that I may make it clear, as I ought to speak." (Col 4:2-4)[18]

Jesus the Teacher

What is, furthermore, definitely striking is that Mark has defined what a gospel book is all about without having it give much attention to the "events" of Jesus' birth and resurrection, which have become the two foci of later endless debates in classical "theology" and two of the major "mysteries" of the classical formulations of Christian belief. The Markan "resurrection" pericope is merely an invitation to Peter and all disciples to proceed away from Jerusalem, where there is merely an empty tomb, into Galilee (16:7) where Jesus preceded them (14:28); the reason is that it is there that he "came… preaching the gospel of God" (1:14) and that he told them: "I will make you become fishers of men." (1:17) Since the gospel is a "word," the book of Mark forms an *inclusio* at both ends of which stands Galilee, and revolves around the teaching of Jesus, and not his "person." Indeed, at his first public appearance the audience's reaction is not "Who is this?" but "What is this?" and its answer is "A new teaching, with authority" (1:27),[19] whose newness lay in that "they were astonished at his teaching, for he taught them as one who had authority, and not as the scribes" (v.22).

---

[18] See also Col 3:16-17; 1 Tim 1:15.
[19] Luke has "What is this *word*?" (4:37), which is a clear reference to the gospel in his double volume Luke-Acts.

That the content of Mark is the "teaching" of Jesus is reflected in the following features of this Gospel. Jesus is referred to essentially as teacher.[20] His followers are known as disciples (44 occurrences) rather than apostles. They are called apostles only in two instances (3:14: 6:30), possibly one. If original,[21] the first time occurs when they are "sent out (*apostellē*) to preach (*kēryssein*) and have authority to cast out demons" (3:14-15). The second time is found upon their return from the mission they were sent out for: "The apostles returned to Jesus [from this mission], and told him all that they had done and *taught*" (6:30). The mission of the apostles is thus first and foremost to "preach (herald the *kērygma*)" and "teach." Indeed, Mark 6:30 is the end of the journey that started thus:

> And he went about among the villages *teaching*. And he called to him the twelve, and began to *send* them out two by two, and gave them authority over the unclean spirits. So they went out and *preached* that men should repent. And they cast out many demons, and anointed with oil many that were sick and healed them. (6:6b-7, 12-13; italics mine)

Put otherwise, is a true apostle the one who teaches the teaching of Jesus.

This is precisely the object of the harsh lesson to which was subjected the first among the twelve, Simon, whom Jesus surnamed Peter (3:16). To the inquiry as to who it is said that Jesus was, Peter replied with the title "Christ" (8:29), that is, "king" and "Son of God," which Jesus was categorically avoiding

---

[20] *Didaskalos* (Mk 4:38; 5:35; 9:17, 38; 10:17, 20, 35; 12:14, 19, 32; 13:1; 14:14) and *rabbi/ouni* (10:51; 11:21; 14:45).

[21] It is not extant in all manuscripts. It may have been added to parallel its occurrence in Lk 6:13. RSV does not include it in Mark.

from beginning to end (Mk 3:11-12; 15:1-5). Peter's reply *sounded* right (8:29) but was wrong, actually "Satanic": "Get behind me, Satan! For you are not on the side of God, but of men." (v.33)[22] The reason for this, according to Mark, is that the eschatological Christ is not dynastic, begetting a kingly progeny while he is living; rather he is the Suffering Servant of Isaiah, whose dynasty is raised after his demise by God himself:

> He was oppressed, and he was afflicted, yet he opened not his mouth; like a lamb that is led to the slaughter, and like a sheep that before its shearers is dumb, so he opened not his mouth. By oppression and judgment he was taken away; and as for his generation, who considered that he was cut off out of the land of the living, stricken for the transgression of my people? And they made his grave with the wicked and with a rich man in his death, although he had done no violence, and there was no deceit in his mouth. Yet it was the will of the Lord to bruise him; he has put him to grief; when he makes himself an offering for sin, he shall see his offspring, he shall prolong his days; the will of the Lord shall prosper in his hand; he shall see the fruit of the travail of his soul and be satisfied; by his knowledge shall the righteous one, my servant, make many to be accounted righteous; and he shall bear their iniquities. Therefore I will divide him a portion with the great, and he shall divide the spoil with the strong; because he poured out his soul to death, and was numbered with the transgressors; yet he bore the sin of many, and made intercession for the transgressors. (Is 53:7-12)

In turn, this is possible because his "seed" (*zera'; sperma*) is like the seed of the word that is taught and that begets children in the

---

[22] Actually, the Greek *ou phroneis ta tou theou all ta tōn anthrōpōn* means: "You do not think/cogitate the way God does, but the way men do" or "You do not have the mind of God, but that of men."

sense of disciples, just as in the wisdom tradition the disciple is referred to as child:

> I do not write this to make you ashamed, but to admonish you as my beloved *children*. For though you have countless guides in Christ, you do not have many fathers. For I became your *father* in Christ Jesus through the gospel. I urge you, then, be imitators of me. Therefore I sent to you Timothy, my beloved and faithful child in the Lord, to remind you of my ways in Christ, as I *teach* them everywhere in every church. (1 Cor 4:14-17; italics mine)

And this is precisely what the Suffering Servant's mission is all about, to teach God's will to all, Gentiles as well as Israel:

> Behold my servant, whom I uphold, my chosen, in whom my soul delights; I have put my Spirit upon him, he will bring forth justice to the nations. He will not cry or lift up his voice, or make it heard in the street; a bruised reed he will not break, and a dimly burning wick he will not quench; he will faithfully bring forth justice. He will not fail or be discouraged till he has established justice in the earth; and the coastlands wait for his law. (Is 42:1-4)

> The Lord God has given me the tongue of those who are taught, that I may know how to sustain with a word him that is weary. Morning by morning he wakens, he wakens my ear to hear as those who are taught. (Is 50:4)

Jesus, the Son of Man

Dissatisfied with the king, who is "Son of God," and the entire kingly institution (palace, temple, temple service), the scriptural God brings their demise through destruction and exile, and chooses as his plenipotentiary representative a mere "son of man" to be his emissary to the exiles scattered among the nations:

In the thirtieth year, in the fourth month, on the fifth day of the month, as I was among the exiles by the river Chebar, the heavens were opened, and I saw visions of God. On the fifth day of the month (it was the fifth year of the exile of King Jehoiachin), the word of the Lord came to Ezekiel the priest, the son of Buzi, in the land of the Chaldeans by the river Chebar; and the hand of the Lord was upon him there. (Ezek 1:1-3)

To be sure, Ezekiel was a priest pertaining to the kingly temple; but the temple was no more and it is as "son of man," that is, not pertaining to the kingly apparatus, that he is chosen to carry the fullness of God's message:

And when I looked, behold, a hand was stretched out to me, and, lo, a written scroll was in it; and he spread it before me; and it had writing on the front and on the back, and there were written on it words of lamentation and mourning and woe. And he said to me, "Son of man, eat what is offered to you; eat this scroll, and go, speak to the house of Israel." So I opened my mouth, and he gave me the scroll to eat. And he said to me, "Son of man, eat this scroll that I give you and fill your stomach with it." Then I ate it; and it was in my mouth as sweet as honey. And he said to me, "Son of man, go, get you to the house of Israel, and speak with my words to them." (2:9-2:4)

Both Ezekiel and Isaiah's Suffering Servant are figures connected to the exile, when Israel was scattered among the nations. This situation corresponded to the one extant at the time of the gospel which was one and assigned to both Peter and Paul, the former as apostle to the Jews of the diaspora and the latter as apostle to the Gentiles (Gal 2:7-8). That is why Mark has Jesus, God's eschatological emissary, introduced early on not only as the Son of God preaching the gospel of God in (the Gentile) Galilee with divine authority (1:11, 14), but also as the Son of man who was preaching the "word (of God)" with the same authority in (the Jewish) Capernaum (Mk 2:2, 10).

What is a Gospel Book?

The conclusion should be clear. Mark is not the story of Jesus, nor is it even about him. It is rather the story-like exposition of his authoritative teaching. Its fabric is of the same fabric as the Old Testament which is neither about God nor his story—let alone the story of Israel or of the (ancient) Jews—but a story-like exposition of God's teaching. This is corroborated by the official designations of the tripartite Old Testament scripture: Torah, Prophets, and Writings. Once more, the teaching is neither about God nor about his messiah. It is rather the teaching *of* God and *of* his messiah to us, for us to hearken to and implement.[23] Unfortunately, later theological endeavors missed the mark.[24] They basically ventured in either one of two directions: finding out what God and his messiah *did* for us or delving into figuring out what the two are (about). In so doing they voided the Gospels of their intended title, and thus meaning, by not realizing that their official title of "Gospels" was intended to put them in line with the Torah, the Prophets, and the Writings, and thus books containing God's word of teaching. Any theological endeavor is bound to betray God's word. Fortunately, on the other hand, there have been church teachers, the like of John Chrysostom, who understood what scripture was

---

[23] Notice, e.g., that the Gospel of John was written so that the hearers might believe in the message in order to accede to the life offered therein (20:30-31), yet, at the same time, this offer will not be implemented unless the teaching is understood as a "commandment" received from God in order to be obeyed (12:49-50; 13:34-35; 15:14, 17).

[24] Pun intended. The Latin *marcus* means "hammer" with which one hits the "mark." See below on Mark's name.

all about and spent their effort into listening to it, then expounding it to others, *as it stands*: a story line challenging us to do God's will and, in so doing, be his witnesses in this world:

> Not every one who says to me, "Lord, Lord," shall enter the kingdom of heaven, but he who does the will of my Father who is in heaven. On that day many will say to me, "Lord, Lord, did we not prophesy in your name, and cast out demons in your name, and do many mighty works in your name?" And then will I declare to them, "I never knew you; depart from me, you evildoers." Every one then who hears these words of mine and does them will be like a wise man who built his house upon the rock; and the rain fell, and the floods came, and the winds blew and beat upon that house, but it did not fall, because it had been founded on the rock. And every one who hears these words of mine and does not do them will be like a foolish man who built his house upon the sand; and the rain fell, and the floods came, and the winds blew and beat against that house, and it fell; and great was the fall of it." And when Jesus finished these sayings, the crowds were astonished at his teaching, for he taught them as one who had authority, and not as their scribes. (Mt 7:21-29)

2

Toward A Scriptural Canon

The Scriptural Paradigm

This pattern of expanding an essential teaching into a work that is of, comparatively, epic proportions, was not created by the New Testament authors. It actually followed the lead of the Old Testament. As I showed in my discussion of the development of the Old Testament, the paradigm itself of scriptural writing originated with the prophetic writings, especially Ezekiel and, for that matter, Second-Isaiah (Is 40-55).[1] In Isaiah and Jeremiah we are told that the prophet's "divine" teaching was committed to writing for the coming ages:

> Hear the word of the Lord, you rulers of Sodom! Give ear to the teaching of our God, you people of Gomorrah! ... Bind up the testimony, seal the teaching among my disciples. I will wait for the Lord, who is hiding his face from the house of Jacob, and I will hope in him. Behold, I and the children whom the Lord has given me are signs and portents in Israel from the Lord of hosts, who dwells on Mount Zion. And when they say to you, "Consult the mediums and the wizards who chirp and mutter, should not a people consult their God? Should they consult the dead on behalf of the living? To the teaching and to the testimony!" (Is 1:10; 8:16-20a)

---

[1] See my *Old Testament Introduction, Volume 1: Historical Traditions*, revised edition (Crestwood, NY: St Vladimir's Press, 2003), 29-40; hereinafter referred to as *OTI₁*.

In the fourth year of Jehoiakim the son of Josiah, king of Judah, this word came to Jeremiah from the Lord: "Take a scroll and write on it all the words that I have spoken to you against Israel and Judah and all the nations, from the day I spoke to you, from the days of Josiah until today." ... Then Jeremiah took another scroll and gave it to Baruch the scribe, the son of Neriah, who wrote on it at the dictation of Jeremiah all the words of the scroll which Jehoiakim king of Judah had burned in the fire; and many similar words were added to them. (Jer 36:1-2, 32)

In Ezekiel, we read that the message is actually not only preordained, but also handed down as an already written scroll to which nothing could be added:

"But you, son of man, hear what I say to you; be not rebellious like that rebellious house; open your mouth, and eat what I give you." And when I looked, behold, a hand was stretched out to me, and, lo, a written scroll was in it; and he spread it before me; and it had writing on the front and on the back, and there were written on it words of lamentation and mourning and woe. And he said to me, "Son of man, eat what is offered to you; eat this scroll, and go, speak to the house of Israel." So I opened my mouth, and he gave me the scroll to eat. And he said to me, "Son of man, eat this scroll that I give you and fill your stomach with it." Then I ate it; and it was in my mouth as sweet as honey. And he said to me, "Son of man, go, get you to the house of Israel, and speak with my words to them." (Ezek 2:8-3:4)

That is to say, the prophetic teaching, as it stands in the scroll (book) of Ezekiel, is itself "the word of God" and thus the "rule" (*kanōn*) by which every subsequent teaching is to be judged. Furthermore, that the prophetic teaching, as it stands in the prophetic scroll, is full and complete, indicates that it is normative and that any outside subsequent or even contemporary comment upon it has a "human," not "divine," origin.[2] The text itself, as it stands in its totality—and not its parts, however lofty or central or essential they may be considered, let alone fabricated formulae—is "the canon of truth." Last, and not least, this prophetic "word of God" committed to writing judges everything and everybody, the nations as well as Israel, and thus does not await any human assessment of its value. Put otherwise, the scriptural canon is not the product of later decisions as to its extent on the basis of a formulaic "rule of faith." Rather, later generations are forced into the choice of either accepting it as such and, in so doing, putting themselves under its authoritative judgment, or refusing it as Hananiah in the book of Jeremiah did. Let me reiterate, the scriptural writings are written in a way that does not allow any decision regarding their authority; they are laid down in writing "with divine authority." One does not judge their value and authority; one's choice is simply to either submit to them or decline to do so. As Matthew put it forcefully, even the children of the kingdom, which is to be found within the confines of the scriptural text describing it (Rev 22:19), can "be thrown into the outer darkness" where "men will weep and gnash their teeth" (Mt 8:12).

---

[2] See, for instance, Ezek 13:1-7 (The word of the Lord came to me: "Son of man, prophesy against the prophets of Israel, prophesy and say to those who prophesy out of their own minds: 'Hear the word of the Lord!' Thus says the Lord God, Woe to the foolish prophets who follow their own spirit, and have seen nothing! Your prophets have been like foxes among ruins, O Israel. You have not gone up into the breaches, or built up a wall for the house of Israel, that it might stand in battle in the day of the Lord. They have spoken falsehood and divined a lie; they say, "Says the Lord,' when the Lord has not sent them, and yet they expect him to fulfill their word. Have you not seen a delusive vision, and uttered a lying divination, whenever you have said, 'Says the Lord,' although I have not spoken?").

The Scriptural Story

From Ezekiel we also learn that the condemning "word of God"
is delivered as a *maśal*, an edifying story that elucidates the "sin"
against God and the subsequent punishment, and the promise of
eventual forgiveness and restoration (Ezek 16, 20, 23).[3] From the
introduction to Psalm 78, which covers in a nutshell the entire
story that runs from Exodus through 2 Kings, i.e., basically the
Torah and the Prior Prophets, we learn that this Ezekelian
edifying story becomes the official scriptural story to be repeated
from generation to generation for Israel to hear it and heed its
teaching:

> Son of man, propound a riddle (*ḥidah*), and speak an allegory
> (*maśal*) to the house of Israel. (Ezek 17:2)

> A Maskil of Asaph. Give ear, O my people, to my *teaching*; incline
> your ears to the words of my mouth! I will open my mouth in a
> parable (*maśal*); I will utter dark sayings (*ḥidot*,[4] riddles) from of
> old, things that we have heard and known, that our fathers have
> told us. We will not hide them from their children, but tell to the
> coming generation the glorious deeds of the Lord, and his might,
> and the wonders which he has wrought. He established a
> testimony in Jacob, and *appointed a law in Israel, which he
> commanded our fathers to teach to their children*; that the next
> generation might know them, the children yet unborn, and arise
> and tell them to their children, so that they should set their hope
> in God, and not forget the works of God, but *keep his
> commandments*; and that they should not be like their fathers, a
> stubborn and rebellious[5] generation, a generation whose heart was

---

[3] See in detail *OTI₁* 23-25.

[4] Plural of *ḥidah*.

[5] The verb *marah* (to be rebellious) is repeatedly used in Ezek 20 (vv. 8, 13, 21) as well
as Ps 78 (vv.8, 17, 40, 56) and its cognate Ps 106 (vv.7, 33, 43).

not steadfast, whose spirit was not faithful to God. (Ps 78:1-8; italics mine)

Consequently, the expanded story of the Pentateuch and the Deuteronomic History is itself an expanded *mašal* intended as "teaching" rather than a historical account. That this is the way these productions were intended is made clear in the choice of the original titles: Torah (instruction; teaching; law) or simply Moses [the prophet] for the first five books, and Prior Prophets for the so-called "historical books" (Joshua, Judges, Samuel and Kings).

The Law and the Prophets

Can one say more about the inner development of the entire gamut of the literature of the Old Testament, especially the Law and the Prophets? A closer look will show that the development was not simply linear, from the *mašal* to a full-fledged story. For such a wide literature to have arisen, there must have been at the same time a "lateral" development.[6] Indeed, scripture does not contain just one prophetic book that was expanded into one major epic, but rather four prophetic scrolls. Furthermore, Ezekiel itself does not consist of the three *mešalim* (parables) found in chapters 16, 20, and 23. The book is rather a complex structure; suffice it to point out the "repetition" of virtually the same *mašal* in chapters 16 and 23.[7] On the other hand, the epical books themselves of the Pentateuch and the Deuteronomic History are replete with similar episodes, which fact betrays a complex structure as well. In other words, the scriptural

---

[6] I prefer the term "lateral" over "internal" since the latter may give the impression that I am speaking of the growth process of one book, whereas I am trying to stress here the production of similar books, epical as well as prophetic.

[7] See also, for that matter, Jer 7 and 26.

production was of an intentionally structured, rather than linear, kind. To be scripture the New Testament writings had no choice but to follow the same pattern. Besides the "linear" trajectory from the "letter" (Galatians) to the "epical gospel" (Mark), there was a concomitant complex production of both an epistolary literature and a gospel-like one.

The Apostle

Within the Pauline corpus, whereas the other letters have a city church as recipient, Galatians is the only letter addressed to the churches of one region (to the churches of Galatia; Gal 2:2). Thus, it is intended as a circular letter with a "universal" validity, so to speak, in the same way as the "letters" of Revelation 2-3 are.[8] Many scholars consider Galatians to be among the first letters written, if not the first. From the New Testament data, one can gather that it was definitely the first among the five major Pauline epistles: Romans, 1 and 2 Corinthians, Galatians, and Ephesians. Romans builds and expands on Galatians. Ephesians is a compendium of the Pauline epistles addressed to churches. The Corinthian correspondence refers formally and materially to Galatians:

> Now concerning the contribution for the saints: as I directed the churches of Galatia, so you also are to do. On the first day of every week, each of you is to put something aside and store it up, as he may prosper, so that contributions need not be made when I come. And when I arrive, I will send those whom you accredit by letter to carry your gift to Jerusalem. (1 Cor 16:1-3)

---

[8] Notice that each of the letters is addressed to all seven churches: "He who has an ear, let him hear what the Spirit says to the churches [plural]." (2:7, 11, 17, 23, 29; 3;6, 13, 22; see also 2:23) The intention is also clear form the fact that all seven letters are part of one book.

The same phrase "the churches of Galatia" is found in Galatians 1:2 and the contribution to the church in Jerusalem was an integral aspect of the agreement between Paul and Barnabas, on the one hand, and the "pillars" of Jerusalem James, Peter, and John, on the other hand (Gal 2:10). One can safely add the expansion in 1 Corinthians 1-2 on the centrality of Jesus Christ's death on the cross as being at the heart of the Pauline gospel, which teaching spans the letter to the Galatians from beginning to end (2:9; 3:13; 5:24; 6:14). It is not an exaggeration to conclude that the content of Galatians is actually the premise on which the other four letters were built.

On the other hand, it is safe to assume that the same applies to Philippians and Colossians. Both contain "hymns" concerning Jesus Christ where his crucifixion takes center stage (Phil 2:5-11; Col 2:15-20). The first contains another passage strongly reminiscent of the thesis of Galatians:

Look out for the dogs, look out for the evil-workers, look out for those who mutilate the flesh. For we are the true circumcision, who worship God in spirit, and glory in Christ Jesus, and put no confidence in the flesh. Though I myself have reason for confidence in the flesh also. If any other man thinks he has reason for confidence in the flesh, I have more: circumcised on the eighth day, of the people of Israel, of the tribe of Benjamin, a Hebrew born of Hebrews; as to the law a Pharisee, as to zeal a persecutor of the church, as to righteousness under the law blameless. But whatever gain I had, I counted as loss for the sake of Christ. Indeed I count everything as loss because of the surpassing worth of knowing Christ Jesus my Lord. For his sake I have suffered the loss of all things, and count them as refuse, in order that I may gain Christ and be found in him, not having a righteousness of my own, based on law, but that which is through faith in Christ, the righteousness from God that depends on faith; that I may know him and the power of his resurrection, and may share his sufferings, becoming like him in his death, that if possible I may attain the resurrection from the dead. (Phil 2:2-11)

The same can be said of Colossians:

Put to death therefore what is earthly in you: fornication, impurity, passion, evil desire, and covetousness, which is idolatry. On account of these the wrath of God is coming. In these you once walked, when you lived in them. But now put them all away: anger, wrath, malice, slander, and foul talk from your mouth. Do not lie to one another, seeing that you have put off the old nature with its practices and have put on the new nature, which is being renewed in knowledge after the image of its creator. Here there cannot be Greek and Jew, circumcised and uncircumcised, barbarian, Scythian, slave, free man, but Christ is all, and in all. Put on then, as God's chosen ones, holy and beloved, compassion, kindness, lowliness, meekness, and patience, forbearing one another and, if one has a complaint against another, forgiving each other; as the Lord has forgiven you, so you also must forgive. And above all these put on love, which binds everything together in perfect harmony. (Col 3:5-14)

If we add the fact that Colossians is akin to Ephesians, and Philippians to Romans (the tenor of both letters reflects the unlikelihood that their author will be able to see his addressees), then it stands to reason to conclude that Galatians is actually the letter that must have "started it all."

The most plausible scenario is something similar to what we have in the Old Testament. I have shown in my revised *Introduction to the OT, vol.1, Historical Traditions*, that Ezekiel[9] forms the kernel around which was woven not only the

---

[9] Together with Second-Isaiah whose message had the exile as its setting.

remaining prophetic literature, but the entire Old Testament. He was in exile and his battle was against his fellows who did not seem to learn the lesson from the collapse of Jerusalem. They were either dreaming of building it up anew or surrendering to the new surrounding by settling under the protection of their new homeland, Babylon, whereas he was inviting them in a totally different direction: becoming the citizenry of a metaphorical city, whose name is "The Lord is there" (Ezek 48:35), meaning a city that lies wherever God is king (rules) over them (Ezek 20:32-33), that is, wherever his will is implemented.

In Galatians, after the Antioch incident (Gal 2:11-14), we find Paul in a similar predicament as Ezekiel. The prophet was to continue his assignment locking horns with Israel (Ezek 3:8-9), speaking the word of the Lord whether the recalcitrant people hear it or refuse to do so (2:5, 7; 3:11). Even more, the same message would have been accepted by outsiders, were it addressed to them:

> For you are not sent to a people of foreign speech and a hard language, but to the house of Israel-- not to many peoples of foreign speech and a hard language, whose words you cannot understand. Surely, if I sent you to such, they would listen to you. But the house of Israel will not listen to you; for they are not willing to listen to me; because all the house of Israel are of a hard forehead and of a stubborn heart. (3:5-7)

However, Second-Isaiah, Ezekiel's "contemporary," taught that the Ezekelian message to Israel would eventually be relayed to the farthest corners of the earth:

> Behold my servant, whom I uphold, my chosen, in whom my soul delights; I have put my Spirit upon him, he will bring forth justice to the nations ... He will not fail or be discouraged till he has

established justice in the earth; and the coastlands wait for his law
... I am the Lord, I have called you in righteousness, I have taken
you by the hand and kept you; I have given you as a covenant to
the people, a light to the nations, to open the eyes that are blind,
to bring out the prisoners from the dungeon, from the prison
those who sit in darkness ... It is too light a thing that you should
be my servant to raise up the tribes of Jacob and to restore the
preserved of Israel; I will give you as a light to the nations, that my
salvation may reach to the end of the earth. (Is 42:1, 4, 6-8; 49:6)

Moreover, not only is the servant who will carry out this mission
said to be "called from the womb" by the Lord (49:1; see Gal
1:15), but the messenger in Second-Isaiah is cast as a messenger
of good news: *mebasser(et)* in the Hebrew text (40:9 [twice];
41:27; 52:7[twice]) and *evangelizomenos* in the LXX (40:9
[twice]; 52:7[twice]). Consequently, Paul, shunned by Jerusalem,
pursued this mission and, like his predecessors Isaiah (8:16),
Jeremiah, and Ezekiel, consigned his "gospel" in a scroll to his
"churches" (Gal 1:2) written "with my own hand" (*tē emē kheiri*;
6:11), that is, with divine authority, just as God's law was
consigned in writing "at the hand of (through) an intermediary"
(*en kheiri mesitou*; 3:19). This course of action was not only
helpful, but necessary. The reason is that, without it, the
Gentiles would have been left completely orphaned and without
any authoritative document after the death of the only remaining
apostle to the nations, given that Barnabas betrayed the gospel
(Gal 2:11-14).

The Producers of the New Testament Literature

Just as the teaching of the three Ezekelian *mᵉšalim* (Ezek 16, 20,
23), and by extension that of the book of Ezekiel, formed the
kernel that was expanded into the biblical epic as well as into the
prophetic literature, Galatians functioned as the kernel for the

development of the New Testament literature as epistles similar to Galatians and as gospel stories similar to the Gospel of Mark. Who would among Paul's disciples qualify for such an endeavor?

A good and safe starting point is the New Testament literature itself, since it is definitely the basis for any later assumptions in the early church tradition regarding this matter. Indeed, besides the authors whose names appear as writers of their books (the epistles and Revelation), all the names that are traditionally associated with the books that do not bear the names of their authors are found in the New Testament: Paul (for the letter to the Hebrews), Matthew (Mt 9:9; 10:3; Mk 3:18; Lk 6:15; Acts 1:13), Mark (Acts 12:12, 25; 15:37, 39; Col 4:10; 2 Tim 4:11; Philem 24; 1 Pet 5:13), Luke (Col 4:14; 2 Tim 4:11; Philem 24), and John (passim). Of all these names Mark and Luke are striking in that they share with the name Paul a Latin, versus an Aramaic,[10] origin. Finding a clue to this feature may be a way to the solution to our question concerning the authorship of the New Testament literature.

Let us begin with Paul. According to Acts this appellation became his recognized name instead of the original Saul (13:9) upon embarking on his "first missionary journey" to the Gentiles (13:2; see 9:15-16). Usually it is assumed that the Apostle decided to take the name of the proconsul Sergius Paulus, but the question remains as to why; and why not Sergius? The answer becomes evident when one realizes that the Latin *paulus* is actually an adjective meaning "little one, small one"; this means that the Latin *Paulus* would be a surname. So the Apostle

---

[10] Or even, for that matter, a Greek origin if one takes into account other close disciples of Paul's the like of Timothy and Epaphras/Epaphroditus.

would actually be Saul "the little one, the lesser one."[11] Whether
the proconsul Sergius was a short person, we shall never know,
but for Paul we have a clear cut reason. From Galatians we learn
that Paul was proud of having been "advanced in Judaism
beyond many of my own age among my people, so extremely
zealous... for the traditions of my fathers" (1:14). But in the
parallel flashing of feathers in Romans (11:1) and Philippians
(3:5) we encounter the addition that he was of the tribe of
Benjamin. The reason is that the first king of Israel was the
Benjaminite Saul, his namesake; Paul may actually have been
named Saul by his parents after King Saul and thus, though from
Tarsus of Cilicia in the diaspora, he was as Israelite as any Jewish
resident of Jerusalem and Judah. Actually the book of Acts has
him as having acquired his Pharisaic training in Jerusalem at the
feet of Gamaliel "a teacher of the law, held in honor by all the
people" (5:34): "I am a Jew, born at Tarsus in Cilicia, but
brought up in this city at the feet of Gamaliel, educated
according to the strict manner of the law of our fathers, being
zealous for God as you all are this day." (22:3) Yet, it is precisely
this glorious CV that was connected in his mind with his fame in
the following manner: "For you have heard of my former life in
Judaism, how I persecuted the church of God violently and tried
to destroy it" (Gal 1:13); "they only heard it said, 'He who once
persecuted us is now preaching the faith he once tried to
destroy.'" (v.23) Consequently, his ego had to be bruised in a
way that would never allow him to boast of his accomplishments
not only on a personal level (But whatever gain I had, I counted
as loss for the sake of Christ; Phil 3:7) but also on a more

---

[11] Compare with *Iakōbou tou mikrou* (Mk 15:40) which RSV translates into "James the
younger," but which could be as well "James the lesser (the small[er])" and thus
"James, the little one," which would entail a derogatory connotation.

objective level. He, the only remaining champion of the true gospel and the one who worked for its sake more than all of them, was the last called among the apostles and thus the "least/littlest" among them:

> ... he [Christ] appeared to Cephas, then to the twelve. Then he appeared to more than five hundred brethren at one time, most of whom are still alive, though some have fallen asleep. Then he appeared to James, then to all the apostles. *Last of all* (*eskhaton*), as to one untimely born, he appeared also to me. For I am *the least* (*ho elakhistos*)[12] of the apostles, unfit to be called an apostle, because I persecuted the church of God. But by the grace of God I am what I am, and his grace toward me was not in vain. On the contrary, I worked harder than any of them, though it was not I, but the grace of God which is with me. (1 Cor 15:5-10; italics mine)

But why use the Latin instead of the Greek? The most immediate explanation is that the surname *Paulus* was used among the Romans[13] and it was fitting that the apostle to the Gentiles would have a Roman surname.[14] This would have been even more understandable if the tradition in Acts as to Paul's being a Roman citizen from Tarsus of Cilicia (22:3) reflected an actuality. There is reason to believe that it was so. It would stand to reason to assume that Paul, a Jew of the diaspora, would have exercised his apostolic activity, at least for a starter, within his home area. We learn from Galatians that this was "the regions of Syria and Cilicia" (1:21). After the agreement struck in Jerusalem, the tension between Paul and the other apostles took place in Antioch (2:11) which lies in the northern part of the

---

[12] The Greek *elakhistos* is the superlative form of *mikros* (small, little).

[13] E.g. Aemilius Paulus in Plutarch.

[14] Besides, there was no correspondent surname in Greek.

Roman province Syria and close to Cilicia. On the other hand, the extreme statement in 1 Corinthians 9:19 (For though I am free from all men, I have made myself a slave to all, that I might win the more) seems to suggest that Paul was indeed a Roman citizen. Tarsus, the main city of Cilicia, was granted the status of "free city" by Marc Anthony, which status was upheld by Augustus; this meant that all those who were born there were automatically Roman citizens.

Mark

According to Acts, Mark is clearly a surname: "John whose other name was Mark" (12:12, 25); "John called Mark" (15:37). Moreover, the thrice occurrence of such an introduction seems to be in preparation for his joining Barnabas on the latter's apostolic journey, where he is referred to simply as Mark (Barnabas took Mark with him and sailed away to Cyprus; 15:39). In other words, John's Hebrew name is changed to the Latin Mark when he embarks on the mission to the Gentiles.[15] This is clearly intentional since it parallels Acts' shift from Saul to Paul, which is linked to Paul's first Gentile missionary journey. The close relation between this John, on the one hand, and Barnabas (see, besides Acts, Col 4:10) and Peter (Acts 12:12; 1 Pet 5:13) on the other hand, militates for his being the same as the John mentioned in Galatians together with James, Peter, and Barnabas (2:9). The New Testament tradition tells us that, at the end, he joined Paul's party, thus endorsing the Apostle's gospel and earning his commendation: "Aristarchus my fellow prisoner greets you, and Mark the cousin of Barnabas (concerning whom you have received instructions—if he comes to you, receive him),

---

[15] Barnabas shares with Paul the apostleship to the Gentiles: Gal 2:9; Acts 11:30; 12:25; 13-14.

and Jesus who is called Justus. These are the only men of the circumcision among my fellow workers for the kingdom of God, and they have been a comfort to me" (Col 4:10-11); "Luke alone is with me. Get Mark and bring him with you; for he is very useful in serving me" (2 Tim 4:11); "Epaphras, my fellow prisoner in Christ Jesus, sends greetings to you, and so do Mark, Aristarchus, Demas, and Luke, my fellow workers." (Philem 23-24) The fact that Mark's name appears in these letters, all addressed to people residing in the Roman province Asia, is an indication that he ended up with the Pauline contingent in the province Asia, whose capital was Ephesus, Paul's headquarters.[16]

It stands to reason that this John spearheaded the production of the gospel story conceived around Paul's gospel as embedded, for the Pauline churches and the ages, in the letter to the Galatians. Moreover, following Paul's lead in Galatians, his gospel story was an explication of, as well as patterned after, the Old Testament scriptures. Indeed, the opening of his work anchors the "beginning of the gospel of Jesus Christ" (Mk 1:1) in the entire Old Testament since his quotation is taken from Deutoronomy, Isaiah, and Malachi: "As it is written in Isaiah the prophet, 'Behold, I send my messenger before thy face [Deut 23:20], who shall prepare thy way [Mal 3:1]; the voice of one crying in the wilderness: Prepare the way of the Lord, make his paths straight [Is 40:3].'" (Mk 1:2-3) In having both Galatians (the word of the apostle) and the Gospel of Mark (the expanded epic) officially read to the Pauline churches alongside the Prophets and the Law, Paul's disciples established a pattern that was to become the rule "in all the churches" for the ages to come. On the other hand, as I showed in my *New Testament*

---

[16] In the Pastoral letters Timothy is introduced as bishop of Ephesus (1 Tim 1:3).

Introduction, vol.1, Mark's intention would have been to vouchsafe the oneness of the gospel (Gal 2:7-8) by opening the door of repentance to Peter after the latter's betrayal of that gospel at Antioch (2:11-14). Put otherwise, Mark functioned as the voice of the repentant Peter who understood that the true Jesus Christ was to be met in (the) Galilee (of the nations) where both Gentiles and Jews shared the same common table.[17] For the listener to the readings the impression is very clear: the end of Mark (16:6-7) indicated that the recalcitrant Peter ended up endorsing the gospel of Paul, or rather, the one gospel that he, Peter, had betrayed. This helped produce the tradition that the church of Antioch, where the infamous incident took place, and the church of Rome, the capital of the empire, are the only churches that boast of having two apostles as their founders. Indeed, the one gospel agreed upon in Jerusalem (Gal 2:7) is preached throughout the entire Roman empire by the power of God's grace that works through the one apostleship of Peter and Paul (2:8). It is worth noting here that the same church tradition ascribes to the third main city of the empire, Alexandria, that it received the gospel at the hand of Mark, the bridge between the two Apostles, sealing metaphorically that the one undivided gospel of Galatians has reached, and been accepted by, the totality of the empire.

Just as in Paul's case, John's Latin surname *Marcus* must have been intended symbolically. The Latin *marcus* means "hammer." A hammer is an instrument with which one nails something in, cementing two pieces together. With a hammer one also "hits

---

[17] That Mark was the "voice" of (the repentant) Peter has been kept in the later traditions concerning the production of that Gospel. This tradition is actually taken from the New Testament itself: "She who is at Babylon, who is likewise chosen, sends you greetings; and so does my son Mark." (2 Pet 5:13).

the nail on the head" and thus makes a "mark," and by extension a "point," as a judge would. This surname fits Mark both personally and functionally. On the one hand, he was the one who, through his repentant attitude, cemented the relation between the two recognized chief Apostles. On the other hand, through his first-of-its-kind literary work, he established the genre "Gospel" that was to become both the "official," and thus binding, presentation of Jesus Christ[18] and, by the same token, the backbone of the New Testament literature. Indeed, the following three works of Luke (the Gospel and Acts), John, and Matthew are patterned after Mark, and these four books not only account for more than two thirds of that literature, but also give the basis for its reading since the canonical New Testament starts with them just as the canonical Old Testament begins with the Law.[19]

I would like to venture here an interesting possibility. The title of the Books of Maccabees comes from the surname *Makkabaios* associated with Judas, the leader of the Jewish revolt against the Seleucids in Palestine (1 Macc 2:4). The most popular explanation is that the Greek is a transliteration of the Hebrew *maqqaby*, which is an adjective whose meaning is "the one of/with the *maqqebet* (hammer)." Since Paul's gospel was critical

---

[18] This is reflected in that the Gospel Book used at liturgy functions as the embodiment of (our knowledge of) Jesus Christ just as the Book of the Law functions as the embodiment (our knowledge of) God: "But if you call yourself a Jew and rely upon the law and boast of your relation to God and know his will and approve what is excellent, because you are instructed in the law, and if you are sure that you are a guide to the blind, a light to those who are in darkness, a corrector of the foolish, a teacher of children, having in the law the embodiment of knowledge and truth..." (Rom 2:17-20)

[19] It is worth noting here that the second part of the New Testament, called liturgically the "Apostle" and which corresponds to the Prophets, has at its head the epistle to the Romans, which is the other scriptural expansion of "the gospel" to the Galatians.

of the Maccabean approach to deal with the Romans through an armed revolt, the surname Mark may well have been given to the writer of the Gospel known by this name in order to establish it as the non-Maccabean and non-zealot "way":

> The beginning of the gospel of Jesus Christ, the Son of God. As it is written in Isaiah the prophet, "'Behold, I send my messenger before thy face, who shall prepare thy *way*; the voice of one crying in the wilderness: Prepare the *way* of the Lord, make his paths straight." John the baptizer appeared in the wilderness, preaching a baptism of repentance for the forgiveness of sins. And there went out to him all the country of Judea, and all the people of Jerusalem; and they were baptized by him in the river Jordan, confessing their sins." (Mk 1:1-5)

It is the way of repentance for one's own sins, which sins brought about the siege of Jerusalem by God as the prophets teach, and not the way of blaming the enemy for the city's destruction. My proposition makes even more sense if one is of the opinion, as I am, that that Gospel was written during the anti-Roman Jewish war of 66-70 A.D.

Luke

When we turn to Luke, we find the following data. First and foremost, his name appears exclusively as Luke, from the Latin root *luc*— meaning "light." Secondly, if one ascribes to the traditional stand that the third canonical Gospel and the Book of Acts are the work of this Luke, then it is definitely interesting that the first occurrence of the first personal pronoun in the plural within the narrative in Acts appears in conjunction with Paul's passing into Macedonia, the land of Alexander, that is, in conjunction with the preaching of the gospel in fully Gentile land for the first time: "And a vision appeared to Paul in the night: a man of Macedonia was standing beseeching him and saying, 'Come over to Macedonia and help us.' And when he had seen the vision, immediately we sought to go on into Macedonia, concluding that God had called us to preach the gospel to them." (Acts 16:9-10) In other words, Luke, together with Timothy who is mentioned for the first time in Acts 16:1, is essentially linked to the mission to the Gentiles. This in turn would explain the choice of his appellation, which is reminiscent of the Isaianic Servant of the Lord who is assigned to be "a light to the nations" (Is 42:6; 49:6). Luke, as it were, is the one who consigned in writing (the apostolic activity of) Paul, the apostle to the Gentiles. Thirdly, the mention of Luke is found exclusively not only in conjunction with that of Mark but also in the same contexts where the latter is "reinstated" by Paul:

Aristarchus my fellow prisoner greets you, and Mark the cousin of Barnabas (concerning whom you have received instructions -- if he comes to you, receive him), and Jesus who is called Justus. These are the only men of the circumcision among my fellow workers for the kingdom of God, and they have been a comfort to me. Epaphras, who is one of yourselves, a servant of Christ Jesus, greets you, always remembering you earnestly in his prayers, that you may stand mature and fully assured in all the will of God. For I bear him witness that he has worked hard for you and for those in Laodicea and in Hierapolis. Luke the beloved physician and Demas greet you. (Col 4:10-14)

Epaphras, my fellow prisoner in Christ Jesus, sends greetings to you, and so do Mark, Aristarchus, Demas, and Luke, my fellow workers. (Philem 23-24)

Henceforth there is laid up for me the crown of righteousness, which the Lord, the righteous judge, will award to me on that Day, and not only to me but also to all who have loved his appearing. Do your best to come to me soon. For Demas, in love with this present world, has deserted me and gone to Thessalonica; Crescens has gone to Galatia, Titus to Dalmatia. Luke alone is with me. Get Mark and bring him with you; for he is very useful in serving me. Tychicus I have sent to Ephesus. (2 Tim 4:8-12)

In comparison with Mark, however, Luke has never faltered. Even more, in the Pauline writings, he is for Paul the (authorial) counterpart of Timothy, Paul's heir. Luke is beloved (*agapētos*; Col 4:14) just as Timothy is (1 Cor 4:7; 2 Tim 1:2). He is Paul's fellow-worker (*synergos*) just as Timothy is (Rom 16:21; 1 Thess 3:2). And above all, he is "alone with me [Paul]" (2 Tim 4:11) just as Timothy is the one of whom Paul writes that "I have no one like him, who will be genuinely anxious for your welfare. They all look after their own interests, not those of Jesus Christ" (Phil 2:20-21). One can easily imagine that, given this special place he had and the fact that he wrote the major work Luke-Acts covering the odyssey of the Pauline gospel of Jesus Christ originating in Galilee and reaching Rome through Jerusalem, that is, covering the Roman empire in its entirety, he was nicknamed *Loukas*. Indeed, in consigning as scripture the teaching of Christ in the Gospel and that of Paul in Acts, he himself became the "literary" "light to the nations" (Is 42:6; 49:6) just as Mark became the "literary" "apostle to the circumcision" (Gal 2:7-8).

Ephesus, the Pauline Headquarters

There is evidence galore pointing toward the Roman province Asia and its capital Ephesus as having been the center of the Pauline missionary activity after the Apostle's break with Antioch (Gal 2:11-14). Let me begin with Acts which covers in broad lines the Pauline itinerary. Antioch is linked to Saul's first mention in conjunction with Barnabas' apostolic activity (11:22-

26) and continues to be at the center of the author's interest in the first part of the book (11:27; 13:1, 14: 14:19, 20, 26; 15:22, 23, 30, 35) during which time Paul and Barnabas were working together. After the break between the two (15:36-41), Antioch disappears completely until its lapidary mention in a context of tension between Paul on the one hand, and Jerusalem and Antioch on the other hand, which reflects that the break was never healed. Indeed, Luke glosses over this episode and Paul's stay at either location is quite short: "When he had landed at Caesarea, he went up and greeted the church, and then went down to Antioch. After spending some time there he departed and went from place to place through the region of Galatia and Phrygia, strengthening all the disciples." (18:22-23) Moreover, this lightning trip to Jerusalem and Antioch is undertaken from Ephesus as his base and where he was active in the same way as he was in Antioch, his "first base":

And they came to Ephesus, and he left them there; but he himself went into the synagogue and argued with the Jews.[20] When they asked him to stay for a longer period, he declined; but on taking leave of them he said, "I will return to you if God wills," and he set sail from Ephesus. (18:19-21)

Thereafter, Ephesus takes center stage up until the end of Paul's apostolic activity (18:24; 19:1, 17, 26, 35; 20:16-17). Indeed, the last mention of Ephesus is connected with Paul's farewell speech to the elders of that church at the beginning of

---

[20] Compare with Acts 9:20-22 (And in the synagogues immediately he proclaimed Jesus, saying, "He is the Son of God." And all who heard him were amazed, and said, "Is not this the man who made havoc in Jerusalem of those who called on this name? And he has come here for this purpose, to bring them bound before the chief priests." But Saul increased all the more in strength, and confounded the Jews who lived in Damascus by proving that Jesus was the Christ).

which he tells them: "You yourselves know how I lived among you all the time *from the first day* that I set foot in Asia" (20:18); during which he tells them: "And now, behold, I know that all you among whom I have gone preaching the kingdom *will see my face no more*" (v.25); and at the end of which Luke writes: "And when he had spoken thus, he knelt down and prayed with them all. And they all wept and embraced Paul and kissed him, sorrowing most of all because of the word he had spoken, *that they should see his face no more*. And they brought him to the ship." (vv.36-38) At any rate, shortly thereafter, starting with his visit to Jerusalem, Paul will be captive until the end of the book.[21] Furthermore, in this same farewell speech, Paul refers to a lengthy stay of three years at Ephesus: "Therefore be alert, remembering that for three years I did not cease night or day to admonish every one with tears." (v.31)

Not only is this information from Acts regarding the momentous centrality of Ephesus and the province Asia for Paul's apostolic activity corroborated by what we find in the Pauline literature, but we also learn from the same that Paul intended them to remain so after his demise. In the Corinthian correspondence, we are told: "But I will stay in Ephesus until Pentecost, for a wide door for effective work has opened to me, and there are many adversaries." (1 Cor 16:8-9) Furthermore, Paul must have stayed enough time for those adversaries to have mustered enough momentum to endanger his life notwithstanding his Roman citizenry: "What do I gain if, humanly speaking, I fought with beasts at Ephesus?" (1 Cor

---

[21] Notice how Luke prepares for Paul's end in conjunction with a visit to Jerusalem already in Acts 18:21 (but on taking leave of them he said, "I will return to you if God wills"). The same is done through the reference to "a vow" (18:18) which is presented as the reason behind his going up to Jerusalem (21:23).

15:32); "For we do not want you to be ignorant, brethren, of the affliction we experienced in Asia; for we were so utterly, unbearably crushed that we despaired of life itself. Why, we felt that we had received the sentence of death; but that was to make us rely not on ourselves but on God who raises the dead; he delivered us from so deadly a peril, and he will deliver us; on him we have set our hope that he will deliver us again." (2 Cor 1:8-10) Also, since the Corinthian correspondence is said to have originated in Asia (1 Cor 16:8 and 19 [The churches of Asia send greetings]), then it stands to reason to assume that the management of the complex affairs of the most (in)famous Pauline church, which warranted an extensive correspondence, took place from Ephesus, which in turn militates for a lengthy stay in that city.[22] If one takes the mention of many possible visits to Corinth by Paul's co-workers as well as by himself (1 Cor 4:17, 19, 21; 16:3, 10, 12; 2 Cor 1:15-16; 9:4; 12:14, 17-18, 20-21; 13:2, 10), of the visits by people from Corinth (1 Cor 1:11; 5:1), and of the many letters (1 Cor 5:9; 2 Cor 7:8) at face value, then this also is an indication for a long sojourn in Asia.[23] That Ephesus remained the headquarters of the Pauline legacy can be gathered from the fact that Timothy, his top aide and heir

---

[22] The close connection between Ephesus and Corinth is also betrayed in Acts. Two of Paul's top helpers, Prisc(ill)a and Aquila (Rom 16:3; 1 Cor 16:19; 2 Tim 4:19), whom he encountered in Corinth (Acts 18:12) relocated to Ephesus (vv.18, 26). Apollos, Paul's colleague at Corinth (1 Cor 1:12; 3:4-6, 22; 4:6; see also 16:12), is introduced in Acts as having been active first at Ephesus (18:24) before he moved to Corinth (19:1).

[23] Even if the mention of these visits and letters is just a literary device, this still puts them in the realm of possibility, which betrays, at least in the mind of the author, both a lengthy stay and a comparatively short distance.

apparent (Phil 2:19-24),[24] is said to have been assigned by Paul
as the bishop of Ephesus (1 Tim 1:3; see also 2 Tim 1:18).

The Form of Scripture

As is clear from the Prophets, the fall of Jerusalem at the
Babylonians' hand is the hinge around which revolves this entire
literature. The story line of the Prior Prophets follows the rise
and fall of Jerusalem and, by extension, its counterpart Samaria,
while giving the reason behind their demise: the disregard of
God's will, of which the king and people are continually
reminded by the prophets. The concern of the Latter Prophets is
to underscore the different facets of this disregard, to announce
God's punishment for such, and to speak of the eventual pardon
and invitation into God's heavenly city, the new Jerusalem. With
the demise of Jerusalem at the Romans' hand in 70 A.D. Paul's
epitomical teaching of Galatians loomed high in the sky of his
Asian churches and so did its epical rendering in Mark's Gospel.
The first underscored that the believers' true mother was the
Jerusalem above of which Isaiah and the prophets spoke, and the
second invited all to realize that its threshold lay in (the) Galilee
(of the nations) where the messiah, its king, was already reigning
in the word preached by Paul.[25] The Pauline churches

---

[24] Notice how Timothy is introduced as co-author of this same letter which functions
as a testament, since it was written from an imprisonment which Paul was not sure to
survive (Phil 1:19-24). As co-author, Timothy is put in a position of authority over the
bishops of the Philippian church (1:1).

[25] See e.g. 1 Cor 15 where we hear that "Christ is preached as raised from the dead ...
Then comes the end, when he [Christ] delivers the kingdom to God the Father after
destroying every rule and every authority and power. For he must reign until he [God]
has put all his enemies under his feet. The last enemy to be destroyed is death." (vv.12,
24-26) That "Christ" is co-extensive with the gospel teaching, just as God is co-
extensive with the Torah, can be gathered from, e.g., the statement "You did not so
learn Christ!" (Eph 4:20).

understood in earnest that the Old Testament was the word of God who resides in the heavenly temple not made by the hand of man, and, as such, was not subject to the interpretation given to it by the authorities of the earthly Jerusalem. Rather, just as God chose Jeremiah (and not the kings and the temple authorities) and Ezekiel (and not the elders of Israel in exile) to carry the true interpretation of his will, so also now, in the (latter) days of the dawn of the new Jerusalem, God chose Paul, who was not taught by man but by God, to teach God's revelation throughout the Roman empire (Gal 1:11-16). The Pauline churches understood that "For though you have countless guides in Christ, you do not have many fathers. For I became your father in Christ Jesus through the gospel" (1 Cor 4:15) and "If to others I am not an apostle, at least I am to you; for you are the seal of my apostleship in the Lord" (1 Cor 9:2). Consequently they became more prone to accept the rule established by Paul's disciples that Galatians and Mark be read at their gatherings as "scripture" alongside the Old Testament readings.

It was then an easy step toward the following stage. Just as the Old Testament scripture was constructed around the prophetic word into a full-fledged literature that was repeatedly read to the congregation, so also, in order for it to be scripture, the New Testament had to follow the same road. The ultimate reason behind this phenomenon is the scriptural premise, based on the prophetic teaching, that, in contradistinction with the other deities that had a statuesque "form" besides their "word of teaching" (*hieros logos*), God in scripture has no statue, let alone temple, and thus his existence is exclusively *logic-al*, that is, expressed through his "word" (*logos*) of instruction. The classic teaching about the difference between the idols and the scriptural God is found in Romans:

> So they are without excuse; for although they knew God they did not honor him as God or give thanks to him, but they became futile in their thinking and their senseless minds were darkened. Claiming to be wise, they became fools, and exchanged the glory of the immortal God for images resembling mortal man or birds or animals or reptiles. Therefore God gave them up in the lusts of their hearts to impurity, to the dishonoring of their bodies among themselves, because they exchanged the truth about God for a lie and worshiped and served the creature rather than the Creator, who is blessed for ever! Amen... But if you call yourself a Jew and rely upon the law and boast of your relation to God and know his will and approve what is excellent, because you are instructed in the law, and if you are sure that you are a guide to the blind, a light to those who are in darkness, a corrector of the foolish, a teacher of children, having in the law the embodiment (*morphōsin*) of knowledge and truth... (Rom 1: 20-25; 2:17-20)

Consequently, his worshippers have not the luxury of "seeing" him, let alone conversing with him as do the Gentiles: "And in praying do not heap up empty phrases as the Gentiles do; for they think that they will be heard for their many words. Do not be like them, for your Father knows what you need before you ask him." (Mt 6:7-8).[26] The only way to make such a *logic-al* God and, for that matter, his *logic-al* messiah, present to the congregants was to "form" him again by "portraying" him through the words of his teaching, since he is—cannot be except—where his word is uttered:

---

[26] One can imagine how difficult it was for Paul to hammer this teaching to his Gentiles who were surrounded by statuesque deities (Acts 17:22-29; Rom 1:22-23; 1 Cor 8:4-6).

The Lord your God will make you abundantly prosperous in all the work of your hand, in the fruit of your body, and in the fruit of your cattle, and in the fruit of your ground; for the Lord will again take delight in prospering you, as he took delight in your fathers, if you obey the voice of the Lord your God, to keep his commandments and his statutes which are written in this book of the law, if you turn to the Lord your God with all your heart and with all your soul. "For this commandment which I command you this day is not too hard for you, neither is it far off. It is not in heaven, that you should say, 'Who will go up for us to heaven, and bring it to us, that we may hear it and do it?' Neither is it beyond the sea, that you should say, 'Who will go over the sea for us, and bring it to us, that we may hear it and do it?' But the word is very near you; it is in your mouth and in your heart, so that you can do it. (Deut 30:9-14)

… thus making it my ambition to preach the gospel, not where Christ has already been *named*, lest I build on another man's foundation. (Rom 15:20; italics mine)

O foolish Galatians! Who has bewitched you, before whose eyes Jesus Christ was publicly portrayed (*proegraphē*, whose literal meaning is "was written in front of you") as crucified? (Gal 3:1; italics mine)

My little children, with whom I am *again in travail* until Christ be *formed* (*morphōthē*, whose literal meaning is "is made to take form, shape") among[27] you! I could wish to be present with you now and to *change my tone* (which can be done only when people are hearing an oral presentation), for I am perplexed about you. (Gal 4:19-20; italics mine)

That is why his worship is also *logic-al*: "I appeal to you therefore, brethren, by the mercies of God, to present your bodies as a living sacrifice, holy and acceptable to God, which is

---

[27] RSV has "in."

your *logic-al* worship (*logikēn latreian*)." (Rom 12:1) And this worship consists not in speaking to or with him, but rather in hearing his word repeatedly throughout the year as consigned in writing "in many and various ways" (Heb 1:1) since the divine word addressed to one church is valid for all:

Therefore I sent to you Timothy, my beloved and faithful child in the Lord, to remind you of my ways in Christ, as I teach them everywhere in every church. (1 Cor 4:17)

This is my rule in all the churches. (1 Cor 7:17)

And when this letter has been read among you, have it read also in the church of the Laodiceans; and see that you read also the letter from Laodicea. (Col 4:16)

To each of the seven churches it is said: "He who has an ear, let him hear what the Spirit says to the churches." (Rev 2:7, 11, 17, 29; 3:6, 13, 22)

And all the churches shall know that I am he who searches mind and heart, and I will give to each of you as your works deserve. (Rev 2:23)

Even more, the New Testament scriptural word is valid for all upcoming generations (And what I say to you I say to all; Mk 13:37) just as the Old Testament scriptural word is (Deut 4:9-10; 6:7-8; 11:19).

Authorship in the Ancient World

When ancient authors published or circulated their writings, many of them did so without attaching their own names or identifying themselves as authors.[28] For the vast majority of

---

[28] For further information, see Kurt Aland, "The Problem of Anonymity and Pseudonymity in Christian Literature of the First Two Centuries," in *The Authorship and Integrity of the New Testament* (London: SPCK, 1965), 1-13; Bruce Metzger,

literary compositions from the ancient Near East and from Greco-Roman antiquity, the names of the authors are simply not explicit. In some cases, the names are left out and the question of authorship is left aside. In others, the works are attributed to well-known figures who did not write them; for example, David and many of the psalms or Solomon and the proverbs. Pseudonymity, or the attribution of "false" names to specific compositions, was exceedingly common in the ancient world. As one scholar has suggested, what must be explained is not the use of false names but rather the reverse: "we need an explanation when the real author gives his name."[29]

Pseudonymity in the ancient world, then, must not be understood as a form of intellectual or personal dishonesty. It was simply part of a conception of authorship that was focused not on the identity of the individual writer but rather on the teacher or school of thought which inspired or instructed him. The individual composition, then, drew its distinctiveness not from the one writing but rather from the traditional authority that the author was writing to explain, defend, or transmit. Many ancient writers, such as those whose works comprise the Bible, did not write out of personal initiative in order to express idiosyncratic beliefs. Rather, they worked in order to set down in writing the teachings of their masters (Baruch and Jeremiah),[30] to locate their particular contribution within a larger tradition (Qoheleth[31] and Solomon), and to honor their masters in a way

---

"Literary Forgeries and Canonical Pseudepigrapha," *Journal of Biblical Literature*, volume 91, no. 1 (March 1972), 3-24; and James Charlesworth, "Pseudonymity and Pseudepigraphy," *Anchor Bible Dictionary* V:540-541.

[29] Aland, *op.cit.* 8.

[30] See especially Jer 36.

[31] The Book of Ecclesiastes.

that, at the same time, conveyed the nature of their "schools of thought" (Plato and Socrates). In this way, authorship was fundamentally a traditional activity.

The Lukan Production

Luke was the major person behind the development of the New Testament. First and foremost he expanded the Gospel of Mark into a major two-volume *magnum opus*. In so doing he hit two birds with one stone. On the one hand, he, the official scriptural voice of Paul, sealed the work of his predecessor Mark as the prototype of any Gospel. On the other hand, he linked forever in the mind of the church Peter (the repentant) and Paul as the Apostles of (the) one (Pauline) gospel, as Paul himself stressed in Galatians 2:7-8. Luke's endeavor is at his clearest in Acts. There we encounter not only a Peter who was spearheading the preaching of the gospel of the Spirit championed by Paul (chs.2-12), but also a Peter who actually championed this cause at the Jerusalem meeting (15:7-11)! However, the basic perspective is maintained: Peter was active in Palestine, the domain of the circumcision, whereas Paul carried the gospel message throughout the confines of the Roman empire and even into Rome itself (chs.13-28).

Upon reading Acts one cannot help but notice that all the churches mentioned therein, where Paul had extensive activity, are those that are recipients of a Pauline letter: Rome, Corinth, Galatia, Ephesus, Philippi, and Thessalonica. The conclusion is clear: there is a close connection between the production of Acts and that of those letters. I discussed Galatians earlier and showed that, most probably, it was the work of Paul and intended as a circular to all the churches of that region. I also showed that most of the other letters built on that letter's premise and content, and that they were probably written in Ephesus, which is, for all intents and purposes, clearly the case for the Corinthian correspondence. Looking closely at the latter, one finds a recurrent motif: Paul is always sending one of his helpers to represent him or speaking of his personal visit as a very remote possibility. This gives the distinct impression that he himself is either not intending or incapable to come himself. Turning to the other letters, one finds the same motif not only in those to Philippi and Ephesus (and Colossae, for that matter) where Paul is writing from prison, but also in those addressed to the Romans and the Thessalonians. Considering that this motif is absent from Galatians, one wonders if it is not actually a literary motif triggered by the fact that Paul was no more alive. The following cumulative argument seems to indicate that this was actually the case and that he most probably died in Ephesus.

First and foremost, as I mentioned earlier, Paul's farewell to the elders of Ephesus in Acts is the beginning of a journey without return (20:16-38), which is confirmed later in that Paul's story ends with his being under house arrest in Rome awaiting either his eventual death or the kingdom, at the end of the book: "And he lived there two whole years at his own expense, and welcomed all who came to him, preaching the kingdom of God and teaching about the Lord Jesus Christ quite openly and unhindered." (28:30-31) Just before the farewell speech to the elders of Ephesus we hear that Paul had just come back to Troas from Philippi (20:5-6), which means that he completed his apostolic journey in the land of the Hellenes, that is, in fully Gentile land, which journey started at Troas where he was called to go to Philippi (16:7-12), the place of the "beginning of the gospel (to the Gentiles)" (Phil 4:15). Troas is mentioned in Acts only at 16:8, 11 and 20:5, 6, and in 2

Corinthians 1:12 we hear that "When I came to Troas to preach the gospel of Christ, a door was opened for me in the Lord." The journey is complete and Paul is ready to depart. Indeed, not only are we told that "Paul had decided to sail past Ephesus, so that he might not have to spend time in Asia; for he was hastening to be at Jerusalem, if possible, on the day of Pentecost" (Acts 20:16) but we also find a setting and a terminology that are reminiscent of those connected with Jesus' death: a Eucharistic meal at night (v.11) in conjunction with the time of Unleavened Bread (v.6), at the end of which "he knelt down and prayed with them all" (v.36; see also "and kneeling down on the beach we prayed and bade one another farewell" in 21:5), and followed by a journey to Jerusalem in order "to die at Jerusalem for the name of the Lord Jesus" (21:13), which was nevertheless undertaken because it was God's will: "And when he would not be persuaded, we ceased and said, 'The will of the Lord be done.'" (v.14)[32] What is compelling about the preceding is that the same kind of specific terminology is linked in Luke-Acts only to the demise of Peter (ch.12) as well as the death of Stephen (ch.7).[33]

If then the Pauline letters to churches, except for Galatians, were written after Paul's death, then the most viable candidate would be the person who wrote Acts, Luke. Indeed, Acts tells us that every church that Paul established would have been honored with a written "gospel" just as the churches of Galatia were. In so doing Luke will have sealed as scripture the teaching of Paul "in all the churches" throughout the entire area of his apostolic activity. In order to do, he resorted to literary devices. The first

---

[32] Compare with Lk 22:42.

[33] Acts 7:60 for "kneeling down" and 12:3 for the mention of the Feast of Unleavened Bread.

was to say that Paul preached the word of God in all parts of the empire and that his teaching was the same:

> Jesus Christ our Lord, through whom we have received grace and apostleship to bring about the obedience of faith for the sake of his name among *all* (*pasin*) the nations, including yourselves who are called to belong to Jesus Christ. (Rom 1:4-6; italics mine)

> But now, since I no longer have *any room* (*mēketi topon*; any place) for work in these regions, and since I have longed for many years to come to you, I hope to see you in passing as I go to Spain, and to be sped on my journey there by you, once I have enjoyed your company for a little. (15:23-24; italics mine)

> Therefore I sent to you Timothy, my beloved and faithful child in the Lord, to remind you of my ways in Christ, as I teach them *everywhere* (*pantakhou*) in every (*pasē*) church ... This is my rule in *all* (*pasais*) the churches. (1 Cor 4:17; 7:17; italics mine)

> When I came to Troas to preach the gospel of Christ, a door was opened for me in the Lord; but my mind could not rest because I did not find my brother Titus there. So I took leave of them and went on to Macedonia. But thanks be to God, who in Christ always leads us in triumph, and through us spreads the fragrance of the knowledge of him everywhere (*en panti topō*). (2 Cor 2:12-14)

> For not only has the word of the Lord sounded forth from you in Macedonia and Achaia, but your faith in God has gone forth everywhere (*en panti topō*), so that we need not say anything. (1 Thess 1:8)

This device made it so that the teaching of any letter was "valid" in any of the churches. This intention is corroborated in the more direct literary request: "And when this letter has been read among you, have it read also in the church of the Laodiceans;

and see that you read also the letter from Laodicea." (Col 4:16)[34]
In 1 Corinthians we have the ultimate step taken to the effect
that this epistle is literarily conceived not only as a circular to the
many churches of the same area, as Galatians was, but actually as
an outright "universal" letter: "To the church of God which is at
Corinth, to those sanctified in Christ Jesus, called to be saints
together with all those who in every place (*en panti topō*) call on the
name of our Lord Jesus Christ, both their Lord and ours." (1
Cor 1:2)

All the preceding sheds a light on the overall device of the
Pauline corpus itself: the choice of the addressee churches. Each
of Corinth and Thessalonica, the capitals of Achaia and
Macedonia, the two main Hellene—and thus quintessentially
Gentile—provinces, are singled out as the recipients of two
letters from the Apostle. The importance of these two provinces
in the Pauline literature as representative of the Gentiles can be
seen in (a) the frequency of their mention, especially Macedonia;
(b) that they are often mentioned together; and (c) the fact that
they are intimately connected with "the collection for the poor"
which was part of the Jerusalem agreement concerning the gospel
as we read in Galatians 2:10. That their status as capitals is of
import can be clearly seen in the following address: "To the
church of God which is at Corinth, with all the saints who are in
the whole of Achaia." (2 Cor 1:1) On the other hand, one can
easily detect the importance of Macedonia specifically in the fact
that it was honored with a letter addressed to another city in it,
Philippi. This is due to the fact that it is the land of the Gentile

---

[34] That the request is a mere literary device can be gathered from the fact that we have
no letter to the Laodiceans in the canon. To say that the letter was lost is an easy cop-
out since the books of the New Testament were kept by the Pauline school that
produced them. See more on this below.

Alexander who conquered Asia Minor and Syria with sword and full armor, and now the Apostle to Alexander's Gentiles is returning the favor with "the word of God," which is "the gospel of peace" and "the sword of the Spirit":

> Therefore take the whole armor of God, that you may be able to withstand in the evil day, and having done all, to stand. Stand therefore, having girded your loins with truth, and having put on the breastplate of righteousness, and having shod your feet with the equipment of the gospel of peace; besides all these, taking the shield of faith, with which you can quench all the flaming darts of the evil one. And take the helmet of salvation, and the sword of the Spirit, which is the word of God. (Eph 6:13-17)

Indeed, "the beginning of the gospel" is linked to the apostolic mission to Philippi (Phil 4:15), the city of Philip, the father of Alexander, which mission brought the message of peace of God, the Father of Jesus Christ.

From this perspective the choice of the remaining three cities can be easily explained. Just as the provinces Macedonia and Achaia were assigned two letters each, so was the province Asia, the base of Paul and his followers. Ephesus and Colossae lie in that province. Ephesus was honored with the letter that is recognized as the compendium of all the other ones. Moreover, according to many important manuscripts, the phrase "in Ephesus" in the letter's address is omitted after "To the saints"; RSV, which follows these manuscripts has: "Paul, an apostle of Christ Jesus by the will of God, to the saints who are also faithful in Christ Jesus." (Eph 1:1) Consequently it was either recognized (if one follows the reading that includes "in Ephesus") or intended (if one considers its omission original) as indeed a universal letter. And if so, then it leaves no room for a second letter to that same city as was the case with Thessalonica and

Corinth. Hence, the other letter to that province was addressed to Colossae. But why that particular city?

Since, unlike the other cities addressed, Colossae occurs only in Colossians 1:1 in the entire New Testament, the most probable explanation is that it was intended metaphorically and thus chosen because of that name's connotation: the Colossus of Rhodes, built at the entrance of the harbor in honor of the deity Helios, the Sun. Given Rome's maritime power and the expanse of the cult of Mithra, the sun god, who was heavily honored in Rome and throughout the empire especially among the soldiers, Colossae was meant to be a stand-in for Rome itself. Another indication of the link between Colossians and Romans is that, according to the New Testament data, these two epistles are addressed to churches Paul had not established nor had previous contacts with. The letter's extolling of Christ over and above any power, heavenly as well as earthly, corroborates my reading. In spite of God's Christ's having been crucified (Col 1:20) by the Roman authorities and of God's ambassador's being fettered (4:18) in a Roman jail, "He [God] disarmed the principalities and powers and made a public example of them, triumphing over them in him [Christ]" (2:15) and "To them [his saints] God chose to make known how great among the Gentiles are the riches of the glory of this mystery, which is Christ among you,[35] the hope of glory" (1:27).

Rome is the capital of the empire and was honored with the most important letter, an expanded version of the one and only "gospel" as laid down for the ages in the epistle to the Galatians. Indeed it is the gospel as inscribed in the holy scriptures (Rom 1:2); that is why it is offered to the Jew—who

---

[35] RSV has "in you."

has the priority because he is "entrusted with the oracles of God" (*ta logia tou theou*; 3:1)—first, but also to the Gentile (1:16), since the scriptural God is the God not only of the Jews, but also of the Gentiles (3:29-30). Moreover this gospel's Apostle is Paul who was specifically assigned for this mission:

> Paul, a servant of Jesus Christ, called to be an apostle, set apart for the gospel of God which he promised beforehand through his prophets in the holy scriptures the gospel concerning his Son ... Jesus Christ our Lord, through whom we have received grace and apostleship to bring about the obedience of faith for the sake of his name among all the nations, including yourselves [citizens of Rome] who are called to belong to Jesus Christ. (1:1-6)

Romans and the Case for the Lukan Production

The probability that the Pauline epistolary collection was Luke's production can be seen at its clearest in the case of Romans. The notorious "abrupt" ending of Acts has puzzled exegetes for centuries and many solutions have been offered. A closer look at this ending, however, will show that it is an introduction to Romans just as the ending of Luke is an introduction to Acts:

> When they had appointed a day for him, they came to him at his lodging in great numbers. And he expounded the matter to them from morning till evening, testifying to the kingdom of God and trying to convince them about Jesus both from the law of Moses and from the prophets. And some were convinced by what he said, while others disbelieved. So, as they disagreed among themselves, they departed, after Paul had made one statement: "The Holy Spirit was right in saying to your fathers through Isaiah the prophet: 'Go to this people, and say, You shall indeed hear but never understand, and you shall indeed see but never perceive. For this people's heart has grown dull, and their ears are heavy of hearing, and their eyes they have closed; lest they should perceive

with their eyes, and hear with their ears, and understand with their heart, and turn for me to heal them.' Let it be known to you then that this salvation of God has been sent to the Gentiles; they will listen." And he lived there two whole years at his own expense, and welcomed all who came to him, preaching the kingdom of God and teaching about the Lord Jesus Christ quite openly and unhindered. (Acts 28:23-31)

This ending is a blueprint of Romans as to both structure and terminology. We are told that Paul tried first to convince the Jews of Rome of his teaching regarding the kingdom of God, and about Jesus from the Law and the Prophets, a teaching which brings about God's salvation on the condition that the recipients believe. Further, we are told that the Jews' refusal prompted him to address the Gentiles of Rome with the same. The thesis of the letter addressed to those in Rome (Rom 1:16) fully corresponds to this scheme: "the gospel, (which he [God] promised beforehand through his prophets in the holy scriptures, concerning his Son [1:2-3]) is the power of God for salvation to every one who has faith, to the Jew first and also to the Greek." Later, after the exposition of that gospel on the basis of God's word in scripture (1:18-8:39), we see in chs.9-11 this pattern developed in detail again according to the same scriptural word. The correspondence in terminology is as impressive; compare the following: (a) "testifying (*diamartyromenos*) … both from the law of Moses and from the prophets" in Acts with "But now the righteousness of God has been manifested apart from law, although the law and the prophets bear witness (*martyroumenē*) to it, the righteousness of God through faith in Jesus Christ for all who believe" (Rom 3:21-22); (b) "And some were convinced (*epeithonto*) by what he said, while others disbelieved (*ēpistoun*)" with "but for those who are factious and do not obey (*apeithousin*) the truth, but obey (*peithomenois*) wickedness, there

will be wrath and fury" (Rom 2:8) and "Then what advantage
has the Jew? Or what is the value of circumcision? Much in every
way. To begin with, the Jews are entrusted with the oracles of
God. What if some were unfaithful (*ēpistēsan*)? Does their
faithlessness (*apistia*) nullify the faithfulness (*pistin*) of God?"
(3:1-3); (c) Paul's statement after the Jews' refusal "Let it be
known to you then that this salvation (*sōtērion*) of God has been
sent (*apestalē*) to the Gentiles; they will listen (*akousontai*)" with
"Brethren, my heart's desire and prayer to God for them [the
Jews] is that they may be saved (*eis sōtērian*)" (Rom 10:1); "So I
ask, have they [the Jews] stumbled so as to fall? By no means!
But through their trespass salvation (*sōtēria*) has come to the
Gentiles, so as to make Israel jealous" (11:11); and "But how are
men to call upon him in whom they have not believed? And how
are they to believe in him of whom they have never heard
(*ēkousan*)? And how are they to hear (*akousōsin*) without a
preacher? And how can men preach unless they are sent
(*apostalōsin*)?" (10:14-15).

On the other hand, Romans is the only letter that combines
two striking features: it is addressed to a city where Paul has not
yet been and it is written in a way that gives the impression to its
hearers that Paul's planned upcoming visit is highly
improbable.[36] Actually it is built on this premise since the
reference to the planned and so much wished for visit form a
literary *inclusio* for the entire letter, which begins with this
literary *topos* (Rom 1:11-15) and ends with it (15:22-32).
Consequently, Romans clearly gives the impression that it was
written as a full-fledged *gospel* to all Romans of the empire in the

---

[36] To be sure, Colossians, which is also addressed to a city Paul had never visited, is
written from jail, but at no point does Paul express his wish or plan to visit that church
as he does so frequently in Romans.

name of the apostle to the Gentiles *because* he was not able to
come and visit in person, that is, because he was dead; notice
how, unlike Ephesians, Philippians, and Colossians, Paul is not
said to be in prison. That the letter was a farewell speech to all
Gentile believers in the empire can be seen from the otherwise
unexplainable ch.16, which includes greetings from all the
Pauline churches of the eastern part of the empire. In other
words, it is, according to Luke, the teaching Paul was
expounding in Acts 28:30-31. This farewell letter corresponds to
the farewell speech to the Ephesians in Acts 17, which would
explain why the letter to the Ephesians, Paul's headquarters, is
formulated as the compendium of all Pauline correspondence as
well as why a few major manuscripts have omitted the reading
"in Ephesus." This omission would make of this letter a circular
"To the saints who are also (*agiois tois ousin kai*) faithful in
Christ Jesus" (Eph 1:1) throughout the Roman empire or, more
specifically, to each of the Pauline communities in that empire
since the Greek *tois ousin* (who are) before *kai* (and) requires a
location and is thus strange before *kai* which the RSV had to
translate as "also" to smoothen the English. Compare with the
parallel simpler phrase in Colossians "To the saints *and* faithful
brethren (*agiois kai pistois adelphois*) in Christ at Colossae" (Col
1:2).

Hebrews

Luke wrote this letter to the Pauline communities of the East at
Timothy's death, as a counterpart of that to the Romans. This is
hinted to in the letter's ending where both Timothy and Italy are
suddenly mentioned for the first and only time: "You should
understand that our brother Timothy has been released, with
whom I shall see you if he comes soon (*takhion*). Greet all your

leaders and all the saints. Those who come from Italy[37] send you greetings." (Heb 13:23-24) Timothy's "release" before his possible "coming soon" seems to refer to his death since Paul, the assumed author, links Timothy's visit to the addressees with his own. But earlier Paul writes: "I urge you the more earnestly to do this in order that I may be restored (*apokatastathō*) to you the sooner (*takhion*)."[38] (v.19) In between the two passages Paul commits his hearers to "the God of peace who brought again from the dead our Lord Jesus, the great shepherd of the sheep, by the blood of the eternal covenant" (v.20). The sudden mention of both "shepherd" and "sheep" (*probatōn*)—both only here in the letter[39]—brings to mind Paul's farewell speech to the elders of Ephesus in Acts 20:28-29 (Take heed to yourselves and to all the flock, in which the Holy Spirit has made you overseers, to care for the church of God which he obtained with the blood of his own Son. I know that after my departure fierce wolves will come in among you, not sparing the flock) which I showed to be a prelude to the Apostle's death.[40] On the other hand, Hebrews' thesis parallels that of Stephen's speech in Acts 7, at the end of which Stephen was "cast out of the city and stoned" (v.58). This same point is brought up for the first time no less than three times at the end of Hebrews:

> For the bodies of those animals whose blood is brought into the sanctuary by the high priest as a sacrifice for sin are burned outside the camp. So Jesus also suffered outside the gate in order to sanctify the people through his own blood. Therefore let us go

---

[37] The original has "those who are from Italy."

[38] These are the only instances of the adverb *takhion* in Hebrews.

[39] The original has *aigeiois* for "sheep" in Heb 11:37.

[40] See *New Testament Introduction, Volume 2: Luke and Acts* (Crestwood, NY: St Vladimir's Press, 2001), 259; hereinafter referred to as *NTI₂*.

forth to him outside the camp and bear the abuse he endured. (Heb 13:11-13)

In turn this example of Christ "outside the walls" is to be followed by all: "For here we have no lasting city, but we seek the city which is to come." (v.14) Indeed, the believers are to remain, as their forbearers were, "strangers and exiles on the earth" (11:13) since, as Paul taught right from the beginning, "the Jerusalem above is free, and she is our mother" and "we, brethren, like Isaac, are children of *promise*" (Gal 4:26, 28)[41]. In other words, we are to walk according to God's will until he comes.

The intention of both Romans and Hebrews is to present the Lukan thesis that the church is not an anti-Roman "revolutionary" movement as that of the Jewish zealots who brought about the destruction of Jerusalem and, in spite of its adherence to a message of liberation for all, it is nonetheless bound to the gospel of peace. Being addressed to the Christians living in the western part of the empire, the language of Romans is appropriately legal; it revolves around the notion of righteousness. Hebrews, on the other hand, being addressed to those living on the shores of the Eastern Mediterranean, is cast in a Platonic-Philonic language befitting the cities of Alexandria and Antioch, the domain of Alexander of Macedon. Addressing himself to the Christians living in the domain of the Jewish

---

[41] See also "our commonwealth is in heaven, and from it we await a Savior, the Lord Jesus Christ, who will change our lowly body to be like his glorious body, by the power which enables him even to subject all things to himself." (Phil 3:20-21).

diaspora, Luke imitated its language which was influenced by Philo.[42]

The Pastoral Epistles

This last corpus of Lukan literature is dedicated to the sealing of the Pauline legacy into a scriptural canon. The epistles are addressed in Paul's name to two of his earliest helpers, the Jew Timothy and the Gentile Titus, as bishops. As expected, Timothy, Paul's official heir (Phil 2:19-22), is the bishop of Ephesus, the Pauline headquarters, and is honored with a letter that functions as Paul's testament:

> As for you, always be steady, endure suffering, do the work of an evangelist, fulfill your ministry. For I am already on the point of being sacrificed; the time of my departure has come. I have fought the good fight, I have finished the race, I have kept the faith. Henceforth there is laid up for me the crown of righteousness, which the Lord, the righteous judge, will award to me on that Day, and not only to me but also to all who have loved his appearing. (2 Tim 4:5-8).

Titus, who is among those who ended deserting Paul,[43] is the bishop of Crete and, as such, relegated to God's judgment. The Greek *Krētēs* is very close to *kritēs* (judge) and both practically sound the same.

One of the most striking features of these epistles is the use of "deposit" (*parathēkē*) instead of "tradition" (*paradosis*) to speak of the gospel message. This shift entails that the churches, including

---

[42] Luke's versatility in using varied literary styles, corresponding to the setting he is dealing with, can be easily seen in his magisterial Luke-Acts.

[43] "For Demas, in love with this present world, has deserted me and gone to Thessalonica; Crescens has gone to Galatia, Titus to Dalmatia. Luke alone is with me." (2 Tim 4:10-11a)

the bishops, are under the authority of the apostolic teaching laid down in writing once and for all in the writings of the New Testament. The "apostolic tradition" is, by definition, the Apostle's teaching which his disciples are to *keep* and not surmise on.

3

The Formation of the New Testament Canon

Was the Old Testament Canon Planned or Haphazard?

Looking at the Old Testament one cannot miss noticing the importance of certain numbers in the overall structure of the Hebrew canon. The Torah is comprised of five books. The Prophets are divided into two sets of four books each: the Prior Prophets (Joshua, Judges, Samuel, Kings) and the Latter Prophets (Isaiah, Jeremiah, Ezekiel, the scroll of the twelve prophets). The *Ketubim* or Writings are made of twelve units (Psalms, Job, Proverbs, Ruth, Song of Songs, Ecclesiastes, Lamentations, Esther, Daniel, Ezra, Nehemiah, Chronicles). The numeral twelve is obviously related to that of the twelve tribes constituting the biblical Israel.

The prologue to the Wisdom of Sirach (Ecclesiasticus), which is the earliest text referring and giving importance to the tripartite structure of the Old Testament, reads thus:

Whereas many great teachings have been given to us through the law and the prophets and the others that followed them, on account of which we should praise Israel for instruction and wisdom; and since it is necessary not only that the readers themselves should acquire understanding but also that those who love learning should be able to help the outsiders by both speaking and writing, my grandfather Jesus, after devoting himself especially to the reading of the law and the prophets and the other books of our fathers, and after acquiring considerable proficiency in them, was himself also led to write something pertaining to instruction and wisdom, in order that, by becoming conversant with this also, those who love learning should make even greater progress in living according to the law.

You are urged therefore to read with good will and attention, and to be indulgent in cases where, despite our diligent labor in translating, we may seem to have rendered some phrases imperfectly. For what was originally expressed in Hebrew does not have exactly the same sense when translated into another language. Not only this work, but even the law itself, the prophecies, and the rest of the books differ not a little as originally expressed.

When I came to Egypt in the thirty-eighth year of the reign of Euergetes and stayed for some time, I found opportunity for no little instruction. It seemed highly necessary that I should myself devote some pains and labor to the translation of the following book, using in that period of time great watchfulness and skill in order to complete and publish the book for those living abroad who wished to gain learning, being prepared in character to live according to the law.

Besides recognizing the tripartite division, the prologue reflects other important features relating to this division. First, there is a fixed order: Law, Prophets and the Other Books (§1, 2 and 3). Secondly, this order clearly reflects some kind of hierarchy, more specifically the primary value of the Law, since the ultimate aim of the instruction and wisdom contained in all three parts is "living according to the law" (§1 and 3). Thirdly, Israel is to be praised (§1) not for having produced the scriptures, rather for having been entrusted with them. As Psalm 78 and Romans aptly make it clear, Israel actually is not only the addressee, but actually the disobedient culprit: "Then what advantage has the Jew? Or what is the value of circumcision? Much in every way. To begin with, the Jews are entrusted with the oracles of God.

What if some were unfaithful? Does their faithlessness nullify the
faithfulness of God? By no means!" (Rom 3:1-4) Indeed, the
Jews are as sinful as the Gentiles: "What then? Are we Jews any
better off? No, not at all; for I have already charged that all men,
both Jews and Greeks, are under the power of sin, as it is written:
'None is righteous, no, not one; no one understands, no one
seeks for God.'" (vv.9-11) The preceding remarks are
corroborated in a fourth feature of the prologue: the scriptures
are for wisdom and instruction not only for the "outsiders" (§1)
but for "those (among the Jews) living abroad" (§3); after all, the
primary aim of the translation from Hebrew into Greek is to
reach the Jews living in Egypt (§3). The reason is that the
biblical Israel is always the one about to be gathered by God
from its dispersion brought about by its disobedience.[1] And
along with those who have been scattered among the nations and
have become like them, the nations themselves are brought into
God's eternal city on his holy mountain:

> For I know their works and their thoughts, and I am coming to
> gather all nations and tongues; and they shall come and shall see
> my glory, and I will set a sign among them. And from them I will
> send survivors to the nations, to Tarshish, Put, and Lud, who draw

---

[1] See, e.g., with Ezekiel: "What is in your mind shall never happen—the thought, 'Let
us be like the nations, like the tribes of the countries, and worship wood and stone.' As
I live, says the Lord God, surely with a mighty hand and an outstretched arm, and
with wrath poured out, I will be king over you. I will bring you out from the peoples
and gather you out of the countries where you are scattered, with a mighty hand and
an outstretched arm, and with wrath poured out ... For on my holy mountain, the
mountain height of Israel, says the Lord God, there all the house of Israel, all of them,
shall serve me in the land; there I will accept them, and there I will require your
contributions and the choicest of your gifts, with all your sacred offerings. As a
pleasing odor I will accept you, when I bring you out from the peoples, and gather you
out of the countries where you have been scattered; and I will manifest my holiness
among you in the sight of the nations." (20:32-24, 40-41)

the bow, to Tubal and Javan, to the coastlands afar off, that have
not heard my fame or seen my glory; and they shall declare my
glory among the nations. And they shall bring all your brethren
from all the nations as an offering to the Lord, upon horses, and in
chariots, and in litters, and upon mules, and upon dromedaries, to
my holy mountain Jerusalem, says the Lord, just as the Israelites
bring their cereal offering in a clean vessel to the house of the
Lord. And some of them also I will take for priests and for Levites,
says the Lord. (Is 66:18-21)

Moreover the ultimate aim of God's salvation is for those whom
he saves to become his people (and he their God) by living
according to his law:

Therefore say, "Thus says the Lord God: I will gather you from
the peoples, and assemble you out of the countries where you have
been scattered, and I will give you the land of Israel." And when
they come there, they will remove from it all its detestable things
and all its abominations. And I will give them one heart, and put a
new spirit within them; I will take the stony heart out of their flesh
and give them a heart of flesh, that they may walk in my statutes
and keep my ordinances and obey them; and they shall be my
people, and I will be their God. (Ezek 11:17-20)

For I will take you from the nations, and gather you from all the
countries, and bring you into your own land. I will sprinkle clean
water upon you, and you shall be clean from all your
uncleannesses, and from all your idols I will cleanse you. A new
heart I will give you, and a new spirit I will put within you; and I
will take out of your flesh the heart of stone and give you a heart
of flesh. And I will put my spirit within you, and cause you to
walk in my statutes and be careful to observe my ordinances. You
shall dwell in the land which I gave to your fathers; and you shall
be my people, and I will be your God. (36:24-28)

It stands to reason, then, to consider together with Sirach's translator that the Writings, twelve in number, function as an invitation to the twelve scattered tribes—and together with them all nations—to return to the God of the Law via the call of the Prophets. This intention is underlined by the fact that, when working one's way from the Writings to the Law, the hearer is faced with the scroll of the twelve prophets.[2]

But what about the numerals four and five, being the basis for the structure of the Prophets and the Law, respectively? Four represents the four directions of the human universe. Consequently, the intention behind the Prophets diptych made of two sets of four books each seems to underscore as well as corroborate my conclusion regarding the use of the numeral twelve. The Prior Prophets is the story of the scattering of the stubbornly disobedient and sinful Israel to the four corners of the universe, the world of the nations (Gen 9-10). The Latter Prophets comprise the indictment of Israel together with the nations, followed by the divine promise to both to be brought back through mere divine compassion into the Noachic covenant that encompasses all mankind (Gen 9), which will be implemented in God's new Jerusalem:

Sing, O barren one, who did not bear; break forth into singing and cry aloud, you who have not been in travail! For the children of the desolate one will be more than the children of her that is married, says the Lord. Enlarge the place of your tent, and let the curtains of your habitations be stretched out; hold not back, lengthen your cords and strengthen your stakes ... For this is like the days of Noah to me: as I swore that the waters of Noah should

---

[2] God's care for *all* Israel, represented through the numeral twelve, is also found in the book of Judges.

no more go over the earth, so I have sworn that I will not be angry with you and will not rebuke you. For the mountains may depart and the hills be removed, but my steadfast love shall not depart from you, and my covenant of peace shall not be removed, says the Lord, who has compassion on you. (Is 54:1-2, 9-10)

As for the Law, it is God's will in the face of the entire world. It is his power expressed through his hand, with its five fingers, with which he saved his people from Pharaoh's hand (Ex 8:19 [finger]; 15:6-12 [hand]; 18:9-11 [hand]) and with which he wrote his law (31:18 [finger]; Deut 9:10 [finger]). Both hand and finger are metaphors for God's power with which he strikes and corrects his people as well as saves them. Thus the numeral five for the Torah is reflective of God's full power, full hand, and is set up over and against the numeral four, reflective of the human universe.

How About the New Testament?

Given, then, that scripture is also a matter of form and not just content, if not basically a matter of form and structure,[3] one would expect that the school that produced and then collected the New Testament writings into a canon had a similar definite plan in mind. To imagine that the canon was the product of a later decision made by some "believers" is not only preposterous, but also actually contradicts the scriptural teaching itself (Jer 36). Indeed, these "believers" would have had to have in hand the text itself in order to take a decision regarding it. But where would they have got it from? From the archives of the church in Corinth or those of the churches of Galatia? Which Galatians in

---

[3] Actually, not only is there no content without form, but understanding the content cannot be done except in the form in which it is handed: a series of texts written in a certain way.

their "right mind" would have preserved as insightful, let alone authoritative, a text that addressed them as "foolish (mindless)" (Gal 3:1)—actually "so foolish (mindless)" (v.3)—and threatened them with anathema if they followed any other teaching even if coming from the other apostles? Which Corinthians in their "right mind" would have cherished and preserved a lengthy text that, from beginning to end, is branding them as "harlots"? Which of Peter's followers would have honored Mark's Gospel and not burned it as Jehoiakim did with Jeremiah's scroll? If the answer is that they repented, then it is the apostolic word as imbedded in the epistle, which would have produced such reaction; consequently, it is the apostolic word, and not their repentance, that is authoritative and the point of reference for any future repentance. If the answer is that they perceived the correctness of the teaching through a revelation from God or their theological insight, then they—and the subsequent "believers"—still stand condemned for their self-righteousness to imagine that they, the "fleshly" babes, can judge the "spiritual" Paul (1 Cor 2:10-3:4). Actually, those who are privy to God's direct revelation or have the divine insight do not need scripture, they can write it themselves! And if so, then why are they worried about scripture at all, let alone exegeting it, in order to found and bolster the correctness of their insight?

The reality is quite different. Just as it is Baruch, Jeremiah's secretary and disciple, who kept the rewritten and edited scroll for the ages (Jer 36:32), and it is Isaiah's disciples who preserved the scroll of his testimony that Israel and Judah refused (Is 8:11-18), so also it is Paul's disciples who kept his correspondence and the Gospels and imposed them on his churches. Whoever later accepted these writings, did so as an authoritative text imposed upon them. Their choice was simply to accept or refuse them, and in no way to appraise their correctness, let alone consider such appraisal as authoritative. One does not choose one's parents, one is produced by them! And scripture is our authoritative parent's word:

> But I, brethren, could not address you as spiritual men, but as men of the flesh, as babes in Christ. I fed you with milk, not solid food; for you were not ready for it; and even yet you are not ready, for you are still of the flesh. (1 Cor 3:1-3)

> I do not write this to make you ashamed, but to admonish you as my beloved children. For though you have countless guides in Christ, you do not have many fathers. For I became your father in Christ Jesus through the gospel. I urge you, then, be imitators of me. Therefore I sent to you Timothy, my beloved and faithful child in the Lord, to remind you of my ways in Christ, as I teach them everywhere in every church. (1 Cor 4:14-17)

> My little children, with whom I am again in travail until Christ be formed in you! (Gal 4:19)

Galatians, Mark, Colossians, and 2 Thessalonians

The letter to the churches of Galatia was conceived as the Pauline gospel in written form, meaning the final authoritative form of the gospel he had preached orally. In other words, this letter was conceived *as* scripture: just as the Law was written by the hand (*en kheiri*) of God's emissary, Moses (3:19), this letter was written by the hand (*en kheiri*) of the Apostle of God (Gal 6:1) making of it the Law of God's eschatological emissary, the messiah (6:2). Already in this letter is planted the seed that will become the thread around which the subsequent literature will build: the gospel is one because it cannot be except one, given that there is one God and one messiah. If some apostles are preaching something else, the reason is not that there are many valid gospels, but rather because they have betrayed the one gospel (1:6-9; 2:1-14). This approach is through and through scriptural as can be seen from the story of Aaron's betrayal and apostasy (Ex 32-34).[4] However, the scriptural story leaves the way of repentance open and reintegrates the fallen so long as they submit to the one and only word of God, the one embedded in scripture itself. This is precisely what Galatians does: after condemning Peter (2:11-14) it relays the content of the gospel (2:15-4:31) and then requires from the addressees to submit unconditionally to it, this being their only way into the kingdom (5:1-6:18).

The Jewish revolutionary war (66-70 A.D.) proved to be an occasion for the testing of the Pauline gospel. Would the apostolic leadership follow the lead of the zealots and use armed revolt against the Romans, or would they follow the gospel of peace and table fellowship, championed by Paul and the Old Testament prophets, leaving the task of vengeance to the Avenger (Rom 12:17-21)? In other words, would one expect God's kingdom or try to "restore the kingdom to Israel" (Acts 1:6) using human agency as many a king of Israel or Judah tried to do? From the perspective of scripture, this question was not to be answered on the basis of the outcome of the war. It was rather to be answered scripturally: to put one's trust in or to refuse God's word *before* the outcome. In this sense the Gospel of Mark functioned as the "prophetic" offer given during the siege of Jerusalem and based on Galatians. It is triggered by the "prophet" John the Baptist's call to repentance and the confession of one's sin (Mk 1:4-5). This John is none else than

---

[4] See also Jer 7:24-26; Ezek 2:3-5; 3:7-9.

John Mark himself who repented by joining the Pauline camp.[5]
He introduces the message of Jesus Christ as taught by Paul in
Galatians: notice the multiple episodes centering around table
fellowship and eating (Mk 2:13-17, 18-22, 23-28; 3:20, 30-44;
7:2, 24-30; 8:1-10, 14-21; 14:3-9, 12-26; compare with Gal
2:11-14) and the centrality of the teaching related to the shame
connected with the cross, which is the stumbling block for Peter
who clearly misunderstands what true messiahship is all about
(Mk 8:27-9:1; compare with Gal 2:15-21). John Mark's appeal
is to invite also Peter to repentance and meet the Christ preached
by Paul in (the) Galilee (of the nations; Mk 16:7) where he
preceded the disciples (14:28) and where all had started (1:9, 14,
16, 28, 39).

This "repentance" of John Mark, which proved to be
momentous in having produced a version of the Pauline gospel
in an epic form for the ages, needed to be introduced and
officially endorsed by the Pauline leadership in order for that
Gospel to become an authoritative reading in the churches. Thus
Colossians was produced, the Pauline charter, itself to be read in
all the churches: "And when this letter has been read among you,
have it read also in the church of the Laodiceans; and see that
you read also the letter from Laodicea." (4:16) Its reliance on
Galatians is evident in the stress on the crucifixion of Christ
(compare Col 1:20 to Gal 1:1 and 6:14-16, and Col 2:13-14 to
Gal 2:18-21) and the equality between Gentile and Jew
(compare Col 3:11 to Gal 3:27-28; 5:6; 6:15). In order to
introduce and endorse the Gospel of Mark, the same Colossians
expanded "all the brethren who are with me" (Gal 1:2) into an
official list of Pauline primary helpers (Col 4:7-17). Among

---

[5] See the Introduction regarding this matter.

these, Mark was integrated as someone related to (the traitor) Barnabas (Gal 2:13), who had repented and was now in the company of Jesus himself, the sole righteous one. Also, Justus, being the Latin for the Greek *dikaios*: "Aristarchus my fellow prisoner greets you, and Mark the cousin of Barnabas (concerning whom you have received instructions—if he comes to you, receive him), and Jesus who is called Justus. These are the only men of the circumcision among my fellow workers for the kingdom of God, and they have been a comfort to me." (Col 4:10-11) At the head of these helpers stands Timothy who is granted the place of honor as Paul's helper par excellence: "Paul, an apostle of Christ Jesus by the will of God, and Timothy our brother." (1:1) The introduction of Timothy and the other helpers was necessary because Paul, if not already dead, was on the way to his end: "I, Paul, write this greeting with my own hand. Remember my fetters. Grace be with you." (4:18)

I strongly believe that 2 Thessalonians was produced at the same time as Colossians which, just as Galatians, is aimed at a church in Asia Minor. Being addressed to the inhabitants of the capital of Macedonia, the land of Alexander and the gateway to the world of the Hellenes, and thus the Gentiles,[6] 2 Thessalonians seals the oneness of the gospel within the Roman empire, beyond the Ionian Sea as well as in Syria and Asia Minor where Judaism traditionally flourished. On the other hand, as the Gospel of Mark did, it underscored the openness of this one gospel to the leaders who were willing to repent. Such was achieved through the inclusion of Silvanus between Paul and Timothy as co-author of the letter (2 Thess 1:2). This Silvanus,

---

[6] *hoi Hellēnes* is, together with *ta ethnē*, the Septuagint translation for *haggoyim* (the nations).

in a Latinized version of the name, is the same as Silas who is
presented as a Jerusalemite leader (Acts 15:22, 27, 32) and Paul's
co-helper strictly in Macedonia (15:40; 16:19-18:5). The fact
that he disappears after Acts 18:5 is an indication that he most
probably split with Paul at that point as John Mark did earlier
(15:38). Still, while in Macedonia, he was a faithful co-worker
and is to be honored as such. The closeness in time between the
Gospel of Mark and 2 Thessalonians can be seen in the handling
of the Lord's coming: in both cases the excitement occasioned by
the Jewish War produced the false teaching of the imminence of
the coming of God's messiah, and in both cases the believers are
prompted not to fall victims to such teaching and to adhere to
that of the one gospel that was from the beginning and remains
unchanged (Mk 13 and 2 Thess 2).

The New Torah

During the testing times of the Jewish War, Mark, Colossians,
and 2 Thessalonians sustained the teaching of God's gospel as
inscribed in Galatians, which is Christ's law to be followed as a
kanōn (rule, Gal 6:16). It stands to reason, then, to imagine that
the Pauline churches, who were bred on scripture, saw in
Jerusalem's fall in 70 A.D. a vindication of the only "true"
apostolic teaching expounded in Galatians (Gal 2:5, 14; 5:7) in
the same way as, in scripture, the earlier fall of Jerusalem in 587
A.D. is presented as a vindication of the teaching of the "true"
Prophets. The connection between these two events is actually
warranted by Paul's teaching in Galatians regarding the two
covenants and the two Jerusalems (4:24-27).

However, the reader of Ezekiel will quickly realize that the
punishment of the recalcitrant Samaria at the hand of the
Assyrians and of the stubborn Jerusalem at the hand of the

Babylonians was not the end of the story. The real danger lying ahead was to submit to the deities of the nations that overcame Jerusalem:

> What is in your mind shall never happen==the thought, "Let us be like the nations, like the tribes of the countries, and worship wood and stone." As I live, says the Lord God, surely with a mighty hand and an outstretched arm, and with wrath poured out, I will be king over you. I will bring you out from the peoples and gather you out of the countries where you are scattered, with a mighty hand and an outstretched arm, and with wrath poured out; and I will bring you into the wilderness of the peoples, and there I will enter into judgment with you face to face. (Ezek 20:32-35)

The fate of the Gentile believers of the Pauline churches was similar at best. Indeed, they were by and large originally Gentile and would find it quite "normal" to slowly slide into submission to another yoke, that of the Romans who actually "liberated" them from the yoke of the earthly Jerusalem (Gal 4:29-5:1). But Paul had forewarned those who were baptized into the one Christ preached by him and have become "Abraham's offspring, heirs according to promise" (3:27-29):

> For you were called to freedom, brethren; only do not use your freedom as an opportunity for the flesh... But I say, walk by the Spirit, and do not gratify the desires of the flesh. For the desires of the flesh are against the Spirit, and the Spirit is[7] against the flesh; for these are opposed to each other, to prevent you from doing what you would. But if you are led by the Spirit you are not under the law. Now the works of the flesh are plain: fornication ... and the like. I warn you, as I warned you before, that those who do

---

[7] RSV has "the desires of the Spirit," which is blatantly incorrect rendition of the original especially in view of the fact that in the preceding verse "desire" is specifically a proclivity of the flesh and is supposed to have been crucified (v.24)

such things shall not inherit the kingdom of God. But the fruit of the Spirit is love ... gentleness ...; against such there is no law. And those who belong to Christ Jesus have crucified the flesh with its passions and desires. If we live by the Spirit, let us also walk by the Spirit. Let us have no self-conceit, no provoking of one another, no envy of one another. Brethren, if a man is overtaken in any trespass, you who are spiritual should restore him in a spirit of gentleness. Look to yourself, lest you too be tempted. Bear one another's burdens, and so fulfill the law of Christ. (5:13-6:2)

Luke-Acts and the Apocalypse

Thus, the Pauline school embarked on a grandiose project that would become the New Torah paralleling the Mosaic Torah. In doing so, it followed the path that produced the latter. The Book of Ezekiel in general, and Ezekiel 20 in particular, is the blueprint of what was to become the Pentateuch, at the heart of which stands Leviticus with its Code of Holiness. Since Israel was in the wilderness and could not have possibly implemented the temple service prescribed in that book,[8] the intention was to challenge the people to understand that this service was the one performed in the heavenly temple (Ex 25:9, 40; 26:30; 27:8; Num 8:4) and nothing less than such could please God when Israel will settle in the earth of the promise. Actually, in order that Leviticus be *imposed* on Israel,[9] it was handed down to the people after they were brought out of Egypt and before they entered Canaan. Before it we have the Book of Exodus and after it, the Book of Numbers. The former underscores the fact that it

---

[8] The prescribed offerings assumed the product of the earth, which is not possible in the wilderness, and the large number of animals that such product would have supported. Add to this the statute of the jubilee year, which is a practical impossibility in actual human life.

[9] Just as later Paul will impose his gospel on the Galatians.

was not Egypt that fed the fledgling Israel, but actually Joseph, who was betrayed by Israel, who sustained both his people and Egypt. To the contrary, Egypt proved to be the oppressor of Israel when "there arose a new king over Egypt, who did not know Joseph" (Ex 1:8) and as the book of Exodus shows, it is actually the God of Joseph who was behind everything: just as he preserved and raised Joseph, he now raises Moses and preserves him. On the other hand, the Book of Numbers pushes the issue further: God is able not only to sustain, but also multiply,[10] his people in the wilderness where there is no bread save God's word.

It is in this vein that the Apocalypse and Luke-Acts were produced. The former describes the heavenly liturgy that takes place in "the temple of the tent of witness" (Rev 15:1) from which God addresses the people in Leviticus (1:1). It is based on Galatians that speaks of the heavenly Jerusalem and expands on the sacrifice of Jesus in Mark, which is introduced with "For the Son of man also came not to be served but to serve, and to give his life as a *ransom (lytron)* for many" (Mk 10:45). Luke-Acts is conceived as a diptych around Revelation in the same way as Exodus and Numbers envelop Leviticus. The parallelism is clearly intended. On the one hand, Luke is not only based on Mark, but is also built around the notion of redemption that forms an *inclusio*: "Blessed be the Lord God of Israel, for he has visited and redeemed (*epoiēsen lytrōsin*) his people ... And coming up at that very hour she gave thanks to God, and spoke of him to all who were looking for the redemption (*lytrōsin*) of Jerusalem" (1:68; 2:38); "But we had hoped that he was the one

---

[10] In Hebrew the name Joseph is from a root meaning "add, multiply."

to redeem (*lytrousthai*) Israel." (24:21)[11] This redemption is
linked to Exodus as is clear from the only other instance of that
term in Luke-Acts: "This Moses whom they refused, saying,
'Who made you a ruler and a judge?' God sent as both ruler and
deliverer (*lytrōtēn*) by the hand of the angel that appeared to him
in the bush. He led them out, having performed wonders and
signs in Egypt and at the Red Sea, and in the wilderness for forty
years." (Acts 7:35-36) On the other hand, it is only in Luke, in
all of the Gospels, Acts, and Revelation, that we encounter the
term "exodus" (Lk 9:31), where it is applied to the preaching
and death of Jesus in Jerusalem, i.e., in relation to the Markan
lytron. As for Acts, it parallels Numbers in that it shows how the
"first word" of Jesus, which is the Lukan gospel (Acts 1:1), bore
fruit in the Evangelist's "second word," i.e., how the gospel word
"multiplied" and the numbers of the believers grew:

> But many of those who heard the word believed; and the number
> of the men came to about five thousand. (Acts 4:4)

> And the word of God increased; and the number of the disciples
> multiplied greatly in Jerusalem, and a great many of the priests
> were obedient to the faith. (6:7)

> Now those who were scattered went about preaching the word.
> Philip went down to a city of Samaria, and proclaimed to them
> the Christ. And the multitudes with one accord gave heed to what
> was said by Philip, when they heard him and saw the signs which
> he did. (8:4-6)

> Now when they had testified and spoken the word of the Lord,
> they returned to Jerusalem, preaching the gospel to many villages
> of the Samaritans. (8:25)

---

[11] These are the only instances of the root *lytr—* in the Gospels (Mt 20:28 is a mere
copy of Mk 10:45).

But the word of God grew and multiplied. (12:4)

The next sabbath almost the whole city gathered together to hear the word of God. But when the Jews saw the *multitudes*, they were filled with jealousy, and contradicted what was spoken by Paul, and reviled him. And Paul and Barnabas spoke out boldly, saying, "It was necessary that the word of God should be spoken first to you. Since you thrust it from you, and judge yourselves unworthy of eternal life, behold, we turn to the Gentiles. For so the Lord has commanded us, saying, 'I have set you to be a light for the Gentiles, that you may bring salvation to the uttermost parts of the earth.'" And when the Gentiles heard this, they were glad and glorified the word of God; and as *many* as were ordained to eternal life believed. And the word of the Lord spread throughout all the region. (13:44-49; italics mine)

So the word of the Lord grew and prevailed mightily. (19:20)

John

While the Lukan contingent was producing the epistolary literature to all corners of the Roman empire and ensuring, through the Pastorals, that the Pauline legacy become the "deposit" for all subsequent generations, the Markan group did something similar by producing the Johannine literature: the Gospel and the three letters. Just as Moses re-issued the Law in Deuteronomy for the new generation that was not privy to the first promulgation of God's will, so did the old Mark revisit his first Gospel but issuing the same word again, assuring his new readers that that word "was since the beginning" (Jn 1:1) and remains the same as a commandment to be followed (12:49-50; 13:34; 15:12) throughout the generations to come, which is none other than the commandment of love as proclaimed in the original gospel, the letter to the churches of Galatia (Gal 5:13-15). "The truth of the gospel" (Gal 2:5, 14; 5:7), which originates with God himself (1:11-16) still rings loud and clear: "Thy word is truth" (Jn 17:17). Just as Deuteronomy was the *book* (*sepher*) of Moses' *dᵉbarim* (words: Deut 1:1), so John is the *book* (*biblion*; Jn 20:30) of the *logos* (word; Jn 1:1) expressed in Jesus' words (*logoi, rhēmata*) as inscribed in the Gospel:

> Now Jesus did many other signs in the presence of the disciples, which are not *written* in this *book*; but these are *written* that you may believe that Jesus is the Christ, the Son of God, and that believing you may have life in his name. (20:30-31; italics mine)

> This is the disciple who is bearing witness to these things, and who has *written* these things; and we know that his testimony is true. But there are also many other things which Jesus did; were every one of them to be *written*, I suppose that the world itself could not contain the *books* that would be *written*. (21:24-25; italics mine)

In other words, just as in Deuteronomy, whatever is necessary and sufficient for salvation was laid down into a "book," which functions as an unchangeable testament.

Matthew and the Integration of the non-Pauline Leadership into the Canon

The last scroll of the Law to be emulated was the Book of Genesis. This is what the Gospel of Matthew, which entitles itself as *biblos geneseōs* (the book of the genesis of...), does. Just as Genesis introduces the entire Old Testament and forms the basis for its reading, so also Matthew puts its stamp on the entire New Testament production and closes its canon. Whereas the Gospel of John reflects a high level of tension between the Pauline leadership and Paul's opponents in the province Asia, that of Matthew presupposes the full break between Pauline Christianity and Judaism. Being now the *ekklēsia* (Mt 16:18; 18:17), the Christian communities are now the target of God's indictments as well as his blessings; hence the excessive harshness against the insiders, which is reminiscent of Paul's harangues against the believers in his letters, and the stress on the coming kingdom whose realm does not fully coincide with that of the church (13:31-43). Until then, everyone is bound by the following rule: "Think not that I have come to abolish the law and the prophets; I have come not to abolish them but to fulfill them. For truly, I say to you, till heaven and earth pass away, not an iota, not a dot, will pass from the law until all is accomplished." (5:17-18) As for this rule, it will stand with no chance that it would change since "Heaven and earth will pass away, but *my words* will not pass away" (24:35).

In order to underscore the perennial primacy of the Old Testament, the original scripture, and not allow any misunderstanding of Galatians (e.g. as happened later with Marcion) the Pauline leadership integrated at this point in their canon the letter of James that was written in response to Galatians. It functions as a reminder that, before and after all, the gospel is "the law of Christ" (Gal 6:2); it is neither a confession of belief nor a theological formula, but a commandment to be followed, a summons to do God's will rather than to pontificate about him since even the demons are good at that (Jam 2:19). In adopting fully the (counter-)epistle of James into the canon, the Pauline school promoted Paul's teaching in Galatians that there is and can be only one gospel, so long as it is not betrayed as in the case of Barnabas.[12] In this same vein we have the two letters ascribed to Peter. Their content is fully Pauline and thus they function as the legacy of the "true" Peter who is none other than Peter "the penitent" as is

---

[12] See below.

clear from the ending of 2 Peter where the writer not only officially endorses *all* the letters of Paul but also considers them on the same level as the Old Testament scriptures:[13]

> But according to his promise we wait for new heavens and a new earth in which righteousness dwells. Therefore, beloved, since you wait for these, be zealous to be found by him without spot or blemish, and at peace. And count the forbearance of our Lord as salvation. So also our beloved brother Paul wrote to you according to the wisdom given him, speaking of this as he does in all his letters. There are some things in them hard to understand, which the ignorant and unstable twist to their own destruction, as they do the other scriptures. (2 Pt 3:13-16)

As for the letter of Jude, the "brother of James," i.e., the leader of the Jerusalemite church after James, it was received into the canon through the intermediacy of 2 Peter, on which it is based. The Johannine epistles, on the other hand, are the testament of the aging John Mark for both Jews and Gentiles, summing up the gospel of Paul that revolves around the love of the neighbor and the table fellowship around the one word of the one Lord. In those epistles we learn that one of the greatest sins is reneging on one's commitment: "They went out from us, but they were not of us; for if they had been of us, they would have continued with us; but they went out, that it might be plain that they all are not of us." (1 Jn 2:19) This indictment applies in an extreme way to an "apostle" who is supposed to function as the ultimate point of reference for God's gospel: "What then is Apollos?

---

[13] Actually, this passage may well be pointing also to the "other" New Testament scriptures. If so, then the "first" apostle is presented as actually canonizing the entire production of the Pauline school: "This is now the second letter that I have written to you, beloved, and in both of them I have aroused your sincere mind by way of reminder; that you should remember the predictions of the *holy prophets* and the commandment of the Lord and Savior through *your apostles*." (3:1-2)

What is Paul? Servants *through whom you believed,* as the Lord assigned to each." (1 Cor 3:5) Consequently, unlike Peter and James who were actually leaders of Judaism, Barnabas was right from the beginning "apostle to the Gentiles" together with Paul (Gal 2:1, 9),[14] yet he betrayed his calling in Antioch (2:13). His fate was that he would not appear at all as the author of any canonical writing.

With Matthew then we have come to the end of a full circle. The gospel genre started with Mark and now Matthew practically canonizes its predecessor as *the* Gospel. Indeed, Matthew follows Mark structurally and materially more closely than either Luke or John. Mark, as I indicated earlier, presents the gospel as being essentially a message of repentance, open for anyone who accepts the message of John the Baptist, a stand-in for John Mark. However, this time around, it is indeed the last chance. Whereas in Mark the teaching of the Baptist (1:7-8) is an introduction to the call of Jesus that the kingdom is at hand (v.15), in Matthew the Baptist's message coalesces with Jesus' call. In this Gospel, both the Baptist and Jesus use the same words: "Repent, for the kingdom of heaven is at hand." (Mt 3:2; 4:17) John's message is none other than Jesus', meaning that Matthew consecrates the full equivalence between the words of the former and those of the latter: to hear John the Baptist is to hear Jesus. That is to say, the Gospel of Mark is itself *the* gospel and there is none other.

In order to seal this full circle, the Matthean school edited the Gospel of Mark by adding after Mark 16:8 verses 9-20 that are made up of post-resurrectional material taken from the other

---

[14] Actually Paul's senior at the beginning of their activity (Acts 11:30; 12:27; 13:1-7).

three Gospels.[15] Consequently, as it stands the canonical Mark looks like the basis or the core that was expanded and commented upon by the other Gospels. It is as though each of these is canonical insofar as it corresponds to the Markan message concerning the one and only valid gospel that was and is forever to be "heralded to the entire creation" (Mk 16:15). Indeed, Matthew proved to be the consummate "scribe who has been trained for the kingdom of heaven," "a householder who brings out of his treasure what is new and what is old" (Mt 13:52), the "old" in this case being the Old Testament scripture, and the "new" the Markan material.[16]

---

[15] Mk 16:9-11/Jn 20:11-18; Mk 16:12-13/Lk 24:13:35; Mk 16:14-18/Lk 24:36-49/Jn 20:19-23; Mk 16:19-20/Lk 24:50-53/Acts 1:3-14.

[16] Notice that the householder brings out both the old and the new from a treasure *that is already there.*

PART II

The Gospel of Matthew

4

Birth and Infancy of the Messiah

The Genealogy of Jesus Christ (1:1-17)

Right from the beginning Matthew defines Christ, identified as the Messiah and thus son of David and new David, primarily as a son of Abraham, the one to whom God's promise was made. Consequently, Jesus is presented as the one in whom that promise is ultimately consummated. Usually genealogies are supposed to be endless, or at least open-ended, especially when in conjunction with kingly dynasties, in order to reflect their stretching into "eternity." In contradistinction to such, Christ's genealogy has a beginning and an end. Its structuring around the numerals three and seven is intended to reflect a divine plan.[1] Three is the number of divine fullness while seven is that of the fullness of the divine order in the creation: it is the combination of the numeral three and the four directions of the created order.[2] The numeral seven is subsumed in the statute regarding the jubilee year (seven times seven) when the created order reverts to the way God made it: the earth belongs to God and thus to everyone who lives on it according to one's needs. Matthew follows here this tradition and views God's plan as preparing for the jubilee year: Christ appears at the beginning of the seventh set of seven. Furthermore, through reference to the Moabite Ruth (Mt 1:5) and the adulterous behavior of Judah,

---

[1] Both these numerals are prominent throughout Matthew.

[2] See e.g. God's seven spirits through which he rules the world (Rev 1:4; 3:1; 4:5; 5:6) and the sets of sevens (seals, trumpets, bowls of wrath) through which he implements his will in the domain of creation.

Salmon, and David (vv.3, 5, 6), the Matthean genealogy makes
it clear that the jubilee is celebrated in spite of the people's sins
and exclusively through God's graceful intervention. Indeed, the
Messiah's name is Jesus "for he will save his people from their
sins" (v.21); he is none other than the Messiah as preached in
Paul's gospel (Gal 1-2). The numeral three overarches the entire
genealogy that is divided in three sets of fourteen generations.
The first one indicates that the promise to Abraham was not
fulfilled in David, the first "beloved,"[3] due to the abhorrent
double sin he committed against his general Uriah the Hittite.[4]
Actually, because of David's sin, Abraham's descendants lost the
gift of the land and were punished with exile, which is the topic
of the second set of fourteen. The third set shows that it is
during the exile in the land where Abraham started, Babylon,
that begins the graceful intervention of God who will forgive his
people by preparing the way for his true "beloved," Jesus the
Messiah.

The symbolic aspect of the genealogy is at its clearest in the
third set. While the first two sets of fourteen are taken from
scripture, the third set, which is the road from captivity into the
heavenly Jerusalem, goes beyond the scriptural data starting with
Zerubbabel. Between the latter and Matthan (Hebrew for
Matthew) we find seven names centered around Zadok from the
Hebrew root *ṣdq* meaning righteousness. The name points both
to the Jerusalemite priesthood whose one of its main
representatives in the times of David was Zadok. Under

---

[3] This is the meaning of the Hebrew root *dwd*.

[4] It is that David, Abraham's descendant, who acted egotistically toward the Hittite
Uriah (2 Sam 11:6-27) when Ephron the Hittite acted magnanimously toward
Abraham and offered to grant him a piece of land for him to bury Sarah (Gen 23:10-
11).

Solomon Zadok is given the place of honor against his rival Abiathar (1 Kg 2:35) and thus his name becomes the patronymic for the Sadducees, the temple priests. On the other hand, righteousness was the rallying cry of the Pharisees. Consequently, in the Matthean genealogy, Zadok is a stand-in for the Judahite leadership in general and, especially, in Palestine. Around this center we have six names detailing the different groups within the Judaism of the time. In order to understand how the names after Zerubbabel work, one is to start with the scriptural triad Jechoniah-Shealtiel-Zerubbabel. The latter, who was the governor of post-exilic Judah (Hag 1:1), came about as a response to the people's prayer to God to implement his promise to (re-)establish Judah: Jechoniah means "God will establish" and Shealtiel "I asked (from) God." The pre-Zadok (Abiud-Eliakim-Azor) and post-Zadok (Achim-Eliud-Eleazar) triads are corresponding with a shift in the order of the first and second names. The first triad refers to the period leading toward the Judaism of Jesus' time: Ezra (Azor)[5] established a very strict Judaism that did not allow any room for diversity (Abiud is the Greek for the Hebrew *'abiyud*, meaning "my father is Judah").[6] Yet, Matthew points out that this was not God's will,[7] which is expressed in Eliakim (from the Hebrew *'eliyaqim* "my God will raise up [true Judaism]") who stands at the heart of the triad. The second triad describes the more diversified Judaism of Jesus' time. It starts with the undefined Achim[8] (Hebrew for "brethren") expressing the different Jewish communities or

---

[5] Both are from the root *'zr*.

[6] *ioud-* is the shortened form of the Greek *Iouda* (Judah) and the Hebrew *yᵉ(h)udah*.

[7] Notice that both Abiud and Azor are not theophoric names, i.e., constructed with "El" or "Yah," whereas Eliakim is.

[8] Close in sound to (Eli)akim.

brotherhoods,[9] then moves to the theophoric Eliud[10] (a Judaism defined not only by Judah, the forefather, but rather by God himself) and finally to the equally theophoric Eleazar (my God is [my] help), expressive of the gospel of divine grace championed by Paul. It is God ultimately who will secure that the brotherhood of the 'aḥim be open like the Pauline communities of Jews and Gentiles alike.

However, it is none of these groups nor even the Jerusalem temple that carried the promise of God to Abraham, realized in the eschatological messiah, but it is rather Matthan, whose name in Hebrew means "gift (of the Lord or God)" and is thus connected with the notion of grace. In other words, the true Abrahamic lineage of the divine promise went beyond the temple and Judaism and was fulfilled through Matthew, the carrier of the Pauline gospel of grace. It is he who fathered the ultimate Jacob, inclusive of both the Northern kingdom of Israel, represented by Joseph, as well as the Southern kingdom of Judah. This lineage is inclusive of all kinds of Judaism, in contradistinction to the Jacob who, in the first third of the genealogy, begets (only) Judah. Whereas Judah ended up fathering David, whose son Solomon ultimately caused the people to be exiled into the foreign land of Babylon, Joseph was the one who, in Genesis, secured their survival in the foreign land of Egypt. My readers are reminded that of the patriarchs only the stories of Abraham and Joseph are not referred to as *toledot* (a genealogy or generation, i.e., a human history). Rather, their stories were, humanly speaking, impossible: the first is granted Isaac only through God's promise, while the second

---

[9] Paul himself will use the appellative "brethren" for his communities to show their validity in the eyes of the Jerusalemite leadership.
[10] The God of Judah.

survived his brothers' plan to eliminate him and became instead the channel of their salvation, again only through God's intervention. Here also, the final Joseph closes the Abrahamic genealogy by foreclosing for himself the possibility of having a *toledot*. Rather, he realizes the fulfillment of the promise to Abraham by associating himself with Mary (the symbol of the Pauline Gentile church) "of whom Jesus was born, who is called Christ." With Jerusalem and its temple having been destroyed, the Jews at large are invited to cling to the Marian messianic community in whose midst Christ reigns. Even Joseph, from whom Christ did not come, is invited to walk the path along with Mary and her child.

The Birth of Jesus Christ (1:18-25)

Nonetheless, Joseph's itinerary is not as straightforward as it looks. It is fraught with a major difficulty: he has to realize that "being just (righteous, *dikaios*)" (Mt 1:19) does not make one a kin of Christ who "came not to call the righteous, but sinners" (9:13). Indeed, Jesus is not part of Joseph's genealogy whose third set counts thirteen, not fourteen, generations (1:12-16);[11] he is rather "generated"[12] through God's Holy Spirit, independently of Joseph who belongs to the Zadok period. Actually, when one follows closely Matthew's terminology one gets the distinct impression that God's plan succeeds in spite of

---

[11] Notice how the 13 generations are centered around Zadok and his righteousness, which Paul has already deemed unfruitful: "Indeed I count everything as loss because of the surpassing worth of knowing Christ Jesus my Lord. For his sake I have suffered the loss of all things, and count them as refuse, in order that I may gain Christ and be found in him, not having a righteousness of my own, based on law, but that which is through faith in Christ, the righteousness from God that depends on faith." (Phil 3:8-9).

[12] Notice the intended use of *genesis* (generation) instead of *gennēsis* (birth) in 1:1 and 18.

Joseph's intentions and actions. Although Joseph, we are told, did not want to disgrace publicly (*deigmatisai*) Mary, he nevertheless "considered" (*enthymēthentos*) "to divorce her secretly/quietly" (*lathra apolysai autēn*), a phrase which can also mean "to dismiss, and thus destroy, by keeping quiet regarding her." Joseph's ill intention is reflected in that both the adverb *lathra* (secretly, quietly) and the verb "considered" have a negative connotation in Matthew. The former describes Herod's plan to destroy Jesus (Mt 2:7)[13] and the latter is used to speak of the negative attitude of Jesus' opponents toward him: "But Jesus, knowing their thoughts (*enthymēseis*), said, 'Why do you think (*enthymeisthe*) evil in your hearts?'" (9:4); "But when the Pharisees heard it they said, 'It is only by Beelzebul, the prince of demons, that this man casts out demons.' Knowing their thoughts (*enthymēseis*), he said to them…" (12:24-25)[14] The one who really protects Mary, and later the child, from Joseph's and Herod's intended or non-intended schemes is the "angel of the Lord," i.e., Paul.[15] The Matthean terminology is thoroughly Pauline. Joseph is addressed as "son of David" and asked to accept that Jesus, the eschatological son of David, is actually from God, his Son through the intervention of the Holy Spirit. This phraseology is reminiscent of Romans:

> Paul, a servant of Jesus Christ, called to be an apostle, set apart for the gospel of God which he promised beforehand through his prophets in the holy scriptures, the gospel concerning his Son,

---

[13] This brings de facto Joseph's action in parallel with that of Herod who will resolve later to "kill" (*apolesai*) the child, especially when one considers the closeness in sound, most probably intended, between the two verbs *apolysai* and *apolesai*.

[14] These account for all occurrences of this root in Matthew.

[15] See my comments on Lk 2:1-21; Acts 5:19; 8:26 in *NTI₂* 33-35, 218. See also my comments on Rev 1:1 in *New Testament Introduction, Volume 3: Johannine Writings* (Crestwood, NY: St Vladimir's Press, 2004), 41; hereinafter referred to as *NTI₃*.

who was descended from David according to the flesh and designated Son of God in power according to the Spirit of holiness by his resurrection from the dead, Jesus Christ our Lord. (1:1-4)

Just as Paul views his gospel in the light of scripture according to the prophets and explicates Jesus in terms of Isaiah's suffering servant,[16] so does Matthew here: "... and you shall call his name Jesus, for he will save his people from their sins."[17] It is in this sense that the same Jesus, whose name means "The Lord will save," becomes also, according to the same book of Isaiah, the realization of the "sign" of Emmanuel, "God with us." On the other hand, by "taking" Mary Joseph endorses the notion of resurrection as "commanded" by the angel of the Lord, Paul.[18] This is evidenced in Matthew's statement that, after the visit of the angel in his dream, Joseph "woke from sleep" (*egertheis apo tou hypnou*). On the one hand, *egertheis* (raise) is the verb Paul uses to refer to God's raising of Jesus from the dead. On the other hand, *hypnou* (sleep) occurs in the rest of the New Testament in conjunction with resurrection (Lk 9:32;[19] Jn

---

[16] Compare (in the original Greek for the New Testament and the Septuagint for the Old) Gal 1:15 with Is 49:1; Phil 2:16 with Is 49:4; 2 Cor 6:2 with Is 49:8; Rom 8:33 with Is 50:8; Rom 10:16 with Is 53:1; Rom 4:25 with Is 53:4-5; 1 Cor 5:7 with Is 53:7; Rom 5:19 with Is 53:11.

[17] Compare to Is 53:10-12: "Yet it was the will of the Lord to bruise him; he has put him to grief; when he makes himself an offering for sin, he shall see his offspring, he shall prolong his days; the will of the Lord shall prosper in his hand; he shall see the fruit of the travail of his soul and be satisfied; by his knowledge shall the righteous one, my servant, make many to be accounted righteous; and he shall bear their iniquities. Therefore I will divide him a portion with the great, and he shall divide the spoil with the strong; because he poured out his soul to death, and was numbered with the transgressors; yet he bore the sin of many, and made intercession for the transgressors."

[18] "Commanded" here is the translation of *prosetaxen* from the verb *prostassō*, from the same root as *diatassō* often found in Paul in conjunction with his directives (1 Cor 7:17; 11:34; 16:1; Tit 1:5).

[19] The reference here is to Jesus' glory connected with his death and thus resurrection.

11:13; Acts 20:9; Rom 13:11-14[20]). The last verse of the
Matthean pericope underscores once more the central statement:
Jesus was born into the Pauline Gentile communities (Mary)
totally independently of Joseph's intervention. Joseph will have
to follow the angel's lead and leave (the Judaism of) Judah for
Egypt and Galilee (2:14, 22), which is the meaning of the
resurrection,[21] just as the Gentile magi will leave for their own
country (vv.12-13).

The Visit of the Magi (2:1-12)

This pericope seems to follow Paul's lead in Romans where the
Apostle hopes that the Gentile's reception of the gospel would
entice the Jews to accept it (Rom 9-11). Here, in Matthew, the
Gentiles, represented by the wise men from the east, accepted the
good news of the gospel while the Jerusalemite leadership (all the
chief priests and scribes of the people) were still inquiring about
its veracity. This led them to search the scriptures since "the
gospel of God" is actually "promised beforehand through his
prophets in the holy scriptures" (Rom 1:1-2). At hearing the
scriptures they find that the gospel followed by the magi leads to
a "king of the Jews" other than Herod, one who, consequently,
does not reside in Jerusalem. Herod "was troubled, and all
Jerusalem with him," in the same way that Zechariah, also
representative of Jerusalem and its temple, was in Luke's gospel
(Lk 1:12). Furthermore, Herod—and with him the political
Jerusalem—was planning to destroy the child born outside
Jerusalem, considering him a challenge to its authority.
However, divine authority is bound to the God of scripture, not

---

[20]The reference here is to the Lord's coming that forms the other side of his
resurrection from the dead.

[21] See my comments on Mk 16:1-6 in *NTI₁* 235-36.

to the earthly Jerusalem. In order to understand scripture, the Jews needed to drop the "veil" from over their eyes (2 Cor 3:13-16) that "kept them from seeing the light of the gospel of the glory of Christ, who is the likeness of God" (4:4). Yet so long as they were in Herod's company, they would not be able to see the "light" of the star that kept eluding them since it appeared only whenever the magi were not in Herod's presence. The (light of the) star "appears" (*tou phainomenou asteros*—the star appeared; Mt 2:7) in the same way as the angel of the Lord did (*ephanē*; 1:20) and will do (*phainetai*; 2:13, 19) to guide Joseph.[22] So the Jewish leadership is invited to follow the lead of the Gentile magi. These learned through their inquiry that it was Jesus, not Herod, who was the true king of the Jews and, as such, worthy of their offerings. Matthew subtly indicates that this discovery was ultimately done through the gospel of Paul. Indeed, it happened "in a dream," i.e., through the same medium used by the angel of the Lord to teach Joseph (Mt 1:20; 2:13, 19). And, just as the Gentile magi learned not to go back to Herod, Joseph the Jew will be warned "in a dream" not return to the Judea ruled by Archelaus, Herod's son (2:23).

The Flight to Egypt (2:13-15)

Though strange, the invitation to go to Egypt can be explained if we consider that location as a stand-in for the Roman empire. This was done in Revelation: "... and their dead bodies will lie in the street of the great city which is allegorically called Sodom and Egypt, where their Lord was crucified." (11:8)[23] The connection to Revelation is strengthened when one considers that (a) the same phrase *eteken huion* (she had borne a son; Mt 1:25) occurs

---

[22] These account for all the instances of this verb in Matthew's infancy narratives.

[23] See my comments in *NTI₃* 81-2.

only once more in the New Testament,[24] in the following
chapter of Revelation (12:5),[25] (b) in both cases mention is made
of "fleeing,"[26] and (c) this is followed by the persecution of
children connected with the new-born child.[27] It is Herod's
enmity toward Jesus that drove the latter into Egypt, and it is
from there that Jesus will be called out with a mission to both
Gentiles (Galilee) and Jews (Jerusalem and Judah).

The Slaying of the Infants and the Return from Egypt (2:16-23)

In the Old Testament, as a result of not abiding by God's will,
the kings end up sacrificing their cities' children to destruction.[28]
Here too, in his stance against the gospel of peace, Herod's
behavior culminates with the destruction of the "children of
Israel," especially those by Rachel, the mother of Joseph, the
main representative of the Northern kingdom of Israel. This
catastrophe is described as the fulfillment of the Lord's words
through Jeremiah: "A voice is heard in Ramah, lamentation and
bitter weeping. Rachel is weeping for her children; she refuses to
be comforted for her children, because they are not." (Mt 2:16;
Jer 31:15) This quotation is taken from the lengthy passage (Jer
31:1-34) that inaugurates Jeremiah's Book of Consolation (Jer
31-33), and culminates with the promise of the new covenant
(31:31-34). Therefore, the scriptural reference functions as a
promise of hope for the future, a promise whose fulfillment is

---

[24]Lk 2:7 has *ton huion autēs ton prōtotokon.*

[25]*eteken huion, arsen* translated into "she brought forth a male child" by RSV in view of
the later *eteken ton arsena* (had borne the male child; v.13).

[26] "Rise, take the child and his mother, and flee to Egypt" (Mt 2:13); "and the woman
fled into the wilderness" (Rev 12:6).

[27] Mt 16-18; Rev 12:17.

[28] See e.g. Ezek 5:17; 16:20-21, 36, 45; 20:39; 36:12-14.

heralded with the safe return of Jesus from Egypt. Just as in Revelation 12, it is Christ's "brethren" that are harmed, but not he. Still the road toward the fulfillment is lengthy. It does not lead directly to "the land of Israel" that is still at war with the gospel message (Mt 2:20-21). Jerusalem and the "land of Israel" will have to receive and accept that the gospel will come from Galilee (of the nations; Mt 4:15) where it found its home (2:22).

Further Reading

Agourides, S. "The Birth of Jesus and the Herodian Dynasty: An Understanding of Matthew, Chapter 2." *Greek Orthodox Theological Review* 37 (1992): 135-146.

Bauer, D. R. "The Kingship of Jesus in the Matthean Infancy Narrative: A Literary Analysis." *Catholic Biblical Quarterly* 57 (1995): 306-323.

Becking, B. "'A Voice Was Heard in Ramah'. Some remarks on the structure and meaning of Jeremiah 31.15-17." *Biblische Zeitschrift* 38 (1994): 229-242.

Brodie, T. L. "Vivid, positive, practical: The systematic use of Romans in Matthew 1-7. An Exploratory Survey." *Proceedings of the Irish Biblical Association* 16 (1993): 36-55.

Eloff, M. "Exile, Restoration and Matthew's Genealogy of Jesus ὁ χριστός." *Neotestamentica* 38 (2004): 75-87.

Erickson, R. J. "Divine Injustice? Matthew's Narrative Strategy and the Slaughter of the Innocents (Matthew 2.13-23)." *Journal for the Study of the New Testament* 64 (1996): 5-27.

Jones, J. M. "Subverting the Textuality of Davidic Messianism: Matthew's Presentation of the Genealogy and the Davidic Title." *Catholic Biblical Quarterly* 56 (1994): 256-272.

Nolland, J. "No Son-of-God Christology in Matthew 1.18-25." *Journal for the Study of the New Testament* 62 (1996): 3-12.

Radermakers, J. "La mère de l'Emmanuel. 'Le Seigneur lui-même vous donnera un signe' (Is 7,14)." *Nouvelle Revue Théologique* 128 (2006): 529-545.

Weaver, D. J. "Rewriting the Messianic Script: Matthew's Account of the Birth of Jesus." *Interpretation* 54 (2000): 376-385.

Weren, W. J. C. "The Five Women in Matthew's Genealogy." *Catholic Biblical Quarterly* 59 (1997): 463-481.

5

The Beginnings of the
Message of the Messiah

The Preaching of John the Baptist (3:1-12)

Matthew's interest in showing that the gospel is the fulfillment of scripture can be seen very clearly in the way he presents John the Baptist as a proto-Jesus. Unlike the previous Gospels, the content of their preaching (*kēryssōn*)[1] in Matthew is verbatim: "Repent, for the kingdom of heaven is at hand." (Mt 3:2; 4:17) Moreover, at the beginning of their public appearance, each of the two *paraginetai* (came; 3:1, 13). However, whereas John the Baptist "comes" to preach the gospel as scripture (and therefore as a promise), Jesus preaches it (4:17) after having "come" to fulfill all scriptural righteousness (3:14) and thus as the one in whom God's full pleasure has been realized (3:17). By the same token, since the repentance required in either case is in view of the kingdom, that kingdom is never to be considered, even in the gospel, as something already realized or even as something taken for granted. Both scripture and the gospel look ahead toward it; the prayer that Jesus taught us, and which is his (see Lk 11:1-4), includes at all times the request "thy kingdom come." This explains why, just as Paul taught in 1 Corinthians 10, the church is to be viewed, as it is in Matthew, as an Israel at the threshold of entering the promised kingdom, just as Israel is always at the threshold of entering the land and, consequently,

---

[1] This is the verb used by Paul to refer to the preaching of the gospel.

potentially still under judgment.[2] In scripture, whenever Israel imagines it possesses the land, it ends up exiled from it; the church is to understand that it is never in possession of the kingdom, lest the church be left outside it just as "the sons of the kingdom will be thrown into the outer darkness" (Mt 8:12). That is why later Matthew will make clear that, before the kingdom comes, not only "not an iota, not a dot, will pass from the law (*nomos*, i.e., *torah*)" (5:18) but also in order to enter into that kingdom the righteousness of the believer in Christ is to surpass that of the strictest followers of the Law (v.20). That is also why he will compare the "children of the kingdom" to a seed that will have to produce fruit in view of the future harvest which will introduce God's kingdom (13:37-43). Since the preaching of the Baptist and that of Jesus are fully equivalent in Matthew, the hearer of this Gospel is already warned of this situation in the Baptist's words to the Pharisees and Sadducees:

> You brood of vipers! Who warned you to flee from the wrath to come? Bear fruit that befits repentance, and do not presume to say to yourselves, "We have Abraham as our father"; for I tell you, God is able from these stones to raise up children to Abraham. Even now the axe is laid to the root of the trees; every tree therefore that does not bear good fruit is cut down and thrown into the fire. I baptize you with water for repentance, but he who is coming after me is mightier than I, whose sandals I am not worthy to carry; he will baptize you with the Holy Spirit and with fire. His winnowing fork is in his hand, and he will clear his threshing floor and gather his wheat into the granary, but the chaff he will burn with unquenchable fire. (3:7-12)

---

[2] A theme expressed most forcefully in Deuteronomy, where the final expression of the law is given to Israel as it stands poised to enter the land.

This motif of being invited while one is still at the threshold is underscored in that John the Baptist preaches "in the wilderness of Judea" (Mt 3:1) where "Jerusalem and all Judea" join "all the region about the Jordan" in *going out* to him in order "to be baptized by him *in the Jordan*" (vv.5-6). This parallels the scriptural journey of Israel, which, led by Joshua, had to cross that river in order to enter the land of the promise. Similarly, here it is Jesus, the eschatological Joshua,[3] who leads the way through the Jordan by fulfilling the righteousness required by the Law (vv.13-15). Indeed, he is the one through whom the Spirit is introduced (v.16).

The Baptism of Jesus (3:13-17)

The (historical) present *paraginetai* (comes) is strange; that is why RSV translates the verb as "came." But Matthew's intention is clear: Jesus is the "coming" one and his coming here is indeed eschatological, in order to fulfill both scripture introduced by John and the righteousness mentioned therein. Moreover, he does so by coming from Galilee, the land of the nations, a location that corresponds to the Ezekelian Babylon. Indeed, at his coming "the heavens were opened" (Mt 3:16) just as it happened when the word of the Lord came to Ezekiel (Ezek 1:1-3)[4]; it is the Spirit, which gives life to the dry bones of Israel before leading them into the land of the new Jerusalem (Ezek 37:1-14), that comes and alights on the one who will lead his followers into the kingdom.

---

[3] The Hebrew *yᵉhošua'* (Joshua) is translated into *Iēsous* (Jesus) in the Septuagint.

[4] The Greek *ēneōkhthēsan hoi ouranoi* (the heavens were opened) is taken from Ezekiel's *ēnoikhthēsan hoi ouranoi*.

The Temptation of Jesus (4:1-11)

Now that Jerusalem and its temple had long since been destroyed and the church is now all on its own after its break with Judaism has been consummated, Matthew rephrases Luke's pericope of Jesus' temptation to accommodate the new situation. Instead of Jerusalem, it is now Rome that is being targeted as the tempting reality. Indeed, the first temptation uses the plural "stones" (Mt 4:3) instead of the singular "stone" (Lk 4:3); the change may have been intended to reflect the many temples of the Roman empire as opposed to the one temple of Jerusalem. Secondly, for Luke, who was writing right after the fall of Jerusalem, the destruction of the temple was still fresh in the people's mind; that is why he gave it weight by linking the last temptation to it. Matthew, on the other hand, rearranges the Lukan order, reserving the final temptation for a reference to the riches of the Roman empire. Furthermore, in Luke, the temptation dealing with the offer of all the kingdoms of the world simply says that "the devil took him up and showed him all the kingdoms of the world in a moment of time" (Lk 4:5). In Matthew, "the devil took him to a very high mountain in order to show him all the kingdoms of the world *and the glory of them*" (4:8).[5]

The Beginning of Jesus' Ministry (4:12-17)

Upon John the Baptist's dismissal from the scene, the gospel, represented by Jesus, "withdrew into Galilee." Yet, its

---

[5] In Luke, this glory is not shown but assumed; it is referred to in the offer itself (Lk 4:6). Besides, Matthew eliminates the Lukan "in a moment of time" (i.e., as in a dream), giving the impression that Jesus was given to see indeed all the riches of the kingdoms and the glory of them, which could be the case only if someone were in Rome.

headquarters moves from Nazareth—the territory of the Gentiles[6]—to Capernaum, the domain of the Jews within Gentile environment.[7] Capernaum here may be a stand-in for Ephesus, a port city that was chosen by the Pauline party as being a convenient place to be the headquarters of the one gospel that would be addressed to Jews and Gentiles alike.[8] This reading is further confirmed in that the move is said to be a fulfillment of a prophetic statement that is addressed to the lands of Zebulon and Naphtali, tribal territories of the Northern kingdom of Israel, and not of Judah.[9] Moreover, the same quotation calls these two lands "Galilee of the nations." In other words, as was the case with Paul, the first—and de facto only—Jews addressed by his gospel[10] were those of the diaspora, outside Palestine,[11] consonant with what the Old Testament teaches: the goods news

---

[6] See *NTI₁* 136-7, 140, 144; *NTI₂* 29, 47-8, 65; *NTI₃* 147-8.

[7] Notice the Matthean addition *parathalassian* (by the sea), that is, at the border of the Roman sea.

[8] See *NTI₁*, 15-16, 88; *NTI₂*, 13-14, 42, 231, 252-6.

[9] Now that the Pauline Gentile communities have become the main component of God's "church" (Greek *ekklēsia;* Hebrew *qahal*) it becomes important to emphasize to them that they have reached their present position only by occupying the place of the original community; this mirrors the statements of Paul and Luke about the Jews in Romans (especially chs. 9-11) and Acts. The purpose here is not to deliver a triumphalistic claim of superiority over the Jews, but rather a message of instruction to the new ecclesial community: just as many of the original inheritors of God's promise have rejected the gospel and thus exiled themselves from God's *qahal*, so the new *ekklēsia* will meet the same fate if it fails to adhere to God's commands. Hence the emphasis on Zebulon and Naphtali over Judah, just as earlier Matthew referred to Rachel's descendants (the Northern kingdom), who were originally ascendant over Jerusalem but were then destroyed due to their transgressions (2:18, which cites Jer 31:15, a passage dealing with the exile of the Northern Kingdom by the Assyrians).

[10] Notice that, in speaking of Jesus' preaching, Matthew uses *ērxato* (began), which I showed to be a reference to the beginning of the gospel; see *NTI₁* 133, 146, 156, 165, 188.

[11] See my comments in *Gal* 69-70 regarding his being apostle to the Gentiles.

of salvation was first addressed to the exiles in Babylon, as witnessed in Isaiah 40-55.

The Calling of the Four Fishermen (4:18-22)

Since the Pauline gospel is the one and only gospel for Jews as well as Gentiles, Peter, the "apostle to the circumcision," together with the other pillars who had accepted Paul and his gospel (Gal 2:7-9), are drafted to carry out its preaching. The numeral four connected with the first disciples is symbolic of the four gates of the heavenly city and its temple, through which all men (Mt 4:19) from all four directions of the universe will be invited to enter. What we find here in Matthew is reminiscent of the imagery found in Revelation:

> It [the holy city Jerusalem] had a great, high wall, with twelve gates, and at the gates twelve angels, and on the gates the names of the twelve tribes of the sons of Israel were inscribed; on the east three gates, on the north three gates, on the south three gates, and on the west three gates. And the wall of the city had twelve foundations, and on them the twelve names of the twelve apostles of the Lamb ... By its light shall the nations walk; and the kings of the earth shall bring their glory into it, and its gates shall never be shut by day -- and there shall be no night there; they shall bring into it the glory and the honor of the nations. (21:12-14, 24-26)[12]

The apostolic ministry is centrifugal because the temple of the heavenly Jerusalem is not a building of stone, but rather it is the ambulatory "temple of the tent of witness" (Rev 15:5) that led the people through the wilderness into the promised land. This

---

[12] See also Acts where Peter and John open the way for all men at one of the temple's gates: "And a man lame from birth was being carried, whom they laid daily at that gate of the temple which is called Beautiful to ask alms of those who entered the temple." (3:2)

universalism of the message and mission is underscored in Matthew when compared with Mark. Indeed, Peter and Andrew are outright *ballontas amphiblēstron* (casting a net) and not *amphiballontas*, whose meaning is also "vacillating."[13] Similarly, there is no mention of the sons of Zebedee being hirelings.[14] In other words, the disciples are shown in a more positive light. This goes hand in hand with the inclusion of all the apostolic brotherhood, except for Barnabas, under the aegis of the one gospel.[15]

Great Multitude (4:23-25)

It is the message of this one gospel, proclaimed and taught by the Pauline Jesus, that spreads among the Gentiles unhindered throughout Syria,[16] whose capital, Antioch, had previously been the site of the pillars' betrayal of Paul and his gospel (Gal 2:11-14). Now the Gentiles from Galilee (i.e., the Roman empire), who join the Jews of the diaspora in accepting it, are included in the open and inclusive range of the mission. It is from the heavenly Jerusalem above (Gal 4:26) that the Messiah declares his law (Gal 6:2), which is the law of the spirit of life (Rom 8:2): love for the neighbor, any and every neighbor. He will soon declare that law from the eschatological mountain (Mt 5-7).

Further Reading

Frankemölle, H. "Johannes der Täufer und Jesus im Matthäusevangelium: Jesus als Nachfolger des Täufers." *New Testament Studies* 42 (1996): 196-218.

---

[13] See *NTI₁* 141.
[14] See *NTI₁* 143.
[15] See Part I on the canon.
[16] Note the change of location to Syria from the Markan "Galilee" (Mk 1:39).

Garlington, D. B. "Jesus, the Unique Son of God: Tested and Faithful." *Bibliotheca Sacra* 151 (1994): 284-308.

Giesen, H. "Galiläa – mehr als eine Landschaft. Bibeltheologisher Stellenwert Galiläas im Matthäusevangelium." *Ephemerides Theologicae Lovanienses* 77 (2001): 23-45.

Meier, J. P. "John the Baptist in Matthew's Gospel." *Journal of Biblical Literature* 99 (1980): 383-405.

Miler, J. "Le travail de l'accomplissement: Matthieu et les Ecritures." *Foi et Vie* 100 (2001): 13-29.

Pilch, J. J. "Imaginary Mountains in Matthew." *Bible Today* 37 (1999): 174-181.

Saucy, M. "The Kingdom-of-God Sayings in Matthew." *Bibliotheca Sacra* 151 (1994): 175-197.

6

The First Book of
the Law of the Messiah

The Beatitudes (5:1-12)

If Jerusalem, already destroyed, may not function as a reference
for the Jews who accepted the gospel, neither may Rome for
the believing Gentiles. Jesus the messiah, preached in the gospel,
is the Lord who is already reigning over all in the heavens. It is
from there, the mount of the heavenly Jerusalem, that he
dispenses his law to the "crowds," i.e., all those who are not yet
members of the messianic community, through his disciples (Mt
5:1 and 7:28). His law is the new law that cannot be dispensed
by the Jewish scribes (7:29) as Paul had indicated in 2
Corinthians 3, but is the law of God's kingdom (5:3, 10). This
law is dispensed in nine blessings: three sets of 3 (see below),
which is the number of divine fullness. This law of God's
messiah (Gal 6:2) is also the law of God's spirit (Rom 8:2): the
entire series of blessings is initiated by this Spirit (Mt 5:3) that
the gospel provides, and culminates with the eschatological joy it
secures (v.12) in spite of and beyond the sufferings such witness
for the gospel entails (v.11).[1] This law neither contradicts nor
supplants the Mosaic Law, but fulfills it (v.17), as taught by
Jeremiah and Ezekiel in conjunction with the new covenant:

---

[1]See 1 Thess 1:6 and my comments thereon in my *I Thessalonians: A Commentary*
(Crestwood, NY; St Vladimir's Seminary Press, 1982), 57-61; hereinafter referred to as
1 Thess.

Behold, the days are coming, says the Lord, when I will make a new covenant with the house of Israel and the house of Judah, not like the covenant which I made with their fathers when I took them by the hand to bring them out of the land of Egypt, my covenant which they broke, though I was their husband, says the Lord. But this is the covenant which I will make with the house of Israel after those days, says the Lord: *I will put my law within them, and I will write it upon their hearts*; and I will be their God, and they shall be my people. (Jer 31:31-33; italics mine)

And I will give them one heart, and put a new spirit within them; I will take the stony heart out of their flesh and give them a heart of flesh, *that they may walk in my statutes and keep my ordinances and obey them*; and they shall be my people, and I will be their God. (Ezek 11:19-20; italics mine)

A new heart I will give you, and a new spirit I will put within you; and I will take out of your flesh the heart of stone and give you a heart of flesh. And I will put my spirit within you, and cause you *to walk in my statutes and be careful to observe my ordinances*. (Ezek 36:26-27; italics mine)

Indeed, it presupposes pursuit of (that Law's) righteousness (Mt 5:6, 10) to the extent of surpassing the effort of the scribes and the Pharisees (v.20). In both these cases Matthew's source is Paul himself:

But if you are led by the Spirit you are not under the law ... But the fruit of the Spirit is love, joy, peace, patience, kindness, goodness, faithfulness, gentleness, self-control; against such there is no law ... If we live by the Spirit, let us also walk by the Spirit. (Gal 5:18, 22-23, 25)

What shall we say, then? That Gentiles who did not pursue righteousness have attained it, that is, righteousness through faith; but that Israel who pursued the righteousness which is based on law did not succeed in fulfilling that law ... For, being ignorant of the righteousness that comes from God, and seeking to establish their own, they did not submit to God's righteousness. For Christ is the end of the law, that every one who has faith may be justified. (Rom 9:30-31; 10:3-4)

For we are the true circumcision, who worship God in spirit, and glory in Christ Jesus, and put no confidence in the flesh. Though I myself have reason for confidence in the flesh also. If any other man thinks he has reason for confidence in the flesh, I have more ... as to righteousness under the law blameless. But whatever gain I had, I counted as loss for the sake of Christ. Indeed I count everything as loss because of the surpassing worth of knowing Christ Jesus my Lord. For his sake I have suffered the loss of all things, and count them as refuse, in order that I may gain Christ and be found in him, not having a righteousness of my own, based on law, but that which is through faith in Christ, the righteousness from God that depends on faith; that I may know him and the power of his resurrection, and may share his sufferings, becoming like him in his death, that if possible I may attain the resurrection from the dead. (Phil 3:3-9)

The Pauline teaching is detectable even in the details of the blessings. The first set revolves around the gift of the land. Care for the poor is required by God in the land he grants Israel, and the breaking of this requirement by the leaders becomes the reason that God punishes his people through exile out of the land (e.g., Jer 7:5-7; 22:3-5; Zech 7:9-14; Mal 3:1-5). Yet these same poor will be taken care of by God himself in his kingdom, the eschatological land in which he will set to rest the new Israel which will be raised through his spirit (Mt 5:1), just as Ezekiel taught. On the other hand, in Paul, the Spirit is in charge of the *paraklēsis* (comfort/consolation) and *klēronomia* (inheritance, heritage) mentioned in the second and third blessings.[2] The second set of blessings revolves around the righteousness (v.6) granted ultimately through mercy (v.7) that allows the heart to see God (i.e., be in his presence) without being burnt through his consuming light (v.8).[3] This is again Paul's teaching, especially in Romans: "Just as you [Gentiles] were once disobedient to God but now have received mercy because of their disobedience, so they [Jews] have now been disobedient in order that by the mercy shown to you they also may receive mercy. For God has consigned all men to disobedience, that he may have mercy upon all." (Rom 11:30-32) Finally, the third set of blessings speaks of the sons of God, his people, who will attain the eschatological peace of his kingdom by suffering for God's righteousness, which alone will secure for them that peace and the joy it entails (Mt 5:9-12).[4]

Salt and Light (5:13-16)

Salt makes an offering acceptable (e.g., Lev 2:13; Num 18:19; Ezek 43:24; 2 Chr 13:5) and the disciples are under judgment if they do not function as such toward the world of "men" (Mt 5:13). The idea that discipleship to the world at large is an offering goes back to Paul himself: "But on some points I have written to you very boldly by way of reminder, because of the grace given me by God to be a minister of Christ Jesus to the Gentiles in the priestly service of the gospel of God, so that the offering of the Gentiles may be acceptable, sanctified by the Holy Spirit" (Rom 15:15-16); "Even if I am to be poured as a libation upon the sacrificial offering of your faith, I am glad and

---

[2] See 1 Cor 14:1-3, 29-32 for *paraklēsis* and Rom 8:15-17; Gal 4:6-7 for *klēronomia*.
[3] See Is 2.
[4] See e.g. Rom 5:1-2.

rejoice with you all." (Phil 2:17) Moreover, the disciples are to be the light of the "world" in order to make out of "men" the "house" of God (Mt 5:14-16), i.e., his temple, as we read in 1 Corinthians 3 and Ephesians 2.[5] This propagation of the gospel can happen only if the disciples are persecuted (Mt 5:10-12) and even die for the cause of the gospel: indeed, the salt melts away without giving out its taste and the light lightens without itself being seen.

The Fulfillment of the Law (5:17-20)

In Matthew the verb *plēroō* (fulfill) is used mainly in conjunction with scripture whereas the verb *katalyō* (undo, destroy) with the temple.[6] Jesus did not come to destroy scripture, but rather to fulfill it through the undoing of the value of the temple and of the leadership connected with it (26:54-61; 27:30-53).[7] After the temple was destroyed in 70 B.C. the Pharisaic rabbis tried to do the same: uphold scripture in spite of the absence of the temple. However, since the words of scripture are fulfilled in the words of the gospel, which is their true interpreter according to Paul (Rom 1:1-2), in Matthew the words of Jesus are to be heeded fully in view of the kingdom of heaven when God "judges the

---

[5]For being light (v.16) see also Eph 5:8-9 (for once you were darkness, but now you are light in the Lord; walk as children of light, for the fruit of light is found in all that is good and right and true); Phil 2:14-15 (Do all things without grumbling or questioning, that you may be blameless and innocent, children of God without blemish in the midst of a crooked and perverse generation, among whom you shine as lights in the world); and 2 Cor 4:6 (For it is the God who said, "Let light shine out [*lampsei*] of darkness," who has shone [*elampsen*] in our hearts to give the light of the knowledge of the glory of God in the face of Christ). *lampo* is the same verb found in Mt 5:15.

[6] See 1:22; 2:15, 17, 23; 4:14; 8:17; 12:17; 13:35; 21:4; 26:54, 56; 27:9 for *plēroō* and 24:1-2; 26:61; 27:40 for *katalyō*.

[7] See later my comments on these passages.

secrets of men according to my gospel" (2:16). Now, the gospel's requirement is to fulfill no less than the entire Law through love for the neighbor (13:8-10). Consequently, if one is to be considered as great in the kingdom, one may not for any reason relax even the littlest of the commandments (Mt 5:19). As a result, the teachers in Matthew's church are to be much stricter than the Pharisees, teachers of the Law.[8]

The Antitheses (5:21-48)

Usually both translations and commentators divide the following antitheses into six sets. I propose that Matthew intended to present Jesus' teaching in five sets, which would make out of them a new Torah. What are generally considered to be the second (vv.27-30) and third (vv.31-32) antitheses should be combined into one. All scriptural references in the antitheses are introduced with "you heard that it was said" (vv.21, 27, 33, 38, 43) except for the one in v.31 where we have "it was also said." This "also" (de) indicates that the quotation in that verse is intended to be connected to the subject that is being discussed. Indeed, the "sin" spoken of in v.32 is referred to with the verb moikheuein (commit adultery),[9] the same term used in the scriptural quotation in v.27. The reversion in v.33 to the full expression "You heard that it was said to the men of old" as found in v.21 indicates that the author wanted to make the transition to another topic clear.[10] My proposed division into five sets creates out of the antitheses a new Torah centered around

---

[8] See further on this matter the invectives of ch.23.

[9] V.32 actually stresses this point by referring to it twice, the second time with the verb moikhasthai.

[10] I believe that it is also intended to draw attention to the third antithesis as the focus as well as center of the new torah. The statement "you heard that it was said to the men of old" is actually introduced with "again" (palin).

the gospel, which revolves around the love for the other. This new Law is linked to the coming kingdom, fulfilling and thus superseding the Old Testament Law.

Anger (5:21-26)

Wrath (*orgē*) is solely God's prerogative,[11] which is why anyone who indulges in it will himself suffer the fire brought about by God's judgment. To the contrary, anyone who is "on the way" (*en tē hodō*),[12] living according to the way of the gospel,[13] is to reconcile with all men before God himself, who is the source of reconciliation[14] and who comes to implement his own justice against those who forsake the gospel by their own anger (Rom 12:19-21; see also Deut 32:35; Prov 20:22).

Adultery and Divorce (5:27-32)

As in the case of anger, this pericope sharpens the demands of the Law by linking the adultery to the heart, which remains under God's scrutiny. Those whose hearts are pure (*katharoi*, clean) will be admitted in God's presence in the kingdom (Mt 5:8). The seriousness of adultery is compounded because it is used so frequently as a metaphor to speak of the people's apostasy in the Old Testament.[15] One is to deal with the member of the body that is the cause of adultery in the same way as Paul ordered that it be done with the church's member who is committing such a sin (1 Cor 5:1-8). Such strictness is required

---

[11] Rom 1:18; 2:8; Eph 5:6; Col 3:6; 1 Thess 2:16.

[12] Omitted in RSV.

[13] See my comments on Mk 10:46-52 in *NTI₁* 201-2; see also *NTI₁*145-6.

[14] See Rom 5:11; 2 Cor 5:18-20.

[15] Is 57:1-5; Jer 13:27; 23:13-14; Ezek 16:32, 38; 23:43, 45; Hos 2:4; 3:1; 4:12-15. In all these instances the root *moikh—* is the same as that found in the Matthean pericope.

because any community member who becomes a stumbling block to the gospel must be excised (Gal 4:30). Actually, the entire Matthean passage is permeated with Pauline terminology. The use of the verb *skandalizei* (scandalizes, causes stumbling)[16] recalls Paul's vocabulary.[17] The verb *sympherei* (it is better) to speak of what is advisable for the body is exactly the one used in conjunction with what is good for the body of Christ (1 Cor 6:12; 10:23); in the same epistle the Apostle uses also the cognate noun *sympheron* (common good) in a context dealing with the same topic (12:7). Finally, *epithymēsai*, translated "lustfully" in RSV, is the verb Paul frequently uses together with the cognate noun *epithymia* to refer to sinful human desire, which is contrary to the will of the Spirit.[18] The only exception to this strict rule is the case of *porneia* (translated as unchastity in RSV) which is to be understood as a non-allowable sexual relationship such as that found in 1 Corinthians 5:1-8 or sexual licentiousness (1 Cor 6:12-20; 7:2). In such a case, separation is to be the rule.

Oaths (5:33-37)

The new Torah's center deals with the "word" of the gospel, which is God's ultimate "yes" to his promises in scripture and in whose service he appointed apostles:

> Was I vacillating when I wanted to do this? Do I make my plans like a worldly man, ready to say Yes and No at once? As surely as God is faithful, our word to you has not been Yes and No. For the Son of God, Jesus Christ, whom we preached among you, Silvanus

---

[16] Translated "causes to sin" in RSV.

[17] 1 Cor 8:13; 2 Cor 11:29 for the verb and Rom 9:33; 11:9; 14:13; 16:17; 1 Cor 1:23; Gal 5:11 for the noun *skandalon*.

[18] Gal 5:16-17, 24-25; Rom 1:24; 6:12; 7:7-8; 13:14.

and Timothy and I, was not Yes and No; but in him it is always Yes. For all the promises of God find their Yes in him. That is why we utter the Amen through him, to the glory of God. But it is God who establishes us with you in Christ, and has commissioned us; he has put his seal upon us and given us his Spirit in our hearts as a guarantee. (2 Cor 1:17-22)

As such, the word of the gospel is self-authenticating and does not need ratification from either heaven or earth (i.e., the universe), which is ruled by Rome and its emperor, or Jerusalem and its leadership. Both are under the aegis of the God preached in the gospel and therefore are insufficient as authoritative witnesses for oaths: "But I say to you, Do not swear at all, either by heaven, for it is the throne of God, or by the earth, for it is his footstool, or by Jerusalem, for it is the city of the great King." (Mt 5:34-35)

Nevertheless, the gospel of grace raises the level of accountability to God, since he is the savior who remains the judge of all: "They [the Gentiles] show that what the law requires is written on their hearts, while their conscience also bears witness and their conflicting thoughts accuse or perhaps excuse them on that day when, according to my gospel, God judges the secrets of men by Christ Jesus." (Rom 2:15-16) Consequently, the other four sets of the new Law are based on the premise that God, beyond the Gentile Roman emperor, is the sole judge.[19] The disciple is not to fear the outsiders but to act with the fear of the judgment of God who saves also the outsiders. From the perspective of the gospel, these are not the threat; the real threat is not living up to God's demands.

---

[19] See below where I discuss in more detail the terminology of the last two sets.

Retaliation (5:38-42)

The fourth set takes up the first antithesis (Mt 5:21-26) and
pushes it a step further by requiring from the believer abstention
from any kind of retaliation against a wrongdoer: "Do not resist
one who is evil." (39a) The reason is presumably the same given
in the first antithesis: God is ultimately the sole judge. Indeed,
Christ's request in both cases revolves around the notion of
judgment:

> But I say to you that every one who is angry with his brother shall
> be liable to judgment ... Make friends quickly with your accuser,
> while you are going with him to court, lest your accuser hand you
> over to the judge, and the judge to the guard, and you be put in
> prison. (vv.22a, 25)

> ... and if any one would sue you[20] and take your coat, let him have
> your cloak as well. (v.40)

Jesus here is not simply creating a new commandment in
opposition to the famous "eye for an eye" commandments of the
Old Testament (Ex 21:23-25; Lev 24:19-21; Deut 19:21), but is
instead juxtaposing this command with other legislation that
limits the boundaries of punishment or profit-taking against a
neighbor. Specifically, his statements play on the restrictions
against taking a garment from a debtor (Ex 22:26-27; Deut
24:10-13, 17-18), withholding payment from laborers (Lev
19:13; Deut 24:14-15), the commandments to provide for the
poor by, among other actions, leaving the gleanings of the field
available for their consumption (Lev 19:9, 23.22; Deut 24:19-
22), and also the statutes delineating proper restitution made to a
neighbor for wrongs (Ex 22:1-15; Lev 6:1-7; Num 5:5-10).

---

[20] The original reads *tō thelonti sou krithēnai* whose literal translation is "the one who
wants that you be judged (brought to judgment)."

More generally, Jesus invokes the prohibitions against slander (Ex 23:1-3; Lev 19:16) and vengeance and grudges (Lev 19:18). The key to these statements is the idea that those who oppress their neighbor, either an innocent one or the one who has made proper restitution, is himself shamed because of the unjust shame that he has brought upon the neighbor (a principle specifically stated in Deut 25:1-3)[21].

Love for Enemies (5:43-48)

This last set is the crowning as well as recapitulation of the previous ones in that it explicates the meaning of the love for the neighbor, which is the heart of the gospel. In this matter the disciple is to be as perfect as the God revealed in the gospel (v.48), who is Father to all (v.45), including those whom the Jews consider "unjust, unrighteous": the Gentiles and the publicans (vv.45-47).

Pauline Terminology

The vocabulary of the last two antitheses betray their origin in Romans 12-13, which speaks of the love for the neighbor in conjunction with the believers' required attitude toward the Roman authorities. An overview of this passage and Matthew 5:38-48 will show the close correspondence between them.

---

[21] The importance of shame in the Bible is especially highlighted in Ezekiel, where both the people of Judah and Jerusalem and the prophet himself (as representative of the nation) are roundly humiliated by God in return for their violation of the commandments. Unleashing such shame on the people is not a gratuitous action, but is intended to drive home the lessons of their rebellion and therefore instruct them in the future regarding the proper fulfillment of the law. Here, the shame inflicted upon the oppressor by the one who turns his cheek is intended to function in a similar fashion.

"Do not resist one who is evil" (Mt 5:39a) recalls "Therefore he who resists the authorities resists what God has appointed, and those who resist will incur judgment" (Rom 13:2). These are the only instances of the verb "resist" (*anthistēmi*) in both books. Moreover, the "evil one" of Matthew 5:39 reappears again in 5:45 in parallel with "unjust, unrighteous," a trademark of the Gentile: "for he makes his sun rise on the evil (*ponērous*) and on the good (*agathous*), and sends rain on the just and on the unjust."

"But I say to you, Love your enemies and *pray* for those who persecute you ... for he makes his sun rise on the evil (*ponērous*) and on the good (*agathous*)" (Mt 5:44-45) is a copy of Paul's series of injunctions: "Let love be genuine; hate what is evil (*to ponēron*), hold fast to what is good (*tō agathō*) ... be constant in prayer ... Bless those who persecute you; bless and do not curse them." (Rom 113:9, 12, 14)

The reference to God as "perfect" (*teleios*) in conjunction with the teaching about neighborly love is encountered only in Pauline literature. In his remarks regarding the behavior required within the church community (Rom 12:3-8) and toward the outsiders (vv.9-21), Paul writes: "I appeal to you therefore, brethren, by the mercies of God, to present your bodies as a living sacrifice, holy and acceptable to God, which is your spiritual worship. Do not be conformed to this world but be transformed by the renewal of your mind, that you may prove what is the will of God, what is good and acceptable and perfect (*teleion*)." (vv.1-2) In his "hymn to brotherly love" he speaks of the perennial value of love beyond faith and hope in the following manner:

Love never ends; as for prophecies, they will pass away; as for tongues, they will cease; as for knowledge, it will pass away. For our knowledge is imperfect (*ek merous*) and our prophecy is imperfect (*ek merous*); but when the perfect (*to teleion*) comes, the imperfect (*to ek merous*) will pass away. Now I know in part (*ek merous*); then I shall understand fully, even as I have been fully understood. So faith, hope, love abide, these three; but the greatest of these is love. (1 Cor 13:8-10, 12a-13)

The Righteousness of the Kingdom (6:1-18)

The following triad dealing with almsgiving, prayer, and fasting takes up the issue of righteousness that was introduced in Matthew 5:20: "For I tell you, unless your righteousness exceeds that of the scribes and Pharisees, you will never enter the kingdom of heaven." The disciple of the kingdom is to remember that his righteousness will be validated by God, the heavenly Father, at the end of times when he will dispense to all their due reward: "Beware of practicing your piety (righteousness, *dikaiosynēn*) before men in order to be seen by them; for then you will have no reward from your Father who is in heaven." (6:1) This is precisely what Paul had taught (1 Cor 4:1-5) and what will indeed take place (Mt 25:31-46). That Matthew had in mind the judgment scene of 25:31-46, where the care for the needy is the cornerstone of the judgment process, is uncovered by his placement of almsgiving before prayer and fasting. These latter two, which are matters between God and us, are outranked by almsgiving, which is a matter between the others and us. The care for the needy becomes so central in the disciple's life that it defines his "prayer," i.e., his stand in God's presence. Just as Paul taught in 1 Corinthians 11:17-34, so for Matthew, God's final judgment is determined by how one behaves toward the others (Mt 6:14). Even if they are indebted to us, we are to dismiss what they owe us because such behavior is only an expression of "our debt" toward God (v.12). Furthermore, this rule is at the heart of being a disciple, since it defines our relation with God even in the solitude in our own inner room (*tameion*) (v.6). Wherever and whenever the disciple is, he is bound by the rule of the kingdom prefigured in the jubilee year (Lev 25:8-55), the year in which all indebtedness to one another is released. Actually, Leviticus clearly explains that the jubilee is a constant reminder to all that they were released freely from their bondage. As for fasting, its value lies now solely in its relation to the kingdom, where God himself will feed us at his table. Here again, just in the case of prayer, fasting is a debt to God who saves us and from whom alone we receive our reward, and not an arrogant demonstration before the eyes of others.

Treasure in Heaven and Earthly Cares (6:19-34)

The consequence of the preceding point, that everything should now be viewed from the perspective of the coming kingdom, is that no treasury on earth is ultimately safe. Now that the temple, which functioned in part as a treasury[22], is no more,[23] the disciple must refuse the temptation to settle for safety in the Roman empire, since it will prove to be as passing as Jerusalem (vv.19-20). The disciple is also reminded that the entire matter lies in his view of reality (vv.22-23).[24] It is up to him to use his "eye"

---

[22] Temples in the ancient world typically contained storehouses where the assets belonging to the temple were stored. Cf. 1 Kg 7:51; 2 Macc 1.11-17.

[23] The irrelevance (and destruction) of the temple is obliquely made in the reference to the passing glory of Solomon, the temple builder par excellence. Solomon's mention is actually at the center of the passage (v.29) if one reads it chiastically (vv.25-28—v.29—vv.30-34).

[24] See my comments on the parallel passage Lk 11:34-36 in *NTI₂* 99-100.

and decide for the God of the gospel, who made his Christ "poor, so that by his poverty you might become rich" (2 Cor 8:9) and his apostles "as poor, yet making many rich; as having nothing, and yet possessing everything" (1 Cor 6:10), against the richness of the Roman empire (Mt 6:24) and, by extension, of any powerful human society. The believer is bound by God's kingdom and its righteousness (v.33) which is to surpass that of the Jerusalem leadership that had put its hope in the temple's survival.

God is the Sole Judge of All (7:1-12)

Now that the believers have been defined independently from both Jerusalem and Rome, they are offered guidelines for the new righteousness that would eventually lead them into the kingdom. First and foremost, they are to follow Paul's injunction not to consider themselves as the judges of the Gentiles by considering them the epitome of sin, as the Jews do: "Judge not, that you be not judged. For with the judgment you pronounce you will be judged, and the measure you give will be the measure you get." (7:1-2) After all, God is the sole judge of the "outsiders" (1 Cor 5:9-13). Indeed, the believers are to worry about their own shortcomings before they look at those of the outsiders (Mt 7:3-5) just as Paul warned the Jew (Rom 2:1-4, 17-24). However, a believer is not to give in to the way of the Gentile world (Do not give dogs what is holy; and do not throw your pearls before swine, lest they trample them under foot and turn to attack you, Mt 7:6)[25] in the same manner as Paul

---

[25] The dogs and swine were considered unclean animals in the Old Testament (Is 66:3); consequently, they were used in Jewish terminology to refer to the Gentiles (see also Mk 7:14-30/Mt 15:21-28).

addressed his Gentile believers (Gal 5:16-21, 24-25; 1 Cor 6:9-11)

Although the path of righteousness (*dikaiosynē*) toward the kingdom is very difficult, hope lies in God's mercy. In his fatherhood for us (through Jesus Christ) he will grant us that righteousness as a gift if we only ask him for it as a child would ask his parent (Mt 7:7-11).[26] The only requirement for obtaining God's mercy is that we love the neighbor (Mt 7:12), an action which is the heart and soul of the Law and the Prophets, as already established by Paul (cf. Lev 19:18). This requirement is non-negotiable; without it our petition for God's gift becomes invalid. Indeed, in the same prayer in which we ask for bread (6:11)—as in 7:9—we also ask that God "forgive us our debts, as we also have forgiven our debtors" (6:12), since "if you forgive men their trespasses, your heavenly Father also will forgive you; but if you do not forgive men their trespasses, neither will your Father forgive your trespasses" (vv.14-15). Consequently, if we do not love the others and grant them their needs, God will not grant us ours.

The Narrow Gate (7:13-14)

Still, this way (*hodos*, road) leading to the life of the kingdom[27] is *tethlimmenē* (hard). This adjective is unique in the New Testament and is the perfect passive participle of the verb *thlibō* (afflict), the root of the noun *thlipsis* (affliction). Literally, the participle means "afflicted" or "under pressure." "Affliction" and "being afflicted" are Paul's trademark when speaking of the way

---

[26] See Rom 5:12, 5, 10 and Phil 3:4-9.

[27] The same verb "enter" used in conjunction with "gate" (7:13) occurs later in the expression "enter the kingdom of heaven" (v.21)

of the gospel.[28] Indeed, later Matthew himself uses the Markan phrase "when tribulation (*thlipseōs*) or persecution arises on account of the *word*" (Mt 13:21/Mk 4:17), a reference to the situation faced by Peter at Antioch (Gal 2:11-14).[29] Here the Evangelist must also have had in mind Peter's attitude later in ch.16 since, in conjunction with "way," he uses "gate" (*pylē*) ("Enter by the narrow gate; for the gate is wide and the way is easy, that leads to destruction, and those who enter by it are many. For the gate is narrow and the way is hard, that leads to life, and those who find it are few." [7:12-13]). This word occurs only once more in this Gospel, in an address to Peter where he is given the true understanding of the gospel of the crucified messiah: "And I tell you, you are Peter, and on this rock I will build my church, and the powers (*pylai*, gates) of death (*hadou*, Hades) shall not prevail against it. I will give you the keys of the kingdom of heaven, and whatever you bind on earth shall be bound in heaven, and whatever you loose on earth shall be loosed in heaven." (16:18-19) The connection is further evidenced in that Hades is the domain of death and destruction, whereas life is linked to the kingdom. The link between these two passages lies in that they both deal with God's judgment against those who do not stand for him under pressure when it comes to upholding "the truth of the gospel" (Gal 2:5, 14).

The Eschatological Judgment (7:15-23)

The decision regarding one's final destination, Hades or the kingdom of heaven, hinges on God's judgment. In its turn, this judgment will be on the basis of the fruits that one will have

---

[28] Rom 5:3; 2 Cor 1:4-8; 6:4; 7:5; Eph 3:13; Phil 1:17; 4:14; 1 Thess 3:4, 7; 2 Thess 1:4-7.
[29] *NTI₁* 158.

produced. In my discussion of the parallel passages in Mark and
Luke, I have shown that the idea of "fruit(s)" is taken from Paul
and that it is the expression of our response to the gospel's call.[30]
Since the Gospel of Matthew is formulated as being God's
eschatological Torah, and Matthew 5-7 are specifically presented
as the messiah's law, "doing" ("bearing")[31] fruits is tantamount to
"doing" God's will (7:21). Consequently, those who do not "do
God's will" are "workers of *lawlessness*/iniquity"[32] (*ergazomenoi
tēn anomian*, v.23).[33] Indeed, one is required to *hear* and *do*
Jesus' words in order to enter the kingdom. Only then is one
"wise" as the wise maidens who join the bridegroom at the
marriage feast, and not "foolish" as the foolish ones who remain
stranded outside after the door is shut (25:10-12). The
connection between these two passages is further corroborated by
the confinement of the phrase "lord, lord" to Matthew 7:21-22
and 25:11. In both instances, the topic is the kingdom of heaven
(7:21; 25:1).

The Two Foundations (7:24-29)

This last pericope ought to be read together with the previous
one. Not only does it start with the conjunction "therefore" but
it also refers to the same topic of hearing Jesus' words and doing
them. At the same time, it uses the term "house" that is found in

---

[30] *NTI₁* 158-9; *NTI₂* 41-42, 70.

[31] The original Greek has all along the verb *poiein* (7:17-19), whose literal meaning is
"do" and which is translated as "bear" in conjunction with fruit(s).

[32] RSV has "evildoers."

[33] The verb *ergazomai* (work) is used equivalently to *poiō* (do): "Why do you trouble
the woman? For she has done (*ērgasato*) a beautiful thing to me. For you always have
the poor with you, but you will not always have me. In pouring this ointment on my
body she has done (*epoiēsen*) it to prepare me for burial. Truly, I say to you, wherever
this gospel is preached in the whole world, what she has done (*epoiēsen*) will be told in
memory of her." (Mt 26:10-13/Mk 14:6-9).

the rest of the Sermon on the Mount only in the opening passage (5:13-16) immediately after the blessings; consequently, it constitutes an *inclusio* with that opening statement and thus functions as a conclusion to the entire Sermon. This conclusion becomes compelling when one adds that the passage 5:14-17 itself stresses the importance of the good works (v.16). On the other hand, the combination of "building" and "rock" (*petra*) occurs only once more in this Gospel: "And I tell you, you are Peter, and on this rock I will build my church, and the powers of death shall not prevail against it" (16:18); nonetheless, it is this same Peter who is branded as "Satan" by Jesus himself a few verses later for betraying his own confession of faith (v.23).

The final conclusion is unavoidable. The two foundations pericope functions as a statement overarching the entire Gospel: this teaching of Jesus, and none other, is to be heeded by the crowds (7:28) as well as disciples (5:1) both of whom will prove to be recalcitrant until the end, where we hear that disciples, with Peter at their head, still "doubted" (28:17). Yet it is through the teaching laid down in the words of this Gospel, again and again refused by his followers, that Jesus will keep building his messianic community, generation after generation, "until the close of the age" (28:20).[34]

---

[34] Compare with 1 Cor 3:11-17 (For no other *foundation* can any one lay than that which is laid, which is Jesus Christ. Now if any one *builds on the foundation* with gold, silver, precious stones, wood, hay, straw— each man's work will become manifest; for the Day will disclose it, because it will be revealed with fire, and the fire will test what sort of work each one has done. If the work which any man *has built on the foundation survives, he will receive a reward.* If any man's work is burned up, he will suffer loss, though he himself will be saved, but only as through fire. Do you not know that you are God's temple and that God's Spirit dwells in you? If any one destroys God's temple, God will destroy him. For God's temple is holy, and that temple you are) and 4:15-17 (For though you have countless guides in Christ, you do not have many

Further Reading

Baxter, W. "The Narrative Setting of the Sermon on the Mount." *Trinity Journal* 25 (2004): 27-37.

Broer, I. "Das Ius Talionis im Neuen Testament." *New Testament Studies* 40 (1994): 1-21.

Draper J. A. "The Genesis and Narrative Thrust of the Paraenesis in the Sermon on the Mount." *Journal for the Study of the New Testament* 75 (1999): 25-48.

Dumbrell, W. J. "The Logic of the Role of the Law in Matthew v 1-20." *Novum Testamentum* 23 (1981): 1-21.

Harrington, D. J. "Not to abolish, but to fulfill." *Bible Today* 27 (1989): 333-337.

Harrington, D. J. "The Sermon on the Mount. What Is It?" *Bible Today* 36 (1996): 280-286.

Hemer, C. "*Epiousios*." *Journal for the Study of the New Testament* 22 (1984): 81-94.

Hill, D. "The Meaning of the Sermon on the Mount in Matthew's Gospel." *Irish Biblical Studies* 6 (1984) 120-133.

Janzen, D. "The Meaning of *Porneia* in Matthew 5.32 and 19.9: An Approach from the Study of Ancient Near Eastern Culture." *Journal for the Study of the New Testament* 80 (2000): 66-80.

Knowles, M. P. "Once More 'Lead Us Not *Eis Peirasmon*." *Expository Times* 115 (2004): 191-194.

Matera, F. J. "Jesus and the Law: Matthew's View." *Bible Today* 39 (2001): 271-76.

Minear, P. S. "The Salt of the Earth." *Interpretation* 51 (1997): 31-41.

---

fathers. For I became your father *in Christ Jesus through the gospel.* I urge you, then, be imitators of me. Therefore I sent to you Timothy, my beloved and faithful child in the Lord, to remind you of *my ways in Christ, as I teach them everywhere in every church*).

Murphy-O'Connor, J. "The Prayer of Petition (Matthew 7:7-11 and par.)." *Revue Biblique* 110 (2003): 399-416.

Powell, M. A. "Matthew's Beatitudes: reversals and rewards of the Kingdom." *Catholic Biblical Quarterly* 58 (1996): 460-479.

Thiessen, G. "Die Goldene Regel (Matthäus 7:12//Lukas 6:31): Über den Sitz im Leben ihrer positive und negative Form." *Biblical Interpretation* 11 (2003): 386-99.

Viljoen, F. P. "Jesus' Teaching on the *Torah* in the Sermon on the Mount." *Neotestamentica* 40 (2006): 135-155.

Whitters, M. F. "'The Eye Is the Lamp of the Body': Its Meaning in the Sermon of the Mount." *Irish Theological Quarterly* 71 (2006): 77-88.

Worth, R. H. *The Sermon on the Mount: Its Old Testament Roots.* New York/Mahwah, NJ: Paulist Press, 1997.

7

The Second Book of
the Law of the Messiah

Now that the messianic law has been laid down, in order to show its efficacy Matthew introduces in chapters 8 and 9 three sets of three miracles each. Since the messianic law is the Pauline gospel, Jesus' path in these chapters follows the itinerary of Paul's apostolic activity.

The First Set of Miracles (8:1-17)

To underline right from the beginning that the gospel is one and includes Gentiles as well as Jews, Matthew moves the Markan pericope of the cleansing of a leper (Mk 1:40-45) to the forefront (Mt 8:1-4), before the healing of many people (Mk 1:29-34/ Mt 8:14-17). The border line between clean and unclean, and thus between Israel and the Gentiles, is crossed since leprosy is punished with exclusion from God's community (Lev 13:45-46; Num 5:2-3). Furthermore, in asking the leper to "show yourself to the priest, and offer the gift that Moses commanded", Jesus witnesses against his opponents (Mt 8:4)[1] that he is not abolishing the Law but actually fulfilling it (Lev 14:2-3).

In order to further underscore that the gospel to Israel is none other than the one preached to and accepted by the Gentile "outsiders" (Rom 9-11) Matthew continues with the Lukan pericope of the healing of the centurion's servant in Capernaum

---

[1] See my comments on Mk 1:45 in *NTI₁* 145-6.

(Lk 7:1-10) which occurs in Luke much later than that of the cleansing of the leper (Lk 5:13-16). Compared to Mark, where Jesus' first activity in Capernaum was in a synagogue (Mk 1:21),[2] in Matthew the second miracle, although in Capernaum, targets the servant of a Gentile Roman centurion. Moreover, in Matthew the noun *pais* in the singular is reserved for sons of Gentiles (8:6, 8, 13 and 17:18) and to the quotation from Isaiah concerning the Lord's suffering servant:

> Behold, my servant (*pais*) whom I have chosen, my beloved with whom my soul is well pleased. I will put my Spirit upon him, and he shall proclaim justice to the Gentiles. He will not wrangle or cry aloud, nor will any one hear his voice in the streets; he will not break a bruised reed or quench a smoldering wick, till he brings justice to victory; and in his name will the Gentiles hope. (Mt 12:18-21; LXX Is 42:1-4)

The hearer of Matthew cannot help but perceive that the Gentile child becomes through the gospel similar to Jesus himself, as Paul taught in Romans:

> For all who are led by the Spirit of God are sons of God. For you did not receive the spirit of slavery to fall back into fear, but you have received the spirit of sonship. When we cry, "Abba! Father!" it is the Spirit himself bearing witness with our spirit that we are children of God, and if children, then heirs, heirs of God and fellow heirs with Christ, provided we suffer with him in order that we may also be glorified with him. (Rom 8:14-17)

As a member of the messianic community, he is fully entitled to sit at Abraham's fellowship table even to the exclusion of the insiders (Mt 8:11-12). That is why the attitude of the Gentiles is given as an example to follow by the Jews, should they seek

---

[2] The same is found in Luke 4:16-31.

salvation: "Truly, I say to you, not even in Israel have I found such faith." (v.10) Notice, in this regard, how the only other paralytic in Matthew is a Jew from Jesus' "own city" (Mt 9:1) who will be saved through faith (v.20) just as the centurion's servant was (8:13)

In line with his generalizing approach, Matthew rephrases Luke's statement from Luke 13:28-29. Whereas Luke had written, "There *you* will weep and gnash your teeth, when *you* see Abraham and Isaac and Jacob and all the prophets in the kingdom of God and *you* yourselves thrust out. And men will come from east and west, and from north and south, and sit at table in the kingdom of God" (Lk 13.28-29), Matthew writes, "I tell you, many will come from east and west and sit at table with Abraham, Isaac, and Jacob in the kingdom of heaven, while *the sons of the kingdom* will be thrown into the outer darkness; there men will weep and gnash their teeth." (Mt 8:11-12) and juxtaposes it with Jesus' reference to the Gentile centurion's faith. Taking into consideration that, in Matthew, the phrase "sons of the kingdom" applies to the believers in the gospel (13:38; see also 5:3, 10),[3] the conclusion is clear: Jesus brings to fruition the Baptist's teaching—that God could raise from the stones children to Abraham—in response to those whose boast was "We have Abraham as our father" (3:9). However, since in Matthew the "sons of the kingdom" include those in the church, this passage also stands as a warning to all of those, whether Jew or Gentile, who consider themselves to be part of Abraham's inheritance. *Any* member of Abraham's family may be cast out of the kingdom if they fail to produce the fruits of Abraham's faith.

---

[3] The Hebrew phrase "sons of" is a general expression meaning "those who pertain to."

Now that the Pauline gospel has reached and been accepted by the Gentiles, the meeting with the Jerusalem church, symbolized by Peter's mother-in-law, follows.[4] From the standpoint of the gospel, as Paul explained in Romans, the Jews are in the same position as the Gentiles: stretched out on a sickbed. [Peter's mother-in law (8:14), the Jewish paralytic (9:2), and the centurion's servant (8:6) are all found in this position, linked by the use of the perfect form of the verb *ballō*.[5]] Matthew makes it clear that it is the gospel word which is the sole way for healing of all Jews: "... he cast out the spirits with a word,[6] and healed all who were sick." (8:16). Both "with a/the word" and "all" (typical of Romans) are found in Matthew, but not in Mark and Luke. Finally, the healer of the Jews is none other than the "servant (*pais*) of the Lord" who healed the centurion's son. Indeed, Mt 8:17 makes reference to the same suffering servant who is mentioned in Mt 12:18-21 .The parallelism between the two passages can be seen in the similar phraseology:

> That evening they brought to him *many* who were possessed with demons; and he cast out the spirits with a word, and *healed all* who were sick. *This was to fulfil what was spoken by the prophet Isaiah*, "He took our infirmities and bore our diseases." (8:16-17)

> And *many* followed him, and he *healed them all*, and ordered them not to make him known. *This was to fulfil what was spoken by the prophet Isaiah*: "Behold, my servant whom I have chosen..." (12:15-18)

---

[4] See my comments on Mk 1:30-31 in *NTI₁* 144. One may also surmise that the Greek *penthera* (mother-in-law) brings to mind the Greek number *pente* (five) recalling the five books of the Law and thus the Mosaic Law to which Peter and his community were bound.

[5] These are the only three instances of the passive perfect (*beblē-*) of *ballō* (throw [down]) in Matthew.

[6] The Greek *logō* may also be understood as "with the word."

On Following Jesus (8:18-22)

Thus, the message begun with the leper goes to the Gentile centurion and then to Peter and through him to all Israel. It is this gospel that is offered to all who will have to follow Jesus "on the other side" (8:18), away from Jerusalem and into the Roman sea (v.24). Notice how Matthew makes clear this centrifugal direction of the gospel preaching away from Jerusalem into the Roman empire. Whereas Luke places Jesus' teachings on discipleship during Jesus' ascent to Jerusalem (Lk 9:51-62) Matthew positions them between the time that Jesus "gave orders to go to the other side" (Mt 8:18) into the area of the Gentile Gadarenes (v.28) and the time "he got into the boat" where "his disciples followed him" (v.23). Jesus' true followers in the domain of the Roman sea are to heed his caveat: from the perspective of the gospel there is no difference between Jew and Gentile.

The scribe is to understand that to follow Jesus means to follow the Son of man who came to implement the forgiveness of sins (9:2, 6) and consequently he is to be prepared not to be scandalized as the scribes will be (v.3). In order to do that, the Jewish scribe will have to admit that he himself is a sinner just as the exiled Jews who were addressed by the son of man Ezekiel (Ezek 2-3) and thus that he is no better than the Gentiles:

> Son of man, go, get you to the house of Israel, and speak with my words to them. For you are not sent to a people of foreign speech and a hard language, but to the house of Israel—not to many peoples of foreign speech and a hard language, whose words you cannot understand. Surely, if I sent you to such, they would listen to you. But the house of Israel will not listen to you; for they are not willing to listen to me; because all the house of Israel are of a hard forehead and of a stubborn heart. (Ezek 3:4-7)

Furthermore, to follow the Son of man who "has nowhere to lay his head" means not to worry about any edifice linked to Judaism, whether it be the temple or any burial place, since all edifices are bound to destruction just as human beings are bound to death; hence, the true follower of the Son of man is to heed Jesus' other call to "leave the dead bury their own dead." The disciple of Jesus is to invite others to become true children of Abraham whose God is "not God of the dead, but of the living" (22:32), the God whose Messiah is "able to destroy the temple of God, and to build it in three days" (26:61)

The Second Set of Miracles (8:23-9:8)

After the call to heed the requirements of true discipleship we see Jesus crossing over into the domain of the Gentiles, in spite of the storm, and then returning to heal the paralytic in "his own city" where he faces a controversy with the leaders of Judaism. This presentation fits perfectly with what we read in Galatians 1:11-2:14.

The second set of miracles is presented against the background of the Galatians controversy. The episode of the calming of the storm follows upon the preceding pericope: "But Jesus said to him, '*Follow me*, and leave the dead to bury their own dead.' And when he got into the boat, his disciples *followed him*." (Mt 8:22-23) This passage away from Jerusalem to the "other side," across the Roman sea, prepares for the apostolic mission as outlined in ch.10 through the use of the verb *kalyptō* (cover) which occurs in Matthew only in these two passages. While Matthew borrows the terminology of "sleeping" (*ekatheuden*)[7]

---

[7] See "Awake, O sleeper (*katheudōn*), and arise from the dead, and Christ shall give you light" (Eph 5:14).

and "waking" (*ēgeiran*)[8] (8:24-25) from Mark and Luke, "being swamped" by the waves, exclusive to Matthew, is the translation of the Greek *kalyptesthai* found later in Mt 10:26: "So have no fear of them; for nothing is covered (*kekalymmenon*) that will not be revealed, or hidden that will not be known." The intent to refer to the apostolic mission outside the realm of Judaism can be further seen in that the pericope of the calming of the storm is a literary foreshadowing of Jesus' death in Judah and his resurrectional epiphany in the Galilee of the Gentiles (28:16). Indeed, Matthew refers to the storm as *seismos* ([earth]quake, 8:24), a term that occurs later only in conjunction with Jesus' death (27:54) and resurrection (28:2).

It is then with the message of the word (of the cross and resurrection) that Jesus moves "to the other side, to the country of the (Gentile) Gadarenes" to perform his healing among the Gentiles and release them from the demons that rule them (8:28). Jesus' intervention resulted in the healing of the two demoniacs and the cleansing of the Gentile land of the Gadarenes: the land was rid of the swine, which are symbolic of the uncleanness of the Gentiles (8:31-32). The result was that the gospel news[9] reached the city of the Gentiles,[10] which "came out" (*exēlthen*) in its entirety to "meet" (*eis apantēsin*) Jesus. The

---

[8] See "Besides this you know what hour it is, how it is full time now for you to wake (*egerthēnai*) from sleep. For salvation is nearer to us now than when we first believed; the night is far gone, the day is at hand" (Rom 13:11-12a).

[9] The verb *apēngeilan* (translated "told" in RSV) is from the verb *apangello*—from the same root as *euangelion* (gospel)—which is used in some cases in conjunction with the proclamation of the good news (Mt 11:4; 28:8, 10; Mk 5:19; Lk 7:22; 24:9; 1 Thess 1:9).

[10] Very probably "the city" here is symbolic of Rome, the capital city of the empire. In Matthew, we have in 8:33-34 the only two instances of the phrase "the city," without any qualification, outside the references to Jerusalem.

only other instance of this phrase in Matthew occurs to describe
the virgins who "went [out] (*exēlthon*) to meet (*eis apantēsin*) the
bridegroom" (25:2). In other words, "all the city" of the Gentiles
went out to meet Jesus just as Roman cities went out to meet the
emperor during his visits (*parousia*) to them. Yet surprisingly, no
sooner have the inhabitants gone to meet Jesus than they
"begged him to leave (*metabē*) their neighborhood." Why did
they ask him to do so?

The verb *metabainō* (move to another place) occurs in
Matthew five times, four with Jesus as subject. Besides the
passage under discussion here, Jesus moves in order to "teach and
preach" (11:1), to enter a synagogue (12:9) in order to heal a
man with a withered hand and teach the audience the true
meaning of the sabbath (vv.10-13), and to sit on the mountain
along the Sea of Galilee (15:29) in order to heal (the outsider)
"great crowds" (v.30). The fifth occurrence is the following: "For
truly, I say to you, if you have faith as a grain of mustard seed,
you will say to *this mountain*, 'Move (*Metaba*) from here to
there,' and it will move (*metabēsetai*); and nothing will be
impossible to you." (17:20). This mountain is none other that
the mount of transfiguration (17:1-19), which is the Mount of
Olives where the Lord shall come in glory to judge Israel and the
nations.[11] Through faith in the gospel word, the scriptural Lord
can relocate anywhere he wishes, just as the Ezekelian God did
through the prophetic word of scripture. The conclusion is that
the verb *metabainō* in Matthew is always used in reference to the
preaching of the gospel. Consequently, one may understand the
petition of the Gadarenes, who accepted the messiahship of
Jesus, as a request that he move from their territory in order to

---

[11] Zech 14.

continue spreading the gospel word. My understanding is corroborated in that Jesus' following action is to cross again by boat and go to "his own city," where he will heal the "Jewish" paralytic just as he had healed the Gentile one.[12] This is the itinerary of Paul's gospel as described in Romans: the gospel to the Gentiles together with the news of its acceptance is to be relayed to Israel.

The healing of the paralytic, the third miracle of the second set, relays to us how the Jewish leadership was scandalized at the message of forgiveness of sins offered to the Jews free of charge by the same Son of man who had offered it in this way to the Gentiles. The difficulty of this offer lies in the fact that the Jew would have to admit that he also is a sinner. Otherwise, he will not be able to take part in the table fellowship around Jesus who "came not to call the righteous, but sinners" (Mt 9:9-13).

Calling of Matthew (9:9-13)

Now that the Pauline gospel, established in the first triad of miracle stories, has spread to both Gentiles and Jews in the second triad, we are introduced to his "follower" (Mt 9:9) who will carry out the propagation of the gospel as scripture among the upcoming generations of church leaders. He is a publican, in the service of the Roman empire, and, if Jewish, a sinner in the Pharisee's eyes. Yet, in Jesus' eyes he is the exemplary follower, since he shares table fellowship with him merely through God's grace. This feature is suggested in the very name "Matthew": the Hebrew *mattan* means "gift". Thus, through God's mercy

---

[12] See my comments above on Mt 8:1-8.

(v.13a) anyone[13] is invited to join the company of "disciples" (v.10) around the "teacher" Jesus (v.11). Since Jesus came for sinners and not the righteous (v.13b), it is exclusively as sinner that one is granted God's salvation. The terminology of salvation through grace and mercy, combined with the statement that all those who are saved are sinners, is clearly Paul's teaching in Romans, which is the classical written presentation of the gospel to the Jerusalemite leaders, represented here by the Pharisees (v.11). Notice the stress on mercy, which is the main point of Paul's conclusion regarding Jews and Gentiles, in the quotation from Hosea 6:6:

> Just as you were once disobedient to God but now have received mercy because of their disobedience, so they have now been disobedient in order that by the mercy shown to you they also may receive mercy. For God has consigned all men to disobedience, that he may have mercy upon all. (Rom 11:30-32)

The Question of Fasting (9:14-17)

In Matthew Jesus is the teacher as Messiah.[14] As Messiah he is the bridegroom who is coming to initiate the eschatological feast in the new heavenly Jerusalem. His followers, who are not bound to the earthly Jerusalem, need not fast in conjunction with its destruction, as was the case in Jeremiah's time (Jer 36:5-9). Their time of fasting is to be determined in conjunction with the bridegroom. So long as he is with them, they are to rejoice. When he is taken from them, then they will fast. Still their fasting will be looking ahead toward the new Jerusalem, and in no way looking back at the old one. Indeed, we are dealing here

---

[13] Notice how, besides changing the name from Levi (as in Mark and Luke) to Matthew, the Evangelist Matthew refers to the publican as *anthrōpon* (a man).

[14] See my comments on 5:1 and the Sermon on the Mount.

with new garments and new wine, reflective of the new feast in the new Jerusalem that lies ahead.

The Gospel Is Proclaimed to All

I pointed out earlier that the call to Matthew is in preparation for the carrying on of the proclamation of the gospel elucidated in Romans throughout the Roman empire. The subsequent three stories (Mt 9:18-34) follow the sequence underlined in Romans: the gospel is first announced to the Jews (9:18-26), then through Jews who accepted it (9:27-31) to the Gentiles (9:32-34). In Romans, Paul repeatedly stresses that the gospel is *first* (*prōton*) to the Jews and then also to the Gentiles,[15] through him, "an Israelite, a descendant of Abraham, a member of the tribe of Benjamin" (Rom 11:1).[16] On the other hand, since Paul is the apostle to the Gentiles, his message is intended to all those living throughout the Roman empire:

> ... we have received grace and apostleship to bring about the obedience of faith for the sake of his name among all the nations, including yourselves who are called to belong to Jesus Christ ... I am under obligation both to Greeks and to barbarians, both to the wise and to the foolish: so I am eager to preach the gospel to you also who are in Rome. (Rom 1:5-6, 14-15)

> For I will not venture to speak of anything except what Christ has wrought through me to win obedience from the Gentiles, by word and deed, by the power of signs and wonders, by the power of the Holy Spirit, so that from Jerusalem and as far round as Illyricum I have fully preached the gospel of Christ, thus making it my ambition to preach the gospel, not where Christ has already been

---

[15] Rom 1:16; 2:9-10.

[16] Notice how Paul is healed of his blindness to become Christ's apostle to the Gentiles in the work of Luke (Acts 9:1-19).

named, lest I build on another man's foundation, but as it is written, "They shall see who have never been told of him, and they shall understand who have never heard of him." This is the reason why I have so often been hindered from coming to you. But now, since I no longer have any room for work in these regions, and since I have longed for many years to come to you, I hope to see you in passing as I go to Spain, and to be sped on my journey there by you, once I have enjoyed your company for a little. (15:18-24)

Matthew follows suit by adding, when compared to Mark and Luke, at the end of each of the first two stories: "And the report of this went *through all that district*" (Mt 9:26); "But they went away and spread his fame *through all that district*" (v.31).

A Ruler's Daughter and the Woman with a Hemorrhage (9:18-26)

I explained in my comments on the Markan passage that these two women represent Judaism as centered around Jerusalem.[17] Whereas in Mark the young girl is ailing (5:23), in Matthew, who follows Luke, Jerusalem is already destroyed and thus the young girl is already dead (Lk 8:42; Mt 9:18). In Luke, however, the petitioner, Jairus, is "a ruler of the synagogue," whereas in Matthew he is not named and presented as *heis arkhōn* (a [certain] ruler). Instead of being indeed the "a guide to the blind, a light to those who are in darkness" as a Jew should be (Rom 2:19), Jairus (the Hebrew *ya'ir* means enlightener) loses de facto his Jewishness and, instead of being a ruler of a synagogue (Mk 5:22/Lk 8:41), becomes just a chieftain as any other. The message's universal intent is further corroborated in that Matthew's rendition of the Markan (and Lukan) story is very

---

[17] See *NTI₁* 166.

succinct and completely eliminates the lengthy passage in which Jesus takes Peter, James, and John with him into the young girl's room. Unlike Mark and Luke who wrote in conjunction with the fall of Jerusalem, Matthew's purview does not include a special attention to the Jewish leadership. His addressees are the members of the church, Gentile as well as Jew, and the gospel lessons apply indiscriminately to either. Indeed, not only does Matthew keep the same requirement of faith from the (Jewish) woman with a hemorrhage (Mt 9:22/Mk 5:34/Lk 8:48)[18] but, unlike Mark ("For this saying you may go your way"; 7:29), he will apply the same rule later to the Canaanite woman ("great is your faith"; Mt 15:28).

Healing of Two Blind Men (9:27-31)

The Markan story of the blind man in Jericho (Mk 10:46-52), which Matthew preserves in its original position (Mt 20:29-34), is duplicated here and rephrased. It is basically generalized: we do not hear of Jericho and there is no mention of a crowd. This generalization goes hand in hand with that underscored in the previous pericope. The parallelism in intent of the two pericopes can also be seen in that the main point of the original story—it is due to faith that the blind's eyes are opened (Mk 10:52/Lk 18:42)—is kept here (Mt 9:28, 29) but not in Matthew 20:29-34 in order to correspond to what was said to the Jews in the previous story (9:22).

The doubling of the blind man is done to show that Jesus' action was witnessed by two persons and thus valid in the eyes of the Law (Deut 17:6; 19:15). This device serves a double purpose:

---

[18] In all three cases it is the same wording *hē pistis sou sesōken se* (your faith has made you well).

to underscore that the gospel does not abolish scripture but fulfills it (Mt 5:17), and to spotlight Jesus' false condemnation by the Pharisees (Mt 9:34).

Healing of the Dumb Demoniac (9:32-34)

To complete his triad Matthew duplicates here this story, which he copies in 12:22-24 from Luke (11:14-15). There are two main changes that were required from its positioning here. The first is its link with the proclamation of the gospel by the healed blind men through the addition to the original story of the phrase "As they were going away": "But they went away (*exelthontes*) and spread his fame through all that district. As they were going away (*exerkhomenōn*), behold, a dumb demoniac was brought to him." (9:31-32) The Greek verb *exerkhomai* actually means "go out" and corresponds perfectly to the idea of going out in order to proclaim the good news.[19] The second change is also an addition to the Lukan original. The crowd's amazement is expressed in their "saying, 'Never was anything like this seen in Israel'" (Mt 9:33b). Indeed, Israel witnessed that a (Gentile) dumb becomes a witness to the gospel: the verb *elalēsen* (translated as "spoke" in RSV) is from *laleō*, meaning "to speak the gospel word."[20] However, the Jewish leaders, Paul's opponents, accused Jesus of being Satan, not God's subject (v.34). The falseness of their accusation is evident, since Jesus' power was already validated by two witnesses. Their attack was triggered by the fact that his power of healing reached also the Gentiles.

---

[19] See *NTI₁* 145, 187.
[20] See *NTI₁* 147, 163, 180.

The Harvest is Great (9:35-38)

It is the Pauline gospel to the Gentiles that is now proclaimed throughout the Roman empire to Jews and Gentiles alike. We have here the repetition of Matthew 4:23 which I showed to be a reference to this open mission:

> And he went about all Galilee, teaching in their synagogues and preaching the gospel of the kingdom and healing every disease and every infirmity among the people. (Mt 4:23)

> And Jesus went about all the cities and villages, teaching in their synagogues and preaching the gospel of the kingdom, and healing every disease and every infirmity. (9:35)

Furthermore, the reason given is Jesus' compassion (9:36a), the expression of God's mercy which is the object of the gospel in Romans.[21] Indeed, the gospel is aimed at the needy sheep (v.36b; also 10:6). That is why the disciples are informed of the difficult task (9:37) with the view of sending them out to continue Jesus' work until the end of times, for which purpose he asks them to pray that God keep finding new laborers for his harvest (v.38). In Matthew, the harvest is clearly linked to the end times:

> He who sows the good seed is the Son of man; the field is the world, and the good seed means the sons of the kingdom; the weeds are the sons of the evil one, and the enemy who sowed them is the devil; the harvest is the close of the age, and the reapers are angels. Just as the weeds are gathered and burned with fire, so will it be at *the close of the age*. (Mt 13:37-40; italics mine)

---

[21] Rom 11:30-32. See above my comments on the Call of Matthew (Mt 8:9-13).

Prolegomena to the Mission of the Twelve

Mark's foremost interest was the mission to the Judeans exhorting them to repent and accept the gospel of peace before the imminent fall of Jerusalem.[22] Luke, writing after the fall of that city, has two sendings, one to Israel by the twelve (Lk 6:13-19) and the other to all nations by the seventy (10:1-17).[23] By the time of the writing of Matthew, the division was between the Pauline churches, composed mainly of Gentiles but also Jews, and the followers of Paul's opponents, who continued to adhere to Jewish practice. Yet, although the basic matrix of the church was Gentile, the one gospel in Matthew remains open to the Pharisees as a last call, just as we read in Romans: first the Jew, and then the Gentile. Consequently, in Matthew 10 there is an intended collocation between the two missions: the gospel is addressed to both Jew and Gentile in one voice. By design, Matthew brings organization to what is spread over the Gospel of Mark, and at the same time produces a merger of Luke's two sendings.[24] By the same token, what Matthew keeps unchanged from his sources, he also does so by design.

The gospel to the Gentiles (Mt 4:23), which was offered to the Jews (9:35), is to be carried by Jesus' disciples to both Israel and the nations in the same terms found earlier: "And he called to him his twelve disciples and gave them authority over unclean

---

[22] *NTI₁* 121-7.

[23] *NTI₂* 84.

[24] Notice especially how Matthew 10:26-36 is taken from Lk 12:2-9 and 51-52, verses I have shown to be injunctions pertaining to the gospel (*NTI₂* 102-3, 111) More importantly, the passage Matthew 10:17-23 has it source in Mark 13:9-13 and Luke 21:12-29, which are part of Jesus' eschatological discourse during which he instructs his apostles concerning the preaching of the gospel throughout the Roman empire, to Jews as well as Gentiles. Add to this that Matthew himself includes some of this material in his chapter 24, which is his version of Jesus' eschatological discourse.

spirits, to cast them out, and to heal every disease and every infirmity." (10:1; compare with 4:23 and 9:35). Since the stress is on the one gospel to both, the Matthean program of evangelization follows the agreement established at the Jerusalem meeting (Gal 2:1-10):

> ... when they saw that I had been entrusted with the gospel to the uncircumcised, just as Peter had been entrusted with the gospel to the circumcised (for he who worked through Peter for the mission [*apostolēn*, apostleship] to the circumcised worked through me also for the Gentiles), and when they perceived the grace that was given to me, James and Cephas and John, who were reputed to be pillars, gave to me and Barnabas the right hand of fellowship, that we should go to the Gentiles and they to the circumcised. (vv.7-9)

Indeed, Matthew's strict reliance on Galatians is betrayed in the way he handles the commissioning of the twelve. The twelve disciples (Mt 10:1) are called "the twelve apostles" (v.2), which is the only instance where Matthew uses the noun "apostle" in his entire gospel; otherwise, he systematically uses "disciple" to refer to the general discipleship as well as to any of the twelve. Moreover, in the list, Peter is referred to as "first" only in Matthew; he is thus the representative of the apostleship dealt with in this chapter. Peter and his fellows are restricted to the mission to Israel (v.5), because the mission to the Gentiles is Paul's domain.

On the other hand, the apostle Matthew's position in the list is altered, when compared to the ones in Mark and Luke. He is moved from seventh to eighth place and is specifically called "the publican" (v.3). In my comments on the apostolic list in Mark, I indicated that the last four names – James the son of Alphaeus, Thaddaeus, Simon the Cananaean, and Judas Iscariot – reflected the attitude of betrayal to the gospel by Peter and James and their followings.[25] Matthew follows suit by copying Mark:

> James the son of Alphaeus, and Thaddaeus, and Simon the Cananaean, and Judas Iscariot, who betrayed him. (Mk 3:18b-19a)

> James the son of Alphaeus, and Thaddaeus; Simon the Cananaean, and Judas Iscariot, who betrayed him. (Mt 10:3b-4a)

The implication is clear. Matthew the publican, the prototype of the consummate disciple, *closes* the part of the list that reflects the stand taken originally by Peter and James at the Jerusalem meeting. In so doing, the Evangelist Matthew himself, for whom Matthew the publican is a stand-in,[26] is underscoring that Jesus' teaching in Matthew 10 is the last word to Israel. By extension, the entire gospel is the message of salvation to Israel as it is to the Gentiles. From the perspective of the gospel, as Paul taught in Romans, Israel is comprised of "lost sheep" (10:6) as much as the "crowds" are (9:36). In his presentation Matthew follows Isaiah's teaching on the Suffering Servant, whose mission is first to Israel, but also to the nations (Is 49:5-6) and whom Matthew later uses as prototype to sum up Jesus' mission (12:15-21; quoting Is 42:1-4).

Mission of the Twelve (10:1-42)

The commission to the twelve is very clear: go only to the cities of Israel. The finality of the mission to Israel is emphasized. It is an exclusive offer that is made in a categorical way: Israel is not God's kingdom; rather the kingdom of the heavens is at hand and the children of Israel are to be ready for it. The initial

---

[25] *NTI*, 153-54.
[26] See above my comments on Mt 9:9-13.

exclusivity—only to Israel—is immediately qualified in terms of the Pauline gospel: "You received without paying (*dōrean*), give without pay (*dōrean*)." (Mt 10:8b) Although common in Paul, the adverb *dōrean* is found in Matthew only in this verse, where it is used twice. Since the kingdom is a gift to Israel, which comes to them from outside, they will have to carry it to those outside, and in the act of doing so they will in fact encounter the kingdom. In scripture, God's gift starts while Israel is in the land of exile. Here, since the gospel represents God's last call to his people, it is, as Paul insistently taught, a message of final judgment (*krisis*) and possible condemnation (*katakrima*)[27] whereby not only the individual house, but the entire city will be eliminated:

And whatever town or village you enter, find out who is worthy in it, and stay with him until you depart. As you enter the house, salute it. And if the house is worthy, let your peace come upon it; but if it is not worthy, let your peace return to you. And if any one will not receive you or listen to your words, shake off the dust from your feet as you leave that house or town. Truly, I say to you, it shall be more tolerable on the day of judgment for the land of Sodom and Gomorrah than for that town. (Mt 10:11-15)

At this point where mention is made of eventual refusal and condemnation, Matthew includes the nations in the same mission. The same testimony to the Jews applies to the Gentiles:

Behold, I send you out as sheep in the midst of wolves; so be wise as serpents and innocent as doves. Beware of men; for they will deliver you up to councils, and flog you in their synagogues, and you will be dragged before governors and kings for my sake, to bear testimony before them and the Gentiles. (vv.16-18)

---

[27] See e.g. Rom 2:14-16; 1 Cor 11:28-32.

Again, as Paul taught, the source of the gospel is not the Jewish apostles, but God's spirit (vv.17-18). However, according to Ezekiel, this Spirit which brings about the new Torah for Israel originates in the land of exile, while Israel is scattered among the nations. That is why the eschatological Torah emanating from the new spirit poured in the new heart (Ezek 36:26-27) applies *as is* to the Gentiles, with all its implications: destruction if one refuses the offer but also life for the one who accepts it "to the end" (Mt 10:22a; see Ezek 18:31).

The underscoring of the fact that the gospel brings about God's final judgment can be seen in the constant interplay between destruction or death, on the one hand, and life, on the other hand, throughout Jesus' speech. The root *apollymi* (destroy, lose) brackets the entire speech as an *inclusio*: "but go rather to the lost (*apolōlota*) sheep of the house of Israel" (Mt 10:6); "He who finds his life (soul) will lose (*apolesei*) it, and he who loses (*apolesas*) his life (soul) for my sake will find it" (v.39) and "And whoever gives to one of these little ones even a cup of cold water because he is a disciple, truly, I say to you, he shall not lose (*apolesē*) his reward" (v.42). In v.28 this same verb is used in parallel with *apokteinō* (kill): "And do not fear those who kill (*apokteinontōn*) the body but cannot kill (*apokteinai*) the soul; rather fear him who can destroy (*apolesai*) both soul and body in hell." The message is clear: whoever is worried about preserving himself and his world will meet the same fate as Jerusalem, which fell to the Romans. Only the one who follows the lead of God's spirit and not his own self (soul)[28] and accepts

---

[28] In the Bible the human *psychē* (soul, self) is always in contradistinction to the divine *pneuma* (spirit). See, e.g., the classic Pauline statement: "It is sown a physical body, it is raised a spiritual body. If there is a physical body, there is also a spiritual body. Thus it is written, 'The first man Adam became a living being'; the last Adam became a life-

the gospel's call to open up for the needs of one's neighbor will find the true life granted by God's spirit. This, in turn, is seen in how Matthew uses the opponents' *topoi* (literary topics) of peace and war to turn their value around. Whereas the Romans bring peace through the sword of destruction, Jesus' disciples, unlike the Jewish revolutionaries, will bring God's peace through the mission assigned to them, which entails the sword of judgment based on mercy for, and service to, others.[29]

Further Reading

Agourides, S. "'Little ones' in Matthew." *Bible Translator* 35 (1984): 329-334.

Agourides, S. "The Mission of the Twelve Apostles within a persecuted Church [Matthew 10,1-42." *Deltion Biblikon Meleton* 27 (1998): 5-36.

Alesso Paraná, F. P. "'Vayan y aprendan.' Lectura de Mt 9,9-13 en clave communicativa. Primera Parte." *Rivista Biblica* 68 (2006): 35-71.

Alesso Paraná, F. P. "'Vayan y aprendan.' Lectura de Mt 9,9-13 en clave communicativa. Segunda Parte." *Rivista Biblica* 68 (2006): 133-173.

Allison, D. C. "Matthew 10:26-31 and the Problem of Evil." *St Vladimir's Theological Quarterly* 32 (1988): 293-308.

---

giving spirit. But it is not the spiritual which is first but the physical, and then the spiritual." (1 Cor 15:44-46)

[29] Regarding the gospel being the "sword of peace" see Eph 6:13-17 (Therefore take the whole armor of God, that you may be able to withstand in the evil day, and having done all, to stand. Stand therefore, having girded your loins with truth, and having put on the breastplate of righteousness, and having shod your feet with the equipment of the gospel of peace; besides all these, taking the shield of faith, with which you can quench all the flaming darts of the evil one. And take the helmet of salvation, and the sword of the Spirit, which is the word of God).

Feiler, P. "The Stilling of the Storm in Matthew: A Response to Günther Bornkamm." *Journal of the Evangelical Theological Society* 26 (1983): 399-406.

Gundry, R. H. "On True and False Disciples in Matthew 8.18-22." *New Testament Studies* 40(1994): 433-441.

Kiley, M. "Why 'Matthew' in Matt 9,9-13?" *Biblica* 65 (1984): 347-351

Pappas, H. S. "The Exhortation to Fearless Confession." *Greek Orthodox Theological Review* 25 (1980): 239-248.

Park, E. C. *The Mission Discourse in Matthew's Interpretation.* Wissentschaftliche Untersuchungen zum Neuen Testament, 2. Reihe 81. Tübingen: Mohr-Siebeck, 1995.

8

The Third Book of
the Law of the Messiah

The Pauline Gospel (11:1)

Jesus' teaching to the twelve apostles, which was "finished, completed" (*etelesen*), is none other than the gospel Paul preached. This is betrayed by the verb *diatassōn* (instructing)—the sole instance of this term in Matthew—which is found in the Pauline literature to speak of the gospel in terms of divine ordinance. On the one hand, it occurs in reference to Paul's directive to his appointed bishop (Tit 1:5) as well as to his instructions to his churches:

> Only, let every one lead the life which the Lord has assigned to him, and in which God has called him. This is my rule (thus I teach/command, *houtōs diatassomai*) in all the churches. (1 Cor 7:17)

> About the other things I will give directions (*diataxomai*) when I come. (11:34b)

> Now concerning the contribution for the saints: as I directed (*dietaxa*) the churches of Galatia, so you also are to do. (16:1)

On the other hand, *diatassōn* is also used to speak of God's Law (Gal 3:19; 1 Cor 9:12-14). This gospel is offered now to John the Baptist and, through him, to all his disciples, as the only way of repentance (Mt 11:20). Thus, Matthew 11 repeats and intensifies the message of ch.10. What Jesus has just taught in ch.10 is nothing else than what God had taught in the Old

173

Testament: the Law and the Prophets (11:13), and the Wisdom Writings (v.19). What Jesus taught is the eschatological law of the Messiah, to whose yoke everyone is called to submit (vv.28-20; compare with Gal 6:2 and Rom 8:2).

Messengers of John the Baptist (11:2-6)

In my discussion of Paul, Mark and Luke, I pointed out that Isaiah was the major scriptural book used by Paul to formulate his gospel.[1] Following Luke's lead (Lk 7:18-23), Matthew states: "The blind receive their sight and the lame walk, lepers are cleansed and the deaf hear, and the dead are raised up, and the poor have good news preached to them."[2] (Mt 11:5) However, he rephrases Luke in a way that reflects even more clearly the reference to the Pauline gospel. Matthew omits the Lukan verses that tell of Jesus' performing in the presence of the Baptist's disciples (Lk 7:20-21): Jesus has just done that through his apostles (Mt 10:8). Indeed, we are told that "John heard in prison about *the deeds of the Christ*" (11:2). Thus, the main point here is that (the Isaianic) scripture is fulfilled in the gospel (11:1). Also, when compared with Luke, Matthew adds that the Baptist was in prison (*desmōtēriō*). In the New Testament, this noun occurs only here and in Acts 5:21, 23 and 26:26, where I showed it to be an oblique reference to the Mosaic Law that Paul had described in terms of imprisonment.[3] On the other hand, in Matthew, the other mention that the Baptist was arrested introduces Jesus' preaching in Galilee (Mt 4:12), exactly as the case is here (11:20-24). This may well be harking back to what Paul said in Philippians, namely that his imprisonment was to be

---

[1] *NTI₁* and *NTI₂*.

[2] Is 26:19; 29:18-19; 35:5-6; 42:18.

[3] *NTI₂* 201-2;

seen as a trigger to the gospel being preached to Rome and thus preparing for the Lord's coming (Phil 1:3-11), which is precisely what we read in Matthew: the Baptist's disciples were to ask Jesus "Are you he who is to come?" and receive the answer from him.

Jesus' Witness Concerning John the Baptist (11:7-19)

This pericope follows the same line of thought: the preaching of the Baptist inaugurates the kingdom of heaven, inasmuch as this preaching is the fulfillment of scripture. Here again, Matthew is clear; he ends the passage with the following addition over Luke:

> From the days of John the Baptist until now the kingdom of heaven has suffered violence, and men of violence take it by force. For all the prophets and the law prophesied until John; and if you are willing to accept it, he is Elijah who is to come. He who has ears to hear, let him hear. (Mt 11:12-15)

First, the beginning statement (From the days… until John) is borrowed from Luke 6:16, a part of a passage comparing the Mosaic Law to the kingdom of God. Secondly, Jesus declares here that the Baptist is Elijah and, as such, the representative of the *entire* Old Testament prophetic literature,[4] which together with the Law accounts, in Matthew, for the entire scripture. Finally, the call "He who has ears to hear, let him hear" occurs elsewhere in Matthew at the end of the two parables depicting the "word" (of the gospel) as a seed that produces fruit (Mt 13:9, 43).

That the preaching of the Baptist is considered to be the gospel inaugurating the kingdom of God puts it on the same footing as

---

[4] Cf. Mal 4.4-6. Notice how Matthew has "*all* the prophets and the law" compared to Luke's "the law and the prophets."

the preaching of Jesus Christ, which is the thesis of Mathew, who alone among the Evangelists fully equates the preaching of Jesus and that of the Baptist:

> In those days came John the Baptist, preaching in the wilderness of Judea, "Repent, for the kingdom of heaven is at hand." (3:1-2)

> From that time Jesus began to preach, saying, "Repent, for the kingdom of heaven is at hand." (4:17)

Since the passage dealing with the Baptist is triggered by his having heard of Jesus' deeds, Matthew ends it with a rephrasing of the Lukan "Yet wisdom is justified by all her children" (Lk 7:35) into "Yet wisdom is justified by her deeds" (Mt 11:19b). As I mentioned earlier, Jesus' deeds actually were performed through the preaching of the gospel he assigned to the twelve. On the other hand, "deeds" fits perfectly the immediately preceding statement "the Son of man came eating and drinking, and they say, 'Behold, a glutton and a drunkard, a friend of tax collectors and sinners!'" In its turn, this behavior reflects the gospel's teaching concerning table fellowship between Jews and Gentiles. The gospel to the Gentiles is the gospel that is to be preached to Israel; yet "*this* generation" (v.16a) is having difficulty submitting to it (vv.16b-19). And whereas, in Luke, "this generation" refers to "the Pharisees and the lawyers" (Lk 7:30-31), the address is generalized in Matthew's gospel to apply to the church, the messianic community of Gentiles and Jews.

Woe to Unrepentant Cities (11:20-24)

That the church membership is the intended audience is corroborated by how Matthew handles the Lukan invective against Chorazin, Bethsaida, and Capernaum (Lk 10:12-15): he introduces it with "Then he began to upbraid the cities where most of his mighty works had been done, because they did not repent" (Mt 11:20). Their lack of repentance puts them under the ultimate divine judgment, exemplified by the destruction of Sodom. However, since repentance in Matthew is the basic condition for the entrance into the kingdom (3:2; 4:17), which can be attained only by "the sons of the kingdom" (13:38) whose "righteousness [is to] exceed that of the scribes and Pharisees" (5:20), the message is clearly intended to the church members.

God's Fatherhood and Christ's Yoke (11:25-30)

Further evidence that the intended audience is the church membership at large is found in the following two statements that are taken from Paul's epistles to the Corinthians and Galatians, which are addressed to the membership of Gentile churches. The terminology of the first passage harks back to 1 Corinthians (see comments on Lk 10:21-22).[5] The second, concerning the "yoke" of Christ who is "gentle (*praus*) and lowly (*tapeinos*) of heart," follows Paul's teaching in Galatians. There, he asks his addressees not to submit anymore to a "yoke" of slavery, an ironic remark concerning the "yoke" of the Law.[6] He then invites them to abide by "the law of Christ," which requires "gentleness" (Brethren, if a man is overtaken in any trespass, you who are spiritual should restore him in a spirit of gentleness [*prautētos*]. Look to yourself, lest you too be tempted. Bear one another's burdens, and so fulfill the law of Christ; Gal 6:1-2), an essential expression of the fruit of the Spirit who frees us from any law: "But the fruit of the Spirit is love, joy, peace, patience, kindness, goodness, faithfulness, gentleness (*prautēs*), self-control; against such there is no law." (Gal 5:22-23) As for

---

[5] *NTI₂* 87-8.
[6] See comments in *Gal* 265-6.

"lowliness," the source is again Paul, who gives both himself and Christ as types of such behavior and requests that his addressees do likewise:

> I, Paul, myself entreat you, by the meekness (*prautētos*) and gentleness of Christ==I who am humble (*tapeinos*) when face to face with you, but bold to you when I am away!... (2 Cor 10:1)

> I know how to be abased (*tapeinousthai*)... (Phil 4:12a)

> Do nothing from selfishness or conceit, but in humility (*tapeinophrosynē*) count others better than yourselves. Let each of you look not only to his own interests, but also to the interests of others. Have this mind among yourselves, which is yours in Christ Jesus, (Phil 2:3-5)

> Live in harmony with one another; do not be haughty, but associate with the lowly (*tapeinois*); never be conceited. (Rom 12:16)

Plucking Grain on the Sabbath (12:1-8)

Now that the gospel has brought about the eschatological law of Christ, the first item on the Matthean agenda is the showdown that took place at the Jerusalem meeting (Gal 2:1-10). To do so Matthew uses the two Markan stories of the debate around the sabbath, a basic tenet of the Mosaic Law. The following Matthean addition reflects the thesis of his Gospel and betrays clearly the reference to Paul:

> Or have you not read in the law how on the sabbath the priests in the temple profane the sabbath, and are guiltless? I tell you, something greater than the temple is here. And if you had known what this means, 'I desire mercy, and not sacrifice,' you would not have condemned the guiltless. (Mt 12:5-7)

The phrase "I desire mercy, and not sacrifice," encountered earlier in the story of the call of Matthew, is repeated here; I indicated there that mercy was the center of Paul's presentation of the gospel in Romans. The reference to Jesus as greater than the temple goes hand in hand with Matthew's teaching and follows Paul's stress that the Jerusalem above supplants the earthly Jerusalem (Gal 4:21-27). Paul also refers to his apostleship as priesthood: "But on some points I have written to you very boldly by way of reminder, because of the grace given me by God to be a minister of Christ Jesus to the Gentiles in the priestly service of the gospel of God, so that the offering of the Gentiles may be acceptable, sanctified by the Holy Spirit." (Rom 15:15-16) In fulfilling God's will of mercy, Jesus, like the priests, does not contravene the sabbath and thus he, together with his companions, is guiltless[7] just as Paul, in his service to the gospel, was guiltless together with his companion Titus.

Healing the Withered Hand (12:9-14)

Matthew's handling of this pericope may well reflect that he had Titus in mind as a prototype. He has two additions. The first is the example of taking care of a sheep on a sabbath day (v.11-12), although he appropriates here a statement Luke uses on two other occasions (13:15; 14:5) where the reference is to an ox or an ass, not a sheep. In Matthew "sheep" is used extensively to speak not only of lost (9:36; 10:6; 15:24) or scattered (26:31) sheep, which will be saved (25:32-33), but also of disciples who are sent to preach the gospel (10:16).[8] This fits perfectly the case

---

[7] In Mt 12:5-7 we have the only two instances of "guiltless" (*anaitioi*) in the New Testament.

[8] The imagery of sheep in conjunction with an apostle goes back to Paul himself: "Who shall separate us from the love of Christ? Shall tribulation, or distress, or persecution, or famine, or nakedness, or peril, or sword? As it is written, 'For thy sake

of Titus, a lost sheep,[9] who became Paul's companion. The
second addition is "whole (healthy) just like the other" after "his
hand was restored" (12:13); my reader is reminded that the hand
in the Bible stands for power. The stress on full equivalence
reminds of the full equality Paul sought at the Jerusalem meeting
between the Gentile Titus and the other Jews who believed in
Jesus' messiahship.

The Chosen Servant (12:15-21)

Just as in the case of Galatians 2:1-10, where the meeting
between Paul, accompanied by the Gentile Titus, and the pillars
ended up with Paul's open mission to the Gentiles, here also the
"healing" of the man with the withered hand (Mt 12:10) opened
the way for the "healing" of *all the many* [10] (v.15). And here
again Matthew follows Paul in connecting the gospel to Isaiah's
hymns of the "Lord's suffering servant." Indeed, he views the
healing of the Gentiles as the fulfillment of the first such hymn
(Is 42:1-4) which he quotes fully:

> Behold, my servant whom I have chosen, my beloved with whom
> my soul is well pleased. I will put my Spirit upon him, and he shall
> proclaim justice to the Gentiles. He will not wrangle or cry aloud,
> nor will any one hear his voice in the streets; he will not break a

---

we are being killed all the day long; we are regarded as sheep to be slaughtered.'" (Rom
8:35-36)

[9] Notice the direct connection of the man with the withered hand with the sheep in
the strictly Matthean addition "Of how much more value is *a man* (*anthrōpos*) than a
sheep!" At the beginning of the story the ailing person was introduced as "a man"
(*anthrōpos*).

[10] Some major manuscripts (among them B and ℵ) have "many crowds," which is a
clear reference to the outsiders, mainly the Gentiles.

bruised reed or quench a smoldering wick, till he brings justice to victory; and in his name will the Gentiles hope. (Mt 12:18-21)[11]

It is worth noting that the positioning of this quotation at this juncture may well have to do with the fact that the last Isaianic hymn of the suffering servant speaks of him thus:

All we like *sheep* have gone astray; we have turned every one to his own way; and the Lord has laid on him the iniquity of us all. He was oppressed, and he was afflicted, yet he opened not his mouth; like a lamb that is led to the slaughter, and like a *sheep* that before its shearers is dumb, so he opened not his mouth ... by his knowledge shall the righteous one, my servant, make *many* to be accounted righteous; and he shall bear their iniquities ... yet he bore the sin of *many*, and made intercession for the transgressors. (Is 53:6-7, 11, 12)

The reference to us as well as to the servant as sheep links the fulfillment of Isaiah's prophecy to the man with the withered hand, who is likened to a sheep and who was healed just as the many were afterwards. Furthermore, it is the servant, as a sheep, who heals the sinners just as the apostle, as a sheep, brings the message of healing to those to whom he is sent (Mt 10:16).

Jesus and Beelzebul (12:22-32)

The healing brought about by the gospel to the Gentile Titus and, with him, to all Gentiles, finds its culmination in the healing (v.22) of the blind and dumb demoniac. Although this episode originates with Luke (11:14-23) and is borrowed by Matthew who uses it twice, earlier in 9:32-34 and here, its rendition in this last instance is peculiar. First, only here do we

---

[11] The express mention of the Gentiles may have prompted some copyists to add "crowds" in v.15.

have the express mention that Jesus "healed" the demoniac, which betrays Matthew's intention to link this pericope with the previous two. On the other hand, the combination blind-dumb is unique in the gospels. The addition "blind" is clearly intentional since Luke has only "dumb," which is precisely the way Matthew's second reference to the demoniac states: "Then a blind and dumb demoniac was brought to him, and he healed him, so that the dumb man spoke and saw." In other words, we have here someone who is both Jewish (blind) and Gentile (dumb).[12] That is to say, that someone is the representative of the Matthean church, which is made now of both Gentiles and Jews. Still, just as in the case of the man with the withered hand, the Evangelist may well have had in mind a prototype in Timothy. Indeed, in Acts, Timothy is introduced in the following way: "And he came also to Derbe and to Lystra. A disciple was there, named Timothy, the son of a Jewish woman who was a believer; but his father was a Greek." (Acts 16:1) The introduction of Timothy in Acts follows the break between Barnabas and Paul (15:36-41) and the latter proceeding on his own into fully Gentile land (16:6-10). In Matthew, the healing of the blind and dumb demoniac is the trigger for a complete schism between Jesus and the Pharisees, representing the Jerusalemite leadership, who de facto declare him anathema in that he is viewed as being under Satan's aegis. In this case, Jesus has no other option than a total break: "He who is not with me is against me, and he who does not gather with me scatters." (Mt 12:30)

---

[12] I have indicated that a Jew is someone who has the Law but does not "see," i.e., understands it, whereas the Gentile cannot "speak" the scriptural word since he does not know it. See *NTI*, 185.

A Tree and its Fruits (12:33-37)

Nearing the middle of the Gospel book, which culminates with the author's "signature" (13:51-52),[13] Matthew brings together the main points of his message. Just as he reiterated Hosea's saying about mercy instead of sacrifice (Mt 12:7) with which he ended the "call of Matthew," here he takes up the teaching about the tree and its fruits (7:15-20), which introduces the concluding part of the Sermon on the Mount (vv.24-27) that I showed to be reflective of Paul's confrontation with the temple, locale of the sacrificial offerings. God's will is divine mercy expressed through acceptance of the needy and outsider, rather than sacrifices offered to God, as the prophets had repeatedly taught and the Pauline gospel now underscores (Rom 12:1-2, 6-10; 1 Cor 10:32-33; Gal 5:22-23; 6:7-10; Phil 1:9-11; Col 1:10).

The link to the end of the Sermon on the Mount is corroborated by the fact that the ending of our pericope here (12:35-36) corresponds to Mt 7:21-23. They both revolve around judgment day (7:22; 12:36), when the measuring rod will be the gospel preached by Paul (Rom 2:16). This gospel is precisely the link that brings together two passages that seem, at first instance, to stress two different elements: deeds in 7:21-23 and words in 12:35-36. Indeed the terminology used in both harks back to Romans 9:5-13 that explains how the salvation proclaimed and brought about in the gospel is inclusive of all. The word (*rhēma*) that men utter (*lalēsousin*) is not supposed to be fruitless (*argon*)[14] (Mt 12:36) because it is the word (*rhēma*)

---

[13] See below my comments on those verses.

[14] RSV has "careless." But fruitless, i.e. without any result, corresponds to the only other occurrence of that adjective in Matthew that depicts workers that were left in the market place workless (20:3, 6).

that the apostles preach (*kēryssomen*) (Rom 10:8).[15] Moreover, in both instances it is our words corresponding to that "word" (*rhēma*) that bring justification and salvation from the judge's condemnation (Rom 10:10; Mt 12:37). On the other hand, this "word" is a word of faith (Rom 10:8) which is, according to Paul, to be expressed in deeds that show that we abide by the will of the one whom we consider our lord, i.e. master (Rom 2:1-16), which deeds Paul speaks of as fruit (Gal 5:22; 6:7-10); it is this aspect that was covered in Mt 7:21-23. Finally, these deeds are deeds of mercy toward those in need; indeed the verb "condemn" (*katadikazō*) occurs only once more in Matthew, earlier in conjunction with the Hosean saying on mercy (7:8): Jesus' disciples, who follow this rule, are not liable to this condemnation.

The Demand for a Sign (12:38-42)

Since divine judgment is bound to the Pauline gospel (Rom 2:16), there will be no other sign given to the Jewish authorities except the gospel message itself that is expressive of God's power and wisdom (1 Cor 1:22-24): it was preached "in demonstration of the Spirit and of power, that your faith might not rest in the wisdom of men but in the power of God." (2:4-5). On the other hand, this demonstration of divine power is linked to God's raising his Son according to the spirit of holiness: "the gospel concerning his Son, who was descended from David according to the flesh and designated Son of God in power according to the Spirit of holiness by his resurrection from the dead." (Rom 1:3-4) It is this teaching that is expressed in our Matthean pericope since, in contradistinction to Luke, Matthew expressly

---

[15] Both verbs *laleō* (speak, utter) and *kēryssō* (preach, herald) are usually used in conjunction with the gospel or the apostolic activity.

links the "sign of Jonah" to the resurrection of the Son of man.[16] Those who accepted the message of mercy preached by Jonah[17] will be the sign of condemnation against the evil and adulterous generation that refused the "sign" of the Pauline "preaching" (Mt 12:41).[18]

The Parable of the Sower and the Purpose of the Parables (13:1-23)

The break with the Jerusalemite authorities leads Jesus to "go out of the house," i.e., the temple. This statement is unique to Matthew, who relocates Jesus as messenger of God's kingdom out of the temple precinct into the open sea: "That same day Jesus went out of the house and sat beside the sea." (Mt 13:1) The new home of the messianic community is the "beach" (*aigialon*; v.2); it is there that the new teaching contained in the gospel of Matthew is delivered. Indeed, this term brackets the entire parabolic teaching, which adds to the parable of the sower four others that are special Matthean material; the last parable speaks of the net of the kingdom gathering fish of every kind "ashore" (*eis ton aigialon*; v.48).[19] This new teaching is the Torah of the kingdom, since it includes seven parables and is reported as the teaching of every scribe who has been trained (discipled,

---

[16] The Hebrew *yonah* means dove, which is the form the Spirit takes when the Father "designates" his Son in Matthew (3:16-17).

[17] Notice how Matthew, following Luke, refers to Jonah's preaching as *kērygma* (Lk 11:32; Mt 12:41), the same term used by Paul to speak of the gospel message (1 Cor 1:21; 2:4).

[18] For the following two pericopes "The Return of the Unclean Spirit (Mt 12:43-45)" and "the Mother and brothers of Jesus (vv.46-50)," see my comments on Lk 11:24-26 and 8:19-21 respectively, in *NTI₂* 96-7 and 74.

[19] These are the only two instances of this noun in Matthew.

mathēteutheis) through (by, at)[20] the (school of the) kingdom of heaven; these are to follow by "bringing out of his treasure what is new and what is old" (v.52) since Jesus "came not to abolish, but to fulfill (bring to completion) the law and the prophets"[21] This beach (*aigialon*) corresponds to the one upon which Jesus meets his disciples after the resurrection in John 21:4.[22] This term, utilized by John and Matthew, was launched by Luke in Acts (Acts 21:5; 27:39-44) as the new home of the messianic community after the fall of the Jerusalem temple. Paul considered it the new place of prayer on his way to a Jerusalem that will refuse his message: "And when our days there were ended, we departed and went on our journey; and they all, with wives and children, brought us on our way till we were outside the city; and kneeling down on the beach we prayed and bade one another farewell." (Acts 21:5) It is sealed as the new home of God's people who were saved after the ship carrying them was wrecked (27:39-44). The finality of the refusal by Jerusalem is underscored. Compared to Mark, who wrote with the hope that Jerusalem might accept the gospel and who used a truncated version of Isaiah 6:9-10 (Mk 4:12), Matthew employs the full quotation (13:14-15), just as Luke before him (Acts 28:26-27). Moreover, he introduces it with the verb, unique in his book, *anaplēroutai* (is *completely* fulfilled; Mt 13:14).[23]

---

[20] RSV has "for." The original dative *tē basileia* is to be taken as instrumental. The notion of "in view of" (for) would have been rendered through the preposition *eis* or *pros* followed by the accusative.

[21] See Rom 1:2 where Paul speaks of the gospel of God as that "which he promised beforehand through his prophets in the holy scriptures."

[22] It is the only instance of this noun in John.

[23] From the verb *plēroutai (is fulfilled)* with the preposition *ana* indicating completeness (to the full).

Matthew follows the lead of Luke, who sees in Jerusalem's refusal a door fully open for the mission to the Gentiles (Acts 28:17-31). Earlier he rephrased Luke's pericope of Jesus' rejoicing at the revelation of the gospel to the Gentiles (Lk 10:21-22; Mt 11:25-27) by introducing his own invitation to his hearers to take the yoke of the new Torah (Mt 11:28-30). Instead of the Lukan "Then turning to the disciples he said privately, 'Blessed are the eyes which see what you see! For I tell you that many prophets and kings desired to see what you see, and did not see it, and to hear what you hear, and did not hear it.'" (Lk 10:22-23) Matthew moves the latter passage to follow the Isaianic quotation (Mt 13:16-17). In so doing he invites his hearers to listen to the prophetic message in order to behold the promise of salvation. Yet, for them to be able to do so, they must not only listen but also embrace that message.[24] This aspect of listening is underscored in Matthew, as Jesus prefaces the explanation of the parable with the statement "Hear then the parable of the sower," and begins the explanation with reference to "*any (every) one (pantos)* who hears" (Mt 13:19), thus universalizing Jesus' message.[25] Furthermore, the importance of understanding can be seen in that the one who "bears fruit, and yields, in one case hundredfold, in another sixty, and in another thirty" is none other than "he who hears the word and understands it" (v.23). Finally, that which is to be heard and understood is "the word of the kingdom" (v.19), a unique phrase

---

[24] This double meaning of the term "hear," with connotations of both listening and obeying, is similar to the common Hebrew verb *šm'*. This aspect of the Hebrew term is most conspicuously on display in Deut. 6:4, which has been encapsulated in Jewish liturgical life as the opening portion of the famous morning and evening daily prayer the *š'ma'*.

[25] This universalizing becomes clearer when one notices how Matthew refers to the different kinds of hearers in the singular (13:19, 20, 22, 23) in contradistinction with Mark (4:15, 16, 18, 20) who is followed by Luke (8:12, 13, 14, 15).

in the New Testament. For Matthew, the gospel is essentially an invitation to the kingdom that is coming. In his book, the content of the preaching of the Baptist, Jesus, and the latter's emissaries is uniform: "(Repent, for) the kingdom of God is at hand." (3:2; 4:17; 10:17)

The Parable of the Weeds among the Wheat and its Explanation (13:24-30, 36-43)

Mark's parable of the seed growing "automatically" (4:26-29) had its value when the author was expecting that his appeal to Jerusalem would be heeded and Israel would join the Gentiles in accepting the gospel, thus opening the way for the Lord's coming in glory (see Rom 11:25-36) and the final harvest (Mk 4:29). Matthew, however, fearing that the mainly Gentile church would not hearken to Paul's caveat in Romans 11:17-24 and imagine instead that entry into the kingdom was assured, transforms the Markan parable into that of the weeds among the wheat; the importance he gives it is betrayed in that it is the only parable, besides that of the sower, that is explained by Jesus. In it, the reader is harshly reminded that the harvest will not take place until "the close of the age" and will be performed by the angels (Mt 13:39, 40; see also v.49). The "kingdom of the Son of man," i.e., the world including the church, still has to undergo his judgment (v.41; see 25:31 "When the Son of man comes in his glory, and all the angels with him, then he will sit on his glorious throne.") that will not take place before "the close of the age," which is relegated until after Jesus' teaching—the seed, i.e., "the word of the kingdom"—has been spread:

> And Jesus came and said to them, "All authority in heaven and on earth has been given to me. Go therefore and make disciples of all nations, baptizing them in the name of the Father and of the Son

and of the Holy Spirit, teaching them to observe all that I have commanded you; and lo, I am with you always, to the close of the age." (28:18-20)

The particular stress on the judgment is also borne by the reference to the "barn" (*apothēkēn*) as the place where the wheat will be gathered (13:30), which recalls the only other occurrences of this word in Matthew. The context of the first (3:12) is clearly the judgment scene: "His winnowing fork is in his hand, and he will clear his threshing floor and gather his wheat into the granary (*apothēkēn*), but the chaff he will burn with unquenchable fire." The second (6:26) is a call that one is not to worry about having "barns" (*apothēkas*) since it is the Father who provides, meaning that he is the only one who has the true food and it is his kingdom—and thus his barn— that ultimately matters: "But seek first his kingdom and his righteousness, and all these things shall be yours as well." (v.33)

Three Matthean Parables (13:44-50)

Matthew's new Torah concludes with three parables peculiar to him. The first two underscore the oneness as well as the uniqueness of the "treasure" of the kingdom (compare with 6:19-21), which requires that we give away all our treasures for its sake (compare with 2:11). The last recapitulates the Matthean teaching expressed in the parable of the weeds among the wheat and by pointing more clearly to the judgment that lies ahead:

> So it will be at the close of the age. The angels will come out and separate the evil from the righteous, and throw them into the furnace of fire; there men will weep and gnash their teeth. (13:49-50; compare with vv.39 and 42)

The last statement (men will weep and gnash their teeth) recalls its first use in conjunction with the "sons of the kingdom being

thrown into the outer darkness" (8:12), which is taken over from
Luke (13:28) but transformed into a Matthean refrain (Mt 2:18;
8:12; 13:42, 50; 22:13; 24:51; 25:30) and points to its last
occurrence in 25:30 that precedes the judgment scene (25:31-
46). For Matthew, there is no assuredness whatsoever for the
believer of entry into God's kingdom until the last judgment,
when God's verdict will be based not on correct formulas of
belief that nominally separate "insiders" from "outsiders," but
rather on whether one, any one, will have implemented his will:

> Not every one who says to me, "Lord, Lord," shall enter the
> kingdom of heaven, but he who does the will of my Father who is
> in heaven. On that day many will say to me, "Lord, Lord, did we
> not prophesy in your name, and cast out demons in your name,
> and do many mighty works in your name?" And then will I declare
> to them, "I never knew you; depart from me, you evildoers."
> (7:21-23)

> "Depart from me, you cursed, into the eternal fire prepared for the
> devil and his angels..." And they will go away into eternal
> punishment... (25:41, 46)

Further Reading

Allison, D. C. "Two Notes on a Key Text: Matthew 11:25-30."
Journal of Theological Studies 39(1988): 277-485.

Bailey, M. L. "The Parable of the Tares." *Bibliotheca Sacra* 155
(1998): 266-279.

Du Plessis, J. G. "Pragmatic Meaning in Matthew 13:1-23."
Neotestamentica 21 (1987): 33-56.

Hagner D. A. "New Things from the Scribe's Treasure Box (Mt
13.52)." *Expository Times* 109 (1998): 329-334.

Rudman, D. "The Sign of Jonah." *Expository Times* 115 (2004):
325-328.

Van Aarde, A. "The carpenter's son (Mt 13:55): Joseph and Jesus in the Gospel of Matthew and other texts." *Neotestamentica* 34 (2000): 173-190.

9

The Fourth Book of
the Law of the Messiah

The Rejection of Jesus at Nazareth (13:53-58)

This new Torah is offered to "his own country" (13:53), following Mark 6:1. However, Jesus' "country" here, the Matthean community, is made mainly of Gentiles. This is reflected in the elimination of the reference to the "kin" found in Mark (A prophet is not without honor, except his own country and his own kin (*syngeneusin*)[1] and his own house; 6:4): "A prophet is not without honor except in his own country and his own house." (Mt 13:57) This shift from the first generation Gospel—Mark—that still functioned as an invitation to Paul's "brethren" to a second generation Gospel that was addressed to a primarily Gentile church can be detected in the change from Jesus' being referred to as "the *carpenter*, the son of Mary" (Mk 6:3) to "the *carpenter's son*, whose mother is called Mary" (Mt 13:55). The message that in Mark was still Paul's is now carried and relayed by Paul's disciples. Still, the community addressed by Matthew does not fare much better than the one condemned by Mark. Both are plagued by a lack of faith: "And he could do no mighty work there, except that he laid his hands upon a few sick people and healed them. And he marveled because of their unbelief" (Mk 6:5-6a); "And he did not do many mighty works there, because of their unbelief." (Mt 13:58) This caveat goes

---

[1] In *NTI₁* 167-9, I showed this expression to refer to Paul's "Jewish" brethren, the Jerusalemite leaders.

hand in hand with the teaching of the previous parables, namely that not all church members will be saved.

The Wandering in the Wilderness of the Nations

With the closing of the third Matthean discourse at Matthew 13:53, we have the beginning of the fourth part of Matthew containing the fourth discourse, which corresponds in the Torah to the Book of Numbers, where we read of the wanderings of Israel in the wilderness. This was prepared for in ch.13 in various ways. On the one hand, Jesus leaves the "house" of Judaism and sits besides the Roman "sea" (13:1). On the other hand, the parable of the weeds among the wheat underscores that God's kingdom, corresponding to the land of God's promise to Abraham, is still far ahead and not all the believers will reach it; this is precisely what we encounter in the Book of Numbers. On this lengthy road, where food is scarce and many a leader will falter, the church is to be led by teachers who are well versed in the teaching of Matthew, the "scribe who has been trained for the kingdom of heaven" and "brings out of his treasure what is new and what is old" (13:52). The new is nothing else but the old which applied to Israel, and is made to apply equally to the Gentiles; indeed, Jesus "did not come to abolish the law and the prophets ... but to fulfill them" (5:17). It is precisely in this section (chs.14-18) that we shall find the teachings and the rules that will govern the life of the church made of Jews as well as Gentiles; actually the term "church," which is not found elsewhere in all four Gospels, occurs twice in this section (16:18; 18:17).

The Death of John the Baptist (14:1-12)

This fourth section picks up where the third one ended. John the Baptist, who is in prison in Matthew 11:1, finds his end here: his role is fulfilled after having pointed to the coming one as fulfiller of the Law, Prophets, and Writings. Furthermore, his end comes at the hand of Herod, a stand-in for the earlier Jerusalemite political leadership, who does not accept his message. Herod hears of the *akoē* (fame) of Jesus, the same expression that was used earlier to speak of the gospel news (4:24). However, he hears but does not understand, violating the Isaianic requirement for fully accepting the *akoē* (You shall indeed hear [through hearing the news, *akoē akousete*] but never understand, 13:14) that I showed to be essential in dealing with Jesus' teaching (13:13, 14, 15, 19, 23, 51; see also 15:10).

The disciples, on the other hand, heed the message. After having buried John's *ptōma* (corpse), rather than the *sōma* (body),[2] they "told" (*apēngeilan*) Jesus that they did so. In so doing, they demonstrate that they had understood that Jesus' teaching fulfilled that of John, and consequently that John can rest in the peace of the coming one who has the power of raising him from the dead. Indeed, earlier, in response to their inquiry, Jesus has asked them to go and "tell" (*apangeilate*) John "what they hear and *see*" namely, that "the dead are raised up" (11:4-5). While John the Baptist ultimately dies and passes into oblivion, Jesus remains forever in the *akoē* (fame, news) of the gospel that carries him throughout time, establishing his continual presence

---

[2] See the difference in my comments on Mk 15:45 in *NTI₁* 230-234.

in every new generation of believers. Thus, John's followers become Jesus' disciples.[3]

Walking on the Water (14:22-36)[4]

Indeed, Jesus' invitation to—actually imposition on—his disciples to go out into the Roman sea[5] follows soon. Matthew makes the allusion to the Roman empire even clearer when he uses the term "many stadia" to describe the distance of the boat from the shore. In the parallel pericope in John 6:16-21, we are told that the distance was "twenty-five stadia."[6] The Greek term *stadion* refers to the Greco-Roman race stadium and, by extension, to the running distance in such.[7] By bringing to mind this Greco-Roman institution, the author is inviting his hearers to make the association with the realm of the Roman empire. The same is done in Luke 24:13 where the disciples were away from Jerusalem and its temple, and thus further into the Roman empire[8] where God's temple was the community gathered around the word and the breaking of the bread, wherever that location might be. As for John 11:18 the distance in stadia is that

---

[3] Just as in the Gospel of John (1:35-40).

[4] For the pericope of the feeding of the five thousand, see my comments on Mk 6:32-44 in *NTI₁* 175-6.

[5] See my comments on the verb *ēnankasen* (made)—whose actual meaning is "forced"—to describe his request to his disciples get into the boat and go to the other side, in *NTI₁* 176.

[6] In the first instance RSV uses "furlongs" while it converts the distance into miles in the second instance. It uses the same kind of conversion to render "stadia" in Jn 11:18 and Lk 24:13.

[7] Its source is most probably Paul's reference to the apostolic activity as a race in the stadium (1 Cor 9:24).

[8] Emmaus is the location where the Maccabees fought the Gentiles (1 Macc 4:47-54) and is used in Luke as the locale where Jesus teaches his disciples that they should break bread with any stranger in his name, thus teaching them the way of the gospel instead of that of the sword. See *NTI₂* 181.

between Jerusalem, the temple site, and Bethany, which is "the house of the poor," locale of the messianic community.[9]

It is precisely this invitation to go into the deep of the Roman sea that tests Peter, who was vacillating in his position toward the Pauline mission to the Gentiles. Although he asked Jesus to "order" that he join the Lord on the water (14:28), yet Peter's doubt, and thus little faith (v.31), filled him with fear and he started sinking. The verb *katapontizomai* (go down into in the sea) used here occurs once more in the entire New Testament (Mt 18:6), to describe the punishment of someone who scandalizes one's little brother: "but whoever causes one of these little ones who believe in me to sin (*skandalisē*), it would be better for him to have a great millstone fastened round his neck and to be drowned (*katapontisthē*) in the depth of the sea." (18:6) The noun *skandalon*, from the same root as the verb *skandalisē*, occurs earlier as an address to Peter himself (16:23) upon his refusal to endorse the gospel of the cross (vv.21-22). All this means that Peter here is presented as the prototype of anyone who does not endorse fully the gospel as preached by Paul and which was originally acquiesced to by Peter himself (Gal 2:1-14). Salvation from total destruction within the waters of the Roman sea comes solely through the hand of the Pauline Jesus (14:31), since he alone can control its raging (v.32). Still, for an apostle, this means to join in the mission of Jesus, namely, to cross over into Gentile land in order to heal its citizens (vv.34-36).

---

[9] See *NTI*, 203.

The Tradition of the Elders (15:1-20)

This passage parallels closely the original pericope of Mk 7:1-23, whose roots I showed to be the debate referred to in Galatians 2:11-14 and to the teaching of Galatians in general.[10] Actually Matthew makes explicit the link to that passage. Between Jesus' reply "not what goes into the mouth defiles a man, but what comes out of the mouth, this defiles a man" (Mk 7:15/Mt 15:11-12), which Mark refers to as parable (7:17), and its explanation (Mk 7:18-23/Mt 15:17-20), Matthew inserts the following:

> Then the disciples came and said to him, "Do you know that the Pharisees were offended when they heard this saying?" He answered, "Every plant which my heavenly Father has not planted will be rooted up. Let them alone; they are blind guides. And if a blind man leads a blind man, both will fall into a pit." But Peter said to him, "Explain the parable to us." (15:12-15)

This addition makes it so that the explanation of the parable together with the introductory remonstrance "Are you also still without understanding?" (v.16; see Mk 7:18a) are addressed to Peter specifically. This recalls Galatians 2:14: "I said to Cephas before them all, 'If you, though a Jew, live like a Gentile and not like a Jew, how can you compel the Gentiles to live like Jews?'"

However, the Matthean addition does more than that. First and foremost it continues what Matthew started in 14:22-33, to show Peter in a bad light. The reason is that, as I indicated in the Introduction, this Gospel is addressed to the church as God's biblical Israel and, as such, the church members as well as leaders

---

[10] See my comments in *NTI₁* 177-78.

can commit the sins and mistakes of the latter.[11] Indeed, Peter
here is addressed with the same words intended for the Pharisees.
In other words, the leaders of the church sit in Moses' seat, just
as the Jewish leaders (23:2). The close link between our passage
and ch.23 is corroborated in that the phrase "blind leaders" is
found only in Matthew 15:14; 23:16, 24 in the entire New
Testament. On the other hand, in both cases criticism is leveled
against the misunderstanding, and thus misuse, of God's Torah,
which makes it a source of death instead of life. This intention is
confirmed in that, outside of Matthew 15:14 and its source,
Luke 6:39, the "pit" occurs only once more in the New
Testament: "What man of you, if he has one sheep and it falls
into a pit on the sabbath, will not lay hold of it and lift it out?
Of how much more value is a man than a sheep! So it is lawful to

---

[11] See already in Paul: "I want you to know, brethren, that our fathers were all under
the cloud, and all passed through the sea, and all were baptized into Moses in the
cloud and in the sea, and all ate the same supernatural food and all drank the same
supernatural drink. For they drank from the supernatural Rock which followed them,
and the Rock was Christ. Nevertheless with most of them God was not pleased; for
they were overthrown in the wilderness. Now these things are warnings for us, not to
desire evil as they did. Do not be idolaters as some of them were; as it is written, 'The
people sat down to eat and drink and rose up to dance.' We must not indulge in
immorality as some of them did, and twenty-three thousand fell in a single day. We
must not put the Lord to the test, as some of them did and were destroyed by serpents;
nor grumble, as some of them did and were destroyed by the Destroyer. Now these
things happened to them as a warning, but they were written down for our
instruction, upon whom the end of the ages has come" (1 Cor 10:1-11); "But if some
of the branches were broken off, and you, a wild olive shoot, were grafted in their
place to share the richness of the olive tree, do not boast over the branches. If you do
boast, remember it is not you that support the root, but the root that supports you.
You will say, 'Branches were broken off so that I might be grafted in.' That is true.
They were broken off because of their unbelief, but you stand fast only through faith.
So do not become proud, but stand in awe. For if God did not spare the natural
branches, neither will he spare you. Note then the kindness and the severity of God:
severity toward those who have fallen, but God's kindness to you, provided you
continue in his kindness; otherwise you too will be cut off." (Rom 11:17-22)

do good on the sabbath." (Mt 12:11-12) Moreover, the judgment of the Pharisees, and thus of Peter and any church leader, is the harshest possible: they are plants not planted by the heavenly Father and thus will be rooted up (*ekrizōthēsetai*; 15:13). As such, they are functionally equivalent to the weeds planted by the enemy:

> The kingdom of heaven may be compared to a man who sowed good seed in his field; but while men were sleeping, his enemy came and sowed weeds among the wheat, and went away. So when the plants came up and bore grain, then the weeds appeared also. And the servants of the householder came and said to him, "Sir, did you not sow good seed in your field? How then has it weeds?" He said to them, "An enemy has done this." The servants said to him, "Then do you want us to go and gather them?" But he said, "No; lest in gathering the weeds you root up (*ekrizōsēte*)[12] the wheat along with them. Let both grow together until the harvest; and at harvest time I will tell the reapers, Gather the weeds first and bind them in bundles to be burned, but gather the wheat into my barn." (Mt 13:24-30)

The Canaanite Woman (15:21-28)

This pericope shows how the door that was kept closed by the Pharisees in the face of the Gentiles was stormed by faith. The faith that the disciples were taught after having faltered (14:22-31)—Peter's confessing the lordship of Jesus (v.30) and the disciples' worshipping him and confessing him as son of God, i.e., messiah (v.33)—was displayed by a Gentile woman, without any prompting, upon her encounter with Jesus: "Have mercy on me, O Lord, Son of David"[13] (15:22). Furthermore, her faith

---

[12] This are the only two instances of the verb uproot (*ekrizoō*) in Matthew.

[13] Son of David and Son of God are equivalent in that both are messianic titles.

was tested and was found truthful (vv.26-27) to the extent that it was given as an example to be emulated by the disciples (v.28).[14] On the other hand, through her faith she forced her way into obtaining what was reserved to "the lost sheep of the house of Israel" (v.24) to whom Jesus had sent out his disciples:

> These twelve Jesus sent out, charging them, "Go nowhere among the Gentiles, and enter no town of the Samaritans, but go rather to the lost sheep of the house of Israel. And preach as you go, saying, 'The kingdom of heaven is at hand.' Heal the sick, raise the dead, cleanse lepers, *cast out demons*. You received without paying, give without pay. (10:5-8)

By the same token, by challenging the Canaanite woman, whose daughter was "severely possessed by a demon" (15:22), Jesus was actually pointing out to his disciples that a "lost sheep of Israel," a sinning Jew, is in the same boat as a Gentile, sinner by definition, as Paul taught in Romans 2.[15] Both are saved through God's grace, his free gift that is granted "without pay."

Healing of Many People (15:29-31)

The link I made between the previous pericope and Jesus' sending out of the twelve is corroborated in the way Mathew handles the following passage found in Mark. Not only does he all along speak of the healing of many people instead of that of a deaf mute (Mk 7:31-37), but he replaces Mark's opening statement "Then he returned from the region of Tyre, and went through Sidon to the Sea of Galilee, through the region of the Decapolis" with "And Jesus went on from there and passed along

---

[14] Compare Jesus' reaction to the Gentile woman's faith (O woman, great is your faith!) with his reaction the Gentile centurion's (Truly, I say to you, not even in Israel have I found such faith; 8:10)

[15] See also Gal 2:15: "We ourselves, who are Jews by birth and not Gentile sinners."

the Sea of Galilee. And he went up on the mountain, and sat down there. And great crowds came to him" (Mt 15:29-30a), which corresponds closely to the opening and closing of the Sermon on the Mount:

> Seeing the crowds, he went up on the mountain, and when he sat down his disciples came to him ... And when Jesus finished these sayings, the crowds were astonished at his teaching, for he taught them as one who had authority, and not as their scribes. When he came down from the mountain, great crowds followed him; and behold, a leper came to him and knelt before him, saying, "Lord, if you will, you can make me clean." And he stretched out his hand and touched him, saying, "I will; be clean." And immediately his leprosy was cleansed. (5:1; 7:28-8:3)

It is clear then that, as in the case of 10:5-8, it is the preaching of the word that brings about healing to the crowds who accept it. That is indeed why Matthew concludes his pericope of the healing of many people with the statement that those who were healed "glorified the God of Israel." In other words, those healed come to know and "turn to God from idols, to serve a living and true God" (1 Thess 1:9), i.e., the scriptural   God preached in the gospel.

Feeding of the Four Thousand (15:32-39)

Matthew follows closely Mark 8:1-10[16] except for the region to which Jesus ends up going: instead of the Markan Dalmanoutha, Matthew has Magadan. I understood the former as referring to Dalmatia, the farthest Gentile area reached by Paul in his missionary activity. Since the Matthean church is God's eschatological community of Jews as well as Gentiles, Magadan

---

[16] See my comments in *NTI*, 182-83.

stands for Armageddon, the mount of judgment, whence he would come to judge the entire world as well as his community.

The Teaching of the Pharisees and Sadducees (16:1-4)

Earlier, in Matthew 12:38-42, the Pharisees request a sign for Jesus' teaching authority and they are given the sign of Jonah, which I explained to be mercy to all who are willing to accept God's offer of forgiveness by accepting and following Jesus' teaching. The following section (Mt 12:43-15:39) expands on this premise and culminates with the common meal that includes the Gentiles together with the Jews. Yet the Pharisees still request a sign! They are even joined by the Sadducees, the temple leaders. This appearance of the Sadducees alongside the Pharisees is special to Matthew in the New Testament and is intended to underscore that the entire leadership of Jerusalem—and by extension that of the church—refuses Jesus and his teaching. Indeed, they are first seen in 3:7-17, where the need for repentance by Abraham's children is emphasized, since they are a direct product of God's intervention, manifested through his spirit that is granted through Jesus. The Pharisees and Sadducees who came for baptism are challenged with the only valid baptism, that of Jesus' teachings, which brings about God's righteousness through the gift of the Spirit. The only other time in Matthew that the Pharisees and Sadducees appear together is here in 16:1-12. What they are presented with is nothing else than the same sign of Jonah offered in 12:28-42: the one gospel of mercy, which makes all—including the Ninevites—children of Abraham and thus recipients of God's promised blessing.[17] However, the Pharisees and Sadducees maintain their own

---

[17] In speaking earlier of the sign of Jonah (Mt 12:38-42) I pointed out that the Hebrew *yonah* meant dove, which is the form the Spirit takes at Jesus' baptism (3:16).

teaching, which they present as the bread of life: only in Matthew do we find the express explanation of leaven as referring to their teaching (16:12).[18]

Peter's Confession (16:13-20)

Given the total refusal of the entire Jerusalemite leadership, Jesus concentrates now on teaching the gospel of the cross to his own disciples in Gentile lands.[19] As I showed in my comments on Mark, this pericope reflects the debate at Antioch between Paul and Peter.[20] However, Matthew's reworking of this pericope sets his text quite apart from those of Mark and Luke. First we have the mention of Jeremiah as one of the prototypes of the Son of man. This prophet is mentioned only in Matthew in the New Testament. The reason is twofold. First, he is the prophet par excellence of Judah's and Jerusalem's doom, which came about because the leaders did not hearken to God's message. Second, similarly to Jesus, he was considered by his contemporaries to be a traitor, since he had demanded that they not resist the invading Babylonian armies. He is first mentioned in conjunction with the children's slaughter at the hand of Herod (Mt 2:17) and he will be mentioned at the occasion of Judas' betrayal of Jesus (27:9). Here he appears at the Jerusalemite leadership's refusal of Jesus, which led him to turn to the Gentiles.

---

[18] See also my comments on the parallel passage Mk 8:11-21 in *NTI₁* 184. Besides, the use of the metaphor of leaven may well reflect a purity concern. Leaven is an impure agent that is not acceptable for altar sacrifice (Lev 2:11; 6:17); the reason is that it is a contaminating agent that spreads quickly. The implied analogy in the Gospels is that the teaching of the Pharisees and Sadducees can easily corrupt the pure gospel teaching.

[19] See my comments on Caesarea Philippi in *NTI₁* 187-88.

[20] See my comments on Mk 8:27-30 in *NTI₁* 187-90.

Consequently, when Peter first accepts that Jesus is the messiah, he is considered to have done so as *Bar-Jona*, the Aramaic for "son of Jonah" and a reference to the dove, which is the Holy Spirit. Indeed, the dove is the root of Peter's correct confessional statement, since the scriptural opposite of the divine spirit is the realm of humans, expressed by the phrase "flesh and blood." Moreover, the confession was "revealed" to him "by my Father who is in heaven." This is reminiscent of Paul's statement regarding his becoming an apostle of the gospel in Galatians:

> For I did not receive it from man, nor was I taught it, but it came through a *revelation* of Jesus Christ. For you have heard of my former life in Judaism, how I persecuted the church of God violently and tried to destroy it; and I advanced in Judaism beyond many of my own age among my people, so extremely zealous was I for the traditions of my fathers. But when he who had set me apart before I was born, and had called me through his grace, was pleased to *reveal his Son* to me, in order that I might preach him among the Gentiles, I did not confer with *flesh and blood*, nor did I go up to Jerusalem to those who were apostles before me, but I went away into Arabia; and again I returned to Damascus. (1:12-17; italics mine)[21]

Here in Matthew Peter starts by accepting and endorsing Paul's mission to the Gentiles just as he did in Galatians (1:18; 2:9, 12a), which Pauline mission was under the aegis of the Spirit (3:2-3, 14; 4:6). And it is those who are "led, live, and walk by the Spirit" that "shall inherit the kingdom of God" (5:18, 21, 25). That is why Simon *as Peter* (who endorsed the Pauline

---

[21] The fact that Paul presents himself in terms of Jeremiah in Galatians (see my comments on Gal 1:15 in *Galatians*) could well be another possible reason for Matthew's choice of Jeremiah. The entire passage in Matthew revolves around Peter's condemnation for having first accepted the gospel (preached by Paul) and then reneged on it, just as in Gal 2:1-14, this gospel being that of the cross (Gal 2:20; 3:1).

gospel) is the foundation upon which Jesus' ecclesial community is built.[22] As Peter he is an apostle just as Paul is,[23] and he becomes a teacher who has the power of tying and untying. If Matthew underscores the value of Peter according to Galatians 2:1-10, it is mainly to underscore his fall, recounted in vv.11-14. Consequently, the keys to God's kingdom do not lie in any person's hand—be it Elijah, Jeremiah or the Baptist, let alone Peter—but in the word preached by Paul and enshrined in Galatians.

Jesus Foretells His Death and Resurrection (16:21-28)

Indeed, Matthew follows closely the Markan text where Peter is addressed as "Satan" and is accused of "not being on the side of God, but of men"[24] (Mt 16:23/Mk 8:33).[25] He even adds that Peter is considered a "hindrance (*skandalon*, stumbling block) to me" by Jesus. This accusation is ominous in view of the fact that earlier we were told that the same "Son of man"—who was confessed correctly here by Peter—"will send his angels, and they will gather out of his kingdom all causes of sin (*skandala*) and all

---

[22] Notice the play on the name *Petros* and *petra* (rock) in the original Greek. Compare Jesus' statement here with Mt 7:24-27: "Every one then who hears these words of mine and does them will be like a wise man who built his house upon the rock; and the rain fell, and the floods came, and the winds blew and beat upon that house, but it did not fall, because it had been founded on the rock. And every one who hears these words of mine and does not do them will be like a foolish man who built his house upon the sand; and the rain fell, and the floods came, and the winds blew and beat against that house, and it fell; and great was the fall of it."

[23] See the equivalence endorsed by Paul in Galatians 2:7-8: "but on the contrary, when they saw that I had been entrusted with the gospel to the uncircumcised, just as Peter had been entrusted with the gospel to the circumcised, for he who worked through Peter for the mission to the circumcised worked through me also for the Gentiles."

[24] The Greek literally reads "you do not think (cogitate) the matters of God, but those of men."

[25] See my comments in *NTI₁* 187-90.

evildoers, and throw them into the furnace of fire; there men will weep and gnash their teeth. Then the righteous will shine like the sun in the kingdom of their Father. He who has ears, let him hear" (Mt 13:41-43). Thus, Peter's reneging on the gospel will cause him to be ousted from the kingdom whose keys he was entrusted with!

The Transfiguration of Jesus (17:1-13)

Unlike Luke, who underscores the link with Jesus' test at the Mount of Olives and thus eliminates the Markan passage about Elijah and John the Baptist,[26] Matthew keeps the Markan sequence and yet in his rendition makes the link with Jesus' resurrection and the perpetuity of his teaching until his coming. On the one hand, he keeps the phrase "with whom I am well pleased," as is the case at Jesus' baptism (Mt 3:17/Mk 1:11/Lk 3:22), in conjunction with "This is my beloved Son, listen to him" (17:5), a phrase which is omitted in the other two Gospels (Mk 9:7; Lk 9:35). Thus Matthew underscores that the teaching of Jesus to whom the disciples are to listen is according to God's pleasure and thus his will.

This underscoring of Jesus' teaching can be further seen in how Matthew rephrases Mark regarding the disciples' fear:

And Peter said to Jesus, "Master, it is well that we are here; let us make three booths, one for you and one for Moses and one for Elijah." For he did not know what to say, for they were exceedingly afraid (*ekphoboi*). And a cloud overshadowed them, and a voice came out of the cloud, "This is my beloved Son; listen to him." And suddenly looking around they no longer saw any one with them but Jesus only. (Mk 9:5-8)

---

[26] See *NTI₂* 75-80

And Peter said to Jesus, "Lord, it is well that we are here; if you wish, I will make three booths here, one for you and one for Moses and one for Elijah." He was still speaking, when lo, a bright cloud overshadowed them, and a voice from the cloud said, "This is my beloved Son, with whom I am well pleased; listen to him." When the disciples heard this, they fell on their faces, and were filled with awe (*ephobēthēsan sphodra*, were exceedingly afraid). But Jesus came and touched them, saying, "Rise (*egerthēte*, be raised), and have no fear (*mē phobeisthe*)." And when they lifted up their eyes, they saw no one but Jesus only. (Mt 17:4-8)

Mark links the fear of the disciples to Jesus' transfiguration and the appearance of Moses and Elijah. Matthew contrasts with Mark by pegging their fear to the command of the voice from the cloud to listen to Jesus. It seems that Matthew wished to demonstrate that the disciples' fear was triggered both by Jesus' assumption of the role of supreme teacher that had formerly belonged to Moses the lawgiver and Elijah the prophet, and by the divine notification that this new role was pleasing to God. The messianic duty of Jesus has now been expanded to make of him the plenipotentiary eschatological teacher.[27]

My understanding that the fear, in Matthew, is linked to a lack of trust in Jesus' words is evidenced in that earlier Peter is said to have experienced fear while walking on the waters (14:30), although Jesus had specifically told his disciples not to fear (v.27). The link between Matthew 14:24-33 and 17:1-13 can be further detected in that the accusation of "little faith" against the disciples occurs in conjunction with these two passages (14:31; 17:20). Here again the reason is the lack of trust in Jesus' teaching. Indeed, the disciples' exhibition of little faith in ch.17

---

[27] Notice also how Matthew changes Peter's address to Jesus from "teacher" (*rabbi*, Mk 9:5) and "master" (*epistata*, Lk 9:33) into "Lord" (*kyrie*, Mt 17:4).

happened while Jesus was on the mountain where he was shown as the teacher. This is further confirmed in that the remaining two instances of "little faith" occur at 6:30, again in conjunction with Jesus' teaching about the kingdom and its righteousness (v.33) which is the topic of the entire Sermon on the Mount, and at 16:8 in conjunction with the false teaching of the Pharisees and Sadducees (vv.5-12).

Matthew's interest in Jesus' ultimate authority in matter of teaching makes explicit what Mark had left implicit: that the Baptist was the eschatological Elijah: "Then the disciples understood that he was speaking to them of John the Baptist." (Mt 17:13) On the other hand, this reference to Elijah fits perfectly Matthew's concern, to always keep at bay the church members; indeed Elijah is depicted as the precursor to the Lord's coming in the following terms: "Behold, I will send you Elijah the prophet before the great and terrible day of the Lord comes. And he will turn the hearts of fathers to their children and the hearts of children to their fathers, lest I come and smite the land with a curse." (Mal 4:5-6) This, in turn, may well explain Matthew's insistence that the transfigured Jesus is the Lord, and not just a teacher as in Mark and Luke.

Healing of the Demoniac Boy (17:14-21)

In spite of his compact rendering of the Markan story (eight verses in Matthew compared to the sixteen of Mark), Matthew does refer to the boy, who is one of the "crowd," as "epileptic" (*selēniazetai*), just as the "epileptics" (*selēniazomenous*, 4:24)[28]

---

[28] These are the only instances of the verb *selēniazomai* (be under the influence of the moon) in the entire New Testament.

that Jesus heals in Syria, land of the Gentiles[29] to whom he sends
out his disciples at the end of the Gospel (Mt 28:18-20). Their
lack of success here is accounted to their "little faith"
(*oligopistian*, Mt 17:20). Jesus' calling his disciples "of little faith"
(*oligopiste* in 14:31 and *oligopistoi* in 6:30; 8:26; 16:8) is
systematically in conjunction with the open mission to all.[30] This
would explain the otherwise enigmatic "And when they saw him
they worshiped him; *but some doubted*"[31] (Mt 28:17).

This concern with the open mission can be further detected in
how the verse in which the disciples are accused of little faith is
phrased: "Because of your little faith. For truly, I say to you, if
you have faith as a grain of mustard seed, you will say to this
mountain, 'Move from here to there,' and it will move; and
nothing will be impossible to you." On the one hand, although
Matthew follows Luke by borrowing from him "if you have faith
as a grain of mustard seed" (Lk 17:6a), he parts with Luke's
ending "you could say to this sycamine tree, 'Be rooted up, and
be planted in the sea,' and it would obey you" (Lk 17:6b) and
inserts here "you will say to this mountain, 'Move from here to
there,' and it will move" (Mt 17:20). Given the immediate
context, the mountain is none other than that where Jesus was
just transfigured as the eschatological teacher. The teaching that
took place there "apart" (*kat 'idian*; 17:1) with the three pillars is
to be announced throughout the Roman empire, just as we hear
in Galatians:

---

[29] See my comments earlier on Mt 4:23-25.

[30] See my comments on the respective passages.

[31] Actually the original *oi de adistasan* literally means "yet they doubted," indicating
that *all* the disciples did.

I went up by revelation; and I laid before them (but privately [*kat 'idian*] before those who were of repute) the gospel which I preach among the Gentiles ... but on the contrary, when they saw that I had been entrusted with the gospel to the uncircumcised, just as Peter had been entrusted with the gospel to the circumcised, for he who worked through Peter for the mission to the circumcised worked through me also for the Gentiles. (2:2, 7-8)

The Temple Tax (17:24-27)

This pericope, unique to Matthew, opens up the teaching connected with the second foretelling of the passion and resurrection (Mt 17:22-23). The intention is to invite Peter, and with him the entire church leadership, to endorse the mission to the Gentiles. The story takes place at Capernaum, representing the Judaism of the diaspora.[32] There Peter is challenged by the collectors of the didrachma, the temple tax imposed by the Law (Ex 30:13-16) and secured by the Roman authorities in support of the maintenance of the Jerusalem temple. Just as Peter earlier confessed that Jesus was the messiah, yet misunderstood its true meaning, here also he was right in saying that Jesus did fulfill his duty toward the temple, yet erred in understanding how. The story revolves around a wordplay connected with the Greek root *tel-*. The verb *teleō*, whose meaning is "finish, complete," is used in the sense of both "fulfill, bring to an end" as well as "fulfill one's duty" as in paying taxes (hence *telei ta didrakhma* [half-shekel] means "pays the temple tax"). Consequently, the noun *telos* can mean "end, aim, fulfillment" as in "the end of the Law" (*telos nomou*, Rom 10:4) or "tax, toll" as in "taxes to whom taxes are due" (*tō to telos to telos*, Rom 13:7).

---

[32] *NTI₁* 144; *NTI₂* 63, 86.

First Jesus leads Simon to state the obvious: the earthly kings collected taxes from the strangers, outsiders (*allotriōn*), i.e., the vanquished who were subdued and who, in order to forego slavery and secure their continued welfare under their conquerors, were forced to pay tribute to the latter in money or in kind. As for those of the household or of the conquering nation, they were free from those taxes and benefited from the tribute of the vanquished. The freedom of the children is a central theme in Paul's gospel.[33] Yet, as he himself taught, it is not to be used egotistically, thus ending up being a reason of offense to the weaker brethren: "Therefore, if food is a cause of my brother's falling, I will never eat meat, lest I cause my brother to fall (*skandalizei*)." (1 Cor 8:13)[34] Speaking later of what true apostleship entails he writes:

> Am I not free? Am I not an apostle? ... If we have sown spiritual good among you, is it too much if we reap your material benefits? If others share this rightful claim upon you, do not we still more? Nevertheless, we have not made use of this right, but we endure anything rather than *put an obstacle in the* way of the gospel of Christ ... For though I am free from all men, I have made myself a slave to all, that I might win the more. *To the Jews I became as a Jew, in order to win Jews; to those under the law I became as one under the law—though not being myself under the law—that I might win those under the law.* To those outside the law I became as one outside the law—not being without law toward God but under the law of Christ—that I might win those outside the law. To the weak I became weak, that I might win the weak. I have become all things to all men, that I might by all means save some. *I do it all*

---

[33] Rom 8:1-2; Gal 4:21-5:1.

[34] See also: "Who is weak, and I am not weak? Who is made to fall (*skandalizetai*), and I am not indignant?" (2 Cor 11:29)

for the sake of the gospel, that I may share in its blessings." (1 Cor 9:1, 11-12, 19-23)

Here, in Matthew, Jesus follows the same path: "Then the sons are free. However, not to give offense to (*skandalisōmen*) them, go to the sea and cast a hook, and take the first fish that comes up, and when you open its mouth you will find a shekel; take that and give it to them for me and for yourself." (Mt 17:26-27) Although Jesus and his followers are sons and thus free from paying any taxes, he orders Peter to do so in order "not to give offense to" the Jews. Yet, he implicitly teaches Peter that their offering is none other than the offering of the Gentiles, and thus bound to the gospel and its requirements.[35] This is clear from the wording of Matthew 17:27: Peter is sent (*poreutheis*) to the (Roman) sea just as the apostles will be sent (*poreuthentes*) to make disciples of all nations (Mt 28:19). Earlier he was prohibited to fish in the sea, but now that he has been taught true discipleship, Peter is asked to go fishing again. Compare the terminology of his calling with the one here:

> As he walked by the Sea of Galilee, he saw two brothers, Simon who is called Peter and Andrew his brother, *casting (ballontas) a net* into the sea; for they were fishermen. And he said to them, "Follow me, and I will make you fishers of men." Immediately they left their nets and followed him. (Mt 4:18-20)

> ... go to the sea and *cast (bale) a hook,* and take the first fish that comes up... (Mt 17:27)

If the fish of the sea represent the Gentiles, the shekel that is taken from *its mouth* represents their offering. This offering is acceptable since it is based on the Gentiles' confession of faith as

---

[35] See *NTI₁* and *NTI₂* on the relation between the preaching of the gospel and the offering of the Gentiles.

can be seen from the correspondence between our text and Romans 10:8-10:

> The word is near you, on your lips and in your heart (that is, the word of faith which we preach); because, if you confess with your lips that Jesus is Lord and believe in your heart that God raised him from the dead, you will be saved. For man believes with his heart and so is justified, and he confesses with his lips and so is saved.

It is possible to extract a further conclusion from this text. The fish in the sea are the Gentiles. Taking the first fish is tantamount to taking *any* fish, meaning that the Gentiles are to be accepted as they are without any kind of discrimination. The offering of both Peter and Jesus is one and the same—one shekel instead of two didrachmas (half-shekels)—underscoring the oneness of the gospel, which is the gospel to the Gentiles preached by Paul as evidenced in Galatians: "but on the contrary, when they saw that I had been entrusted with the gospel to the uncircumcised, just as Peter to the circumcised, for he who worked through Peter for the apostleship to the circumcised worked through me also for the Gentiles."[36] Since the numeral four is symbolic of the temple (building),[37] one may also add that the one offering amounting to four drachmas[38] may be intended to say that Jesus' and Peter's one offering was made

---

[36] I am following closely the Greek that does not repeat the terms "entrusted," 'gospel," and "apostleship," stressing thus the oneness of the gospel to both Paul and Peter, namely the one whose content is Paul's preaching to the Gentiles (see my comments on these verses in *Gal* 69-70). RSV waters down the matter: "but on the contrary, when they saw that I had been entrusted with the gospel to the uncircumcised, just as Peter had been entrusted with *the gospel* to the circumcised (for he who worked through Peter for the mission to the circumcised worked through me also for the Gentiles)."

[37] See my comments in *NTI₁* 141-3, 147. See also my comments on Mt 4:18-22.

[38] The drachma was the basic Hellenistic monetary unit (see Lk 15:8-9).

to the temple of the new Jerusalem where the gospel offering was laid:

> But on some points I have written to you very boldly by way of reminder, because of the grace given me by God to be a minister of Christ Jesus to the Gentiles in the priestly service of the gospel of God, so that the offering of the Gentiles may be acceptable, sanctified by the Holy Spirit. (Rom 15:15-16)

My last suggestion fits perfectly with the notion of fulfillment, central in Matthew. Here Jesus fulfills[39] the temple of Jerusalem with the new eschatological one just as he fulfills the Mosaic Law (Mt 5:17) with the eschatological law of the messiah.[40] This in turn is corroborated by the fact that the following text of chapter 18 is itself a compendium of the Messiah's law.

Matthew 18

Although Matthew18 borrows heavily from Mark and Luke, the outcome of his heavy rephrasing and his own additions is a material that is Matthean through and through. After having firmly established that the one gospel is the sole foundation of the church built on Peter, Jesus addresses the church membership, and especially its leadership, with the "law" pertaining to it, which is none other than the "law of the messiah" (Gal 6:2) epitomized in the love for the neighbor. As I showed in my comments on Galatians 6:1-10, Paul's injunctions there are addressed mainly to the church's leadership; moreover, his point of reference is the coming judgment and kingdom.[41] And just as "the law of the messiah" was the final word in the

---

[39] See earlier my comments on Matthew's use of the verb *telei* (fulfills) to speak of the payment of the temple tax.

[40] See earlier my comments on Mt 5:1 and 17.

[41] *Gal* 313-4.

letter to the Galatians, whose content is the gospel to the
Gentiles,[42] here also "the law" of Matthew 18 is the last section
of Jesus' teaching in (the) Galilee (of the Gentiles).

Indeed, Matthew formulates his gospel, the new Torah,
around Jesus' five speeches that all end with a similar formula
"when Jesus had finished (teaching)…" (7:28; 11:1; 13:53; 19:1;
26:1). The formula ending the fourth speech states that, after he
had finished speaking, Jesus left Galilee and entered Judea
(19:1), whereas the one that ended the third claims that Jesus
entered Galilee ("his own country") after he had relayed a series
of parables (13:53-54). That is to say, in the Matthean structure,
the third "teaching material," the central section of the five part
teaching, took place in Galilee (see comments below). It is then
the gospel to the Gentiles whose central message is the love for
the neighbor, which is the subject of Matthew 18, the last word
in Jesus' fourth "teaching."

The Greatest in the Kingdom (18:1-5)

Matthew's rephrasing of Mark betrays the fact that it is the
mainly Gentile Matthean church which is addressed here. It is
Jesus' "disciples" who approach him and their question is as to
who is greater "in the kingdom of heaven"; actually the entire
debate is related to that kingdom (Mt 18:2, 3, 4) to which the
church community is bound. An immature child, (a stand-in for
the Gentiles),[43] is here considered a member of the community
simply on the basis of Jesus "calling" (*proskalesamenos*) him, just
as he earlier "called" his disciples (Mt 10:1; 15:32) and the
"crowd" (15:10). One of the conditions to the entry into that

---

[42] Gal 1:8-9, 15-16.
[43] *NTI,* 194.

kingdom is *straphēte* (turn), which is the literal translation of the Hebrew *šub* meaning turn, return, and often translated in the Septuagint as *metanoō* (repent). In order to fulfill this requirement, the church's leaders must consider themselves like children, immature sinners and thus in need of mercy. This is corroborated in Jesus' demand that the leader humble himself (*tapeinōsei*) since "He who is greatest among you shall be your servant; whoever exalts himself will be humbled, and whoever humbles himself will be exalted" (23:11-12).[44] Moreover, humility is the trademark of the master who holds the yoke of the new Torah: "Take my yoke upon you, and learn from me; for I am gentle and lowly (*tapeinos*) in heart, and you will find rest for your souls." (11:29)

Temptations to Sin (18:6-9)

Paul wrote to the Corinthians: "Give no offense to Jews or to Greeks or to the church of God." (1 Cor 10:32) Just as Jesus taught Peter not to give offense (*skandalisōmen*) to the Jews (Mt 17:27), here he applies the same rule to the church leaders; they are not to give offense to the lesser members of the church of God. The punishment is harsh: "but whoever causes one of these little ones who believe in me to sin (*skandalisē*), it would be better for him to have a great millstone fastened round his neck and to be drowned (*katapontisthē*) in the depth of the sea." The link to Peter, as a representative church leader, is unavoidable. The verb *katapontizomai* occurs only once more in the entire New Testament: "So Peter got out of the boat and walked on the

---

[44] The verb "to humble oneself" here may also reflect the link in Matthew's mind with Gal 6:1-2: "Brethren, if a man is overtaken in any trespass, you who are spiritual should restore him in a spirit of gentleness. Look to yourself, lest you too be tempted. Bear one another's burdens, and so fulfill the law of Christ."

water and came to Jesus; but when he saw the wind, he was afraid, and beginning to sink (*katapontizesthai*) he cried out, 'Lord, save me.'" (Mt 14:29-30)

Parable of the Lost Sheep (18:10-14)

This parable taken over from Luke 15:3-7 is linked to the preceding pericope in Matthew through the phrase "one of these little ones" (Mt 18:6, 10). The injunction not to despise the little ones seems to corroborate the thesis that this entire chapter is about church order; indeed, the same idea of despising the lesser one occurs in Paul in conjunction with the Eucharistic gathering:

> When you meet together, it is not the Lord's supper that you eat. For in eating, each one goes ahead with his own meal, and one is hungry and another is drunk. What! Do you not have houses to eat and drink in? Or do you despise the church of God and humiliate those who have nothing? What shall I say to you? Shall I commend you in this? No, I will not. (1 Cor 11:20-22)

Another indication is that the sheep is referred to as "gone astray" (from the verb *planaō*; v.12 [twice], v.13)—instead of the Lukan "lost" (from the verb *apollymi*)—which is used of the "disciples" in Matthew 24 (vv. 4, 5, 11, 24) who are referred to as "chosen" (vv.22, 24, 31), i.e., those who accepted God's call and thus are insiders (22:14). The emphasis on church order is amplified by the following pericope, an application of the parable of the lost sheep, in which explicit reference is made to the "church" (Mt 18:17) which is, along with 16:18, the only other instance of the noun *ekklēsia* in the Gospels.

A Brother Who Sins (18:15-20)

This is an expansion on Luke 17:3 (Take heed to yourselves; if your brother sins, rebuke him, and if he repents, forgive him), which makes of it a rule for every "church" that is bound by the "keys" handed to Peter (compare Mt 18:18 to 16:19). That the unrepenting brother ends up as "a Gentile" in his status of excommunication points to the fact that this rule is actually based on Paul's teaching:

> It is actually reported that there is *immorality* among you, and of a kind that is not found even among pagans; for a man is living with his father's wife. And you are arrogant! Ought you not rather to mourn? Let him who has done this be removed from among you. For though absent in body I am present in spirit, and as if present, I have already pronounced judgment in the name of the Lord Jesus on the man who has done such a thing. When you are assembled, and my spirit is present, with the power of our Lord Jesus, you are to deliver this man to Satan for the destruction of the flesh, that his spirit may be saved in the day of the Lord Jesus. (1 Cor 5:1-5)

Indeed, later Paul depicts the Corinthians' sinful behaviors as actions governed by the "Gentile' way of living that preceded their acceptance of the gospel:

> Do you not know that the unrighteous will not inherit the kingdom of God? Do not be deceived;[45] neither the *immoral*, nor idolaters, nor adulterers, nor sexual perverts, nor thieves, nor the greedy, nor drunkards, nor revilers, nor robbers will inherit the kingdom of God. And such were some of you. But you were washed, you were sanctified, you were justified in the name of the Lord Jesus Christ and in the Spirit of our God. (1 Cor 6:9-11)

---

[45] Notice that the Greek verb *planōmai* used here is the same as the one that was translated as "went/gone astray" in Mt 18:10-14.

The Unforgiving Servant (18:21-35)

This parable is an expansion on Luke 17:4. Peter is completing his learning process within the "church"; he is a disciple, not the master. And the master's teaching concludes with the same comment he made in conjunction with the Lord's Prayer: "So also my heavenly Father will do to every one of you, if you do not forgive your brother from your heart." (Mt 18:35)[46] This theme of mercy is central to Matthew, as can be seen from his repeated reference to God's injunction through the prophet Hosea: "I desire mercy, and not sacrifice" (Mt. 9:13, 12:7; cf. Hos 6:6). Its centrality in this parable can be detected in the use of the verbs "feel pity for" (*splankhnizomai*, 18:27) and "have patience" (*makrothymeō*, 18:26, 29). The first is typical of Jesus' attitude toward the needy (9:36; 14:14; 15:32; 20:34). The second refers to the practical outcome—patience—of this feeling of pity; in his patience the servant is to emulate his master (18:26, 29) just as the disciples are to emulate the heavenly Father in the matter of forgiving (6:14-15; 18:35). Finally, that no less than divine mercy (should not you have had mercy on your fellow servant, as I had mercy on you? 18:33) is the ultimate basis for the final judgment is clear from the fact that the phrases "settle accounts" (*logon synairein*, v.23)[47] and "wicked servant" (*doule ponēre*, v.32) occur only once more in the New Testament, in the Matthean parable of the talents (25:19, 26, respectively), which deals with the final judgment.[48]

---

[46] Cf. Mt 6.14-15: "For if you forgive men their trespasses, your heavenly Father also will forgive you; but if you do not forgive men their trespasses, neither will your Father forgive your trespasses."

[47] Also as simply *synairein* (reckon) in v.24.

[48] See also 1 Thess 1:10 (wrath to come) and Rom 2:5, 8: 3:5; 5:9; 9:22; Eph 5:6; Col 3:5; 1 Thess 2:16; 5:9; Jn 3:36.

Furthermore, the master's "anger, wrath" (18:34) is reminiscent of the divine "wrath to come" (Mt 3:7/Lk 3:7).

Finally, one should note that this presentation of the messianic law of love for the neighbor in Matthew 18 follows the pericope concerning the freedom of the "sons" from their submission to the Jerusalem temple. This sequence parallels that found in Galatians: the stress on love as being the new rule (Gal 5:2-6:10) is the conclusion Paul draws from his comments regarding the status of the Galatians as children of the Jerusalem above (4:21-30).[49]

Further Reading

Agourides, S. "'Little ones' in Matthew." *Bible Translator* 35 (1984): 329-334.

Carlisle, C. R. "Jesus' Walking on the Water: A note on Matthew 14.22-33." *New Testament Studies* 31 (1985): 151-155.

Carter W. "Paying the Tax to Rome as Subversive Praxis: Matthew 17.24-27." *Journal for the Study of the New Testament* 76 (1999): 3-31.

Cousland, J. R. C. "The Feeding of the Four Thousand *Gentiles* in Matthew? Matthew 15.29-39 as a Test Case." *Novum Testamentum* 41 (1999): 1-23.

Duling, D. C. "Building and Loosing: Matthew 16:19; Matthew 18:8; John 20:23." *Forum* 3 (1987): 3-31.

Hernant, D. "Structure littéraire du 'Discours communautaire' de Matthieu 18." *Revue Biblique* 103 (1996): 76-90.

Kasselouris, H. "The narrative on the confession of Peter (Matth. 16, 13-20 par) and on the anointing of Jesus (Matth.

---

[49] Notice the conjunctions *dio* (so, Gal 4:31) and *oun* (therefore, 5:1).

26, 6-13 par). Parallel Messianic Narratives?" *Deltion Biblikon Meleton* 23 (1994): 27-33.

Marcus, J. "The Gates of Hades and the Keys of the Kingdom (Matt 16:18-19)." *Catholic Biblical Quarterly* 50 (1988): 443-455.

Penner J. A. "Revelation and Discipleship in Matthew's Transfiguration Account." *Bibliotheca Sacra* 152 (1995): 201-210.

Robinson B. P. "Peter and his Successors: Tradition and Redaction in Matthew 16.17-19." *Journal for the Study of the New Testament* 21 (1984): 84-104.

Verseput, D. J. "Jesus' Pilgrimage to Jerusalem and Encounter in the Temple: A geographical Motif in Matthew's Gospel." *Novum Testamentum* 36 (1994): 105-121.

Zucker, D. J. "Jesus and Jeremiah in the Matthean Tradition." *Journal of Ecumenical Studies* 27 (1990): 288-305.

10

The Fifth Book of
the Law of the Messiah

Teaching About Divorce (19:1-12)

"Now when Jesus had finished these sayings, he went away from Galilee and entered the region of Judea beyond the Jordan; and large crowds followed him, and he healed them there." (19:1-2) Here Matthew follows Mark closely except for the rephrasing of the rule against divorce and the addition regarding the eunuchs.[1] One is allowed to divorce only in case of *porneia*, translated as "unchastity" in RSV. The discussion concerning the meaning of this word has been long and thorny, and no consensus has been reached. My understanding of this word in Matthew is based on my exegesis of Mark, where I argued that this passage follows Paul's teaching in 1 Corinthians. In the epistle, *porneia* is used in its scriptural sense, as a metaphor for following the religious way of the Gentiles.[2] It is best then to read the Matthean exception as harking back to Paul's instruction in 1 Corinthians 7:10-15.

Another possible, but less likely, understanding of *porneia* is that it refers to sexual relations with a close blood relative, which is strictly prohibited by the Law. The source in this case would be 1 Corinthians 5:1-5, where the situation of a man living with his father's wife is referred to as *porneia* (v.1). If Matthew is following Paul's teachings in this latter case, the pericope is

---

[1] Cf. Mk 10:1-12.
[2] See *NTI₁* 195-7.

addressing the case of a Gentile who was in such a relationship (or a relationship which ran similarly counter to Old Testament laws governing consanguinity) at the time of accepting the gospel message; according to Matthew, such a liaison would have to be discontinued. In either case, the ultimate source of the Gospel passage is most likely the Pauline correspondence.

Jesus' response to his disciples' objections, in which he speaks of becoming "eunuchs for the sake of the kingdom of heaven," is clearly taken from Paul's invitation in chapter 7 of 1 Corinthians dealing with marriage:[3]

> Now concerning the unmarried, I have no command of the Lord, but I give my opinion as one who by the Lord's mercy is trustworthy. I think that in view of the present distress it is well for a person to remain as he is. Are you bound to a wife? Do not seek to be free. Are you free from a wife? Do not seek marriage. But if you marry, you do not sin, and if a girl marries she does not sin. Yet those who marry will have worldly troubles, and I would spare you that. I mean, brethren, the appointed time has grown very short; from now on, let those who have wives live as though they had none, and those who mourn as though they were not mourning, and those who rejoice as though they were not rejoicing, and those who buy as though they had no goods, and those who deal with the world as though they had no dealings with it. For the form of this world is passing away. I want you to be free from anxieties. The unmarried man is anxious about the affairs of the Lord, how to please the Lord; but the married man is anxious about worldly affairs, how to please his wife, and his interests are divided. And the unmarried woman or girl is anxious about the affairs of the Lord, how to be holy in body and spirit;

---

[3] This fact militates for my understanding of *porneia*. Both Matthean additions in his passage concerning marriage would have their source in the same Pauline chapter that is dealing with marriage.

but the married woman is anxious about worldly affairs, how to please her husband. I say this for your own benefit, not to lay any restraint upon you, but to promote good order and to secure your undivided devotion to the Lord ... So that he who marries his betrothed does well; and he who refrains from marriage will do better. A wife is bound to her husband as long as he lives. If the husband dies, she is free to be married to whom she wishes, only in the Lord. But in my judgment she is happier if she remains as she is. And I think that I have the Spirit of God. (1 Cor 7:25-35; 38-40)

The ending statement of the Matthean passage, "He who is able to receive this, let him receive it," obviously reflects Paul's judgment that it is better not to be married, although this state is not possible for everyone.

Little Children Blessed (19:13-15)

Whereas Mark (10:13-16) teaches that the children, i.e., the Gentiles, are not to be hindered from joining themselves to Christ in their present state, Matthew underscores their full partnership with the Jews in the messianic community, which is reflected in his additional "and pray" (19:13). My reader is reminded that, when it comes to Jesus, "prayer" (*proseukhē*) and "pray" (*proseukhomai*) refer in the Gospels to the messianic community gathered around Jesus outside the boundaries of the Jerusalem temple.[4]

The Rich Young Man (19:16-22)

Since Matthew's community is essentially composed of Gentiles, Jesus' address in Mark to the Jew who knows the commandments (10:19) is here directed to a Gentile, who is

---

[4] See *NTI₁* 144.

asked to "keep" them (Mt 19:17). As Paul taught, keeping the commandments of the Law is summed up in the love for one's needy neighbor (vv.21-22). Since the love for the neighbor (all neighbors, even enemies) is what makes one perfect as the heavenly Father is (5:43-48), Jesus' addressee here is shown the way to perfection (19:21a) which leads to life eternal (vv.16-17).[5] In the interpretation of the event that follows, Jesus emphasizes the link between Israel and the new community that will be composed primarily of Gentiles by invoking the twelve tribes of Israel. The tribes here are clearly a reference to the eschatological community of the church, which will be expected to adhere to the standards set down by Jesus' understanding of the law's implications.

The Workers in the Vineyard (20:1-16)

The Evangelist continues to pursue the topic of the equivalence between Jew and Gentile that he had underlined in ch.19. However, this equivalence is applied here to the Matthean church in its entirety and consequently to all its membership; the original status of the member is disregarded. The "workers" (*ergatai*) referred to here (Mt 20: 1, 2, 8) are none other than the disciples (10:9-10) who work for the final harvest (9:37, 38). The ones who are hired later, and thus work less, are not exempt from receiving the full measure of God's grace. The reason is that the master hires according to his needs throughout the day. Moreover, every time he does so, he chooses some out of many, meaning that those who end up working could not have been hired at all! Thus, the act of hiring itself is an expression of the

---

[5] The adjective *teleios* (perfect) occurs only in Matthew, in these three instances, among the gospels.

householder's mercy; from this perspective all workers are equal and the only reaction on their part ought to be one of gratitude.

This parable recapitulates the teaching of Galatians in that the disciple is ultimately saved through divine grace, and not through his "works." On the other hand, the conclusion "So the last will be first, and the first last" reminds one of the teaching of Romans 11, where the ones that are called first end up last while the ones who are last called end up first.

The Passion of the Son of Man (20:17-19)

The link with Galatians seems to have been on Matthew's mind. Not only is the theme of that letter prominent in the previous parable which is special to that Evangelist, but so also is the mention of the crucifixion in the third announcement of the Son of man's passion. Matthew points back to the gospel of the cross which is at the heart of the scandalous teaching connected with the first announcement of the passion in all three Synoptics (Mt 16:21-24/Mk 8:31-34/Lk 9:22-23) and thus makes of that gospel the theme of the entire passion story through the literary device of *inclusio*. That this is intentional can be seen in that Matthew includes this aspect in his later handling of the fate of Jesus' disciples, especially those in position of leadership: "Therefore I send you prophets and wise men and scribes, some of whom you will kill and crucify, and some you will scourge in your synagogues and persecute from town to town." (23:34)[6] This teaching forms precisely the conclusion of Galatians: "But far be it from me to glory except in the cross of our Lord Jesus

---

[6] The mention of crucifixion is absent from the Lukan parallel: "Therefore also the Wisdom of God said, 'I will send them prophets and apostles, some of whom they will kill and persecute.'" (Lk 11:49)

Christ, by which the world has been crucified to me, and I to the world." (6:14)

The Request of James and John (20:20-28)

Yet, just as earlier Peter did not understand that gospel, so here his colleagues James and John, who will act in opposition to the teaching of the previous parable, follow his lead. They were looking for prominence and preeminence over their colleagues, workers as much as they are, in the kingdom (v.21). Jesus teaches both them and their indignant colleagues (vv.24-25) that the only way to the kingdom is that of the Son of man: service to the others until death (vv.26-28).

The Healing of the Two Blind Men (20:29-34)

Starting with the third foretelling of Jesus' suffering, crucifixion, death, and resurrection as Son of man (20:17-19), the pericope dealing with the request of James and John (vv.20-28), which teaches true discipleship, is followed by that of the healing of the two blind men at Jericho, the function of which is to show that only someone whose eyes have opened through faith in Jesus as Son of man can proceed in the new "way" that leads to the promised land of the Jerusalem above. Indeed, on the one hand, the reader of Matthew cannot help but relate, as two opposites, the two blind men who ultimately see—and thus understand—and follow Jesus, to James and John who ultimately are blinded by their arrogance. On the other hand, the following pericope starts with the sending of two disciples to prepare for Jesus' triumphal entry into Jerusalem (21:1) but also for the eventual path to the cross. The last pair illustrates the proper path of the cross, the stage for which is set by the desperate cry of the two blind men. The intended relation is reflected in that Matthew changes the Markan and Lukan "two of his/the disciples" (Mk 11:1/Lk 19:29) into simply "two disciples" (Mt 21:1). The reader cannot help but perceive that the disciples leading their peers into Jerusalem with Jesus, "the Son of man (who) came not to be served but to serve, and to give his life as a ransom for many" (20:28), are not the likes of James and John, but rather the likes of the two blind men who cried out repeatedly and exclusively for Jesus' "mercy" (vv.29-30).

Triumphal Entry into Jerusalem (21:1-9)

As Jesus later will send his disciples from his eschatological mountain of glory in Galilee in order for them to make disciples of the nations (Mt 28:16-20), here also he sends his two disciples from the Mount of Olives, the eschatological mountain of God,[7] to Jerusalem that lies "opposite (*katenanti*) you" and thus "against you." Although Jerusalem is against him, Jesus brings her the message of salvation. Matthew's approach to the matter is special to him since he introduces new material expanding on the Markan original which is closely followed by Luke.

Already in Mark 11:2, "untying" (loosing; *lysate* from the root *lyō*) the colt that is "tied" (bound; *dedemenon* from the root *deō*) reflects Law terminology. Consequently, Jesus is presented as the one who is going to offer the Jerusalemite Jews the Pauline gospel as expounded in Galatians. Yet, through two major additions (Mt 21:4-5, 10-11) Matthew not only underscores the Markan intention but also remolds this pericope to make it fit within the overall message of his Gospel.

---

[7] See Zech 14 and *NTI₂* 54-6.

1. The quotation stresses Mark's point, namely that the real captivity is the yoke of the Law, which is alluded to in the end of the quotation from Zechariah 9:9, where the term translated "ass" in the RSV is *hypozygiou*, meaning "(a beast) under a yoke."[8]

2. In v. 4, Matthew interjects one of his basic teachings, namely, that whatever Jesus does, he does to fulfill the Law and the Prophets (5:17-18). Just as he does throughout his Gospel, Matthew comments by saying that "This took place to fulfill what was spoken by the prophet" (21:4).

3. The quotation in v.5 is taken from Zechariah 9:9 as well as Isaiah 62:11: "Tell the daughter of Zion, Behold, your king is coming to you, humble, and mounted on an ass, and on a colt, the foal of an ass." The opening "Tell the daughter of Zion" comes from Isaiah 62:11 and takes the place of the opening found in Zechariah 9:9: "Rejoice greatly, O daughter of Zion! Shout aloud, O daughter of Jerusalem!" Both prophetic passages hail the coming King as victorious savior, which is the connotation of the root *yaša'* in Hebrew.[9] Yet, the reference to (the eschatological) salvation is fully dismissed. The elimination of salvation means that the world including

---

[8] "Tell the daughter of Zion, Behold, your king is coming to you, humble, and mounted on an ass (*onon*), and on a colt, the foal of an ass (*hypozygiou*)." (Mt 21:5)
[9] "Say to the daughter of Zion, 'Behold, your *salvation* comes; behold, his reward is with him, and his recompense before him'" (Is 62:11); "Rejoice greatly, O daughter of Zion! Shout aloud, O daughter of Jerusalem! Lo, your king comes to you; triumphant and *victorious* is he, humble and riding on an ass, on a colt the foal of an ass." (Zech 9:9)

the church ("kingdom of the son") is still to be judged. In the original Hebrew source, the King is God himself, whereas here the reference is to the Messiah. In Mt 13, the kingdom of the "Son" is just the prelude to that of God; it corresponds to our world in its totality, including the "church." The kingdom of God (the heavenly Jerusalem/Zion) will include the "nations" together with God's *ekklēsia* (Zech 9:10). Later, the disciples will be sent out [*poreuthentes*] to all nations to carry out that message of peace.

4. Like the ass, the city itself is in captivity; and so is the colt, i.e., the children of Jerusalem, the younger generation of post 70 A.D. Judaism. My understanding is suggested by the fact that the only other use of yoke in this gospel is found in the following text: "Come to me, all who labor and are heavy laden, and I will give you rest. Take my yoke (*zygon*) upon you, and learn from me; for I am gentle and lowly in heart, and you will find rest for your souls. For my yoke (*zygos*) is easy, and my burden is light." (Mt 11:28-30) In the Zechariah quotation Matthew follows the Hebrew over the LXX; by reading the Hebrew literally (on purpose, and not as a synonymic parallelism as the LXX does) he comes up with an ass and a colt instead of just a colt. Furthermore, he introduces this split into the narrative itself, which shows that it is intended. Since in his time, in contradistinction with Mark's, Jerusalem is long gone, the Jews for him are mainly those in the diaspora, especially Asia Minor. So he rephrases Mark by splitting between the "mother" Jerusalem and its child/children, and underscores that the children are definitely

hypozygion (under the yoke) if their allegiance is still to the Mosaic Law.

5. This seems to be corroborated by differences in the Matthean and Lukan accounts. While in Luke, the invitation to Jerusalem to say "Hosanna" (Lk 13:34-35) is realized at Jesus' entry to Jerusalem (Lk 19:28-28), in Matthew the Hosanna of the "mother" at this occasion (Mt 21:9) becomes an example to follow and thus an invitation to her "children"—and by extension to the Christian *ekklēsia*—in Mt 23:37-39. The Lukan sequence is reversed.

6. The second addition Mt 21:10-11 has the function of introducing Jesus, the fulfiller of the Law and the Prophets, as himself "*the* prophet"[10] whom God will raise in the stead of Moses (Deut 18:15, 18). As all his predecessors, he is an outsider (compared to the central authorities), since he is from the domain of the Gentiles. His being a prophet again goes hand in hand with what was said earlier: he does not establish the kingdom, but prepares for it through his "word" (compare with Lk 1:76) that the disciples will carry to the "end of the age" (28:20).

The Cleansing of the Temple (21:10-17)

Matthew closely follows Jeremiah. Just as Jeremiah claimed that the yoke of Babylonian captivity was inflicted on Jerusalem (Jer 27-28) because it had refused God's yoke (2:20; 5:5), so also for

---

[10] Found in the absolute only in John. Although required by "Jesus," still sound-wise it is still "the prophet," which puts Jesus in parallel with all the Matthean "the prophet."

Matthew the yoke of Roman destruction was inflicted on the city because it refused the yoke of God's messiah. As for liberation from the yoke, in both cases it is implemented through God's messiah:

> And it shall come to pass in that day, says the Lord of hosts, that I will break the yoke from off their neck, and I will burst their bonds, and strangers shall no more make servants of them. But they shall serve the Lord their God and David their king, whom I will raise up for them. (Jer 30:8-9)

> O Jerusalem, Jerusalem, killing the prophets and stoning those who are sent to you! How often would I have gathered your children together as a hen gathers her brood under her wings, and you would not! Behold, your house is forsaken and desolate. For I tell you, you will not see me again, until you say, "Blessed is he who comes in the name of the Lord. (Mt 23:37-39)

Indeed, this was the chant intoned by the crowds who confess Jesus as "the prophet from Nazareth of Galilee." On the other hand, the entire city "is stirred" against him just as it "was troubled" earlier at the news of his messiahship (Mt 2:3).[11] That is why, just as Jesus chose (in Matthew 2:22-23) to settle in Galilee instead of Judah, so here he skirts Bethphage, the town of the revolutionaries, on his way to the Mount of Olives (21:1), and lodges in Bethany, the town of the poor and symbol of the church community (v.17), which ensures that "My house shall be called a house of prayer" (v.13).[12]

Matthew's continuing reliance on Jeremiah in this chapter is betrayed by the composite quotation, taken from Isaiah 56:7 and

---

[11] These are the only instances in Matthew where Jerusalem is referred to in conjunction with the Greek modifier *pas* (all, in its entirety).

[12] *NTI*₁ 202-203.

Jeremiah 7:11, explaining Jesus' actions against the temple merchants who are making the temple "a den of robbers" (Jer 7:11).[13] But this quotation also reflects the portion of the text from Isaiah. This passage in Isaiah is concerned with the acceptance of sacrifices from the foreigners who will join themselves to the Lord, at which point "[the Lord's] house shall be called a house of prayer," and reflects the evils of the current users of the temple, who have doomed the present temple to destruction by the Romans by their cultic violations (and, implicit in the Jeremiah passage, through their moral failings). The implied message is that the acceptance of the Gentiles should inaugurate a new era that will transcend the sins of the old generation.

Jerusalem's Refusal and Condemnation (21:18-32)

In the pericope of the cursing of the fig tree (21:18-22) Jerusalem is condemned for not having accepted the prophet from outside Jerusalem (v.11) just as it was condemned for not having hearkened to Jeremiah: faith in the prophet's word was required and was not found (Mt 21:21-22). Jeremiah extensively uses the metaphor of bad figs to speak of the king and inhabitants of Jerusalem who refused the word of the Lord which he, Jeremiah, delivered. Besides Jeremiah 24, where the Judahite exiles in Babylon are likened to good figs while the Judahites still living in the land or having fled to Egypt are likened to bad figs that cannot be eaten, the verdict against the bad figs in 24:9-10 (I will make them a horror to all the kingdoms of the earth, to be

---

[13] In the entire New Testament, Jeremiah is referred to by name only in the gospel of Matthew: at 2:17 and 27:9 in conjunction with Jerusalem's refusal of Jesus' messiahship, and at 16:14 to prepare for Peter's confession of Jesus as the messiah (v.16).

a reproach, a byword, a taunt, and a curse in all the places where I shall drive them. And I will send sword, famine, and pestilence upon them, until they shall be utterly destroyed from the land which I gave to them and their fathers) is reiterated later:

> Thus says the Lord of hosts, Behold, I am sending on them sword, famine, and pestilence, and I will make them like vile figs which are so bad they cannot be eaten. I will pursue them with sword, famine, and pestilence, and will make them a horror to all the kingdoms of the earth, to be a curse, a terror, a hissing, and a reproach among all the nations where I have driven them, because they did not heed my words, says the Lord, which I persistently sent to you by my servants the prophets, but you would not listen, says the Lord. (29:17-19)

Earlier, in ch.8, we hear that the fruitlessness of the fig tree is the outcome of God's curse: "Were they ashamed when they committed abomination? No, they were not at all ashamed; they did not know how to blush. Therefore they shall fall among the fallen; when I punish them, they shall be overthrown, says the Lord. When I would gather them, says the Lord, there are no grapes on the vine, nor figs on the fig tree; even the leaves are withered, and what I gave them has passed away from them." (vv.12-13)

On the other hand, God's harsh verdict against Jerusalem is justified by Jeremiah's position at the end of a long series of prophets, as we hear in 29:19 and as a repeated motto in that book (7:25; 25:4; 26:4-5; 28:8; 35:15; 44:4). Here also the Jerusalemite leadership has no excuse: if it refuses the authority of Jesus, at least it should endorse that of the Baptist (Mt 21:27-33) who was introduced earlier by Jesus himself as Elijah (11:14; 17:10-13), whose final mission "before the great and terrible day of the Lord comes" is to "turn the hearts of fathers to their children and the hearts of children to their fathers, lest I come and smite the land with a curse" (Mal 4:5-6). Furthermore, Matthew alone among the Evangelists follows in the footsteps of Jeremiah by making of John the Baptist the last among a long series of prophets: "For all the prophets and the law prophesied until John." (11:13) Since Matthew 11:23-24 is unique, it betrays his interest in stressing twice the link between Elijah and the Baptist and thus points out the finality of the latter's preaching; indeed, his call to repentance in Matthew is cast in the same words as Jesus': "Repent, for the kingdom of heaven is at hand." (Mt 3:2; 4:17) Consequently, Jesus' call to repentance functions as an iteration of that made by John.

This full equivalence between the two calls is taken up here also, in the parable of the two sons, special to Matthew and added as an appendix to the preceding pericope; this can be seen in that Jesus' main point in both is that "you did not believe him" (21:25, 32). In this parable the will of the Lord—to work in his vineyard (v.28)—is ultimately expressed through the Baptist's preaching (v.32) and the response to the latter is tantamount to one's response to the Lord (vv.29, 32). The close link between the call to repentance in Matthew 3 and 4 on the one hand, and the lesson of this parable, on the other hand, is betrayed in what Jesus says here: "John came to you in the way of righteousness." (21:32) This is also the way he himself had introduced to the Baptist: "Let it be so now; for thus it is fitting for us to fulfill all righteousness." (3:15). Considering that the Baptist is a stand-in for John Mark, who repented and in so doing became the "introducer" of Paul, then what Jesus is offering here is the teaching of Paul as the law of Christ, the Messiah.

The Parable of the Vineyard and the Tenants (21:33-46)

The parable of the two sons actually functions as a bridge between the earlier pericope and the following parable. Indeed, the two brothers are asked to go and work in the vineyard, which is the main subject of the parable of the vineyard and the tenants, which Matthew takes over from Mark. Since the repenting (Gentile) son is the one who ends up working according to God's will in the vineyard, whereas the other son, the Jew, does not hearken to God's invitation, so is it that the Lord's vineyard is given over to the former. However, the Matthean statement, special to him, is phrased in a way that threatens the church itself with such a verdict: "Therefore I tell you, the kingdom of God will be taken away (*arthēsetai*) from you and given to a nation producing the fruits of it." (21:43) Indeed, earlier Jesus has forewarned and again later he will forewarn that "from him who has not, even what he (imagines he) has will be taken away (*arthēsetai*)" (13:12; 25:29). After all, the table of the kingdom is God's and not ours:

> When Jesus heard (the centurion), he marveled, and said to those who followed him, "Truly, I say to you, not even in Israel have I found such faith. I tell you, many will come from east and west and sit at table with Abraham, Isaac, and Jacob in the kingdom of heaven, while the sons of the kingdom will be thrown (*ekblēthēsontai*) into the outer darkness; there men will weep and gnash their teeth." (8:10-12)

However, since now it is the kingdom of heaven itself that will be taken away and given to a "nation," i.e., another Gentile community, which would produce the fruits required by that kingdom, the hearer cannot help but perceive that the chief priests and the Pharisees here function as stand-ins for the church leaders. What applies to the previous leaders of God's *ekklēsia* applies to the actual leaders of the same *ekklēsia*, since the one God has one community (see e.g. Ezek 37:15-28 and 1 Cor 10:1-4).

The Parable of the Marriage Feast (22:1-14)

This parable is a reprise of the previous one, as indicated by the introduction: "And again Jesus spoke to them in parables." This can also be seen in the contrast between Matthew and Luke. Whereas the Lukan original speaks of a banquet, Matthew writes: "The kingdom of heaven may be compared to a king who gave a marriage feast for his son." Matthew's rephrasing of the Lukan original coheres with his overall theme, which is that the message addressed to the Jews applies now to the mainly Gentile church community. This stand can be seen in the addition of *emporia* (business) next to Luke's *agron* (field, farm) (Mt 22:5), to speak of the business that the guests use as an excuse.[14] Since for Matthew the primary point is the attainment of the kingdom, he opts to change Luke's "A man once gave a great banquet" (Lk 14:15) into "a king who gave a marriage feast for his son" (Mt 22:1), which clearly points to the eschatological banquet of the kingdom by playing on numerous scriptural metaphors describing the relationship between God and Israel as a marriage.[15] The invitation for the marriage feast of the son is the last chance for the invitees to be received into the king's favor; the message parallels that of the sending of the son in the previous parable (21:37). The similarity can be seen by the reaction of the people in each case:

---

[14] See *NTI₂* 121 and 125 regarding the connection of the Jew with *agron*.

[15] This image of the marriage between God and his people is also found in Rev 21:9-14, where the new Jerusalem is specifically referred to as the "bride of the Lamb."

When the season of fruit drew near, he sent his servants to the tenants, to get his fruit; and the tenants took his servants and beat one, killed another, and stoned another. Again he sent other servants, more than the first; and they did the same to them. Afterward he sent his son to them, saying, "They will respect my son." But when the tenants saw the son, they said to themselves, "This is the heir; come, let us kill him and have his inheritance." And they took him and cast him out of the vineyard, and killed him. (21:34-39)

But they made light of it and went off, one to his farm, another to his business, while the rest seized his servants, treated them shamefully, and killed them. (22:5-6)

Insiders – church members – should not rest at ease. Just as the Matthean addition to Mark in the previous parable threatened the insiders with expulsion from the kingdom, so here the addition to Luke threatens expulsion from the marriage feast of the kingdom:

But when the king came in to look at the guests, he saw there a man who had no wedding garment; and he said to him, "Friend, how did you get in here without a wedding garment?" And he was speechless. Then the king said to the attendants, "Bind him hand and foot, and cast him into the outer darkness; there men will weep and gnash their teeth." For many are called, but few are chosen. (Mt 22:11-14)

Paying Taxes to Caesar (22:15-22)

From the perspective of the kingdom the teachings of three major Jewish parties are criticized in turn. This pericope questions the ideology of the zealots, the war party that took arms to fight the Romans. The zealots wanted to channel the tax money (*kēnson*, vv.17, 19) away from the temple (17:25)[16] to their own treasury in support of the armed revolution. These three instances are all the occurrences of *kēnson* in Matthew. The only other occurrence in the New Testament is found in Mk 12:14, which is part of his pericope regarding the debate as to whether one is to pay taxes to Rome (vv.13-17). Thus, Matthew's handling of the matter of taxes makes his critique of the zealots even more pertinent in the sense that one can be free of Rome just as Jesus and Peter were free of the Jerusalem temple.[17]

The Resurrection (22:23-33)

After the zealots, the Sadducees are called to accept Jesus' invitation into the kingdom where the earthly temple and its service will be obsolete. Both instances in Acts where the Sadducees are mentioned present them as a group with ties to the temple: "And as they were speaking to the people, the priests and the captain of the temple and the Sadducees came upon them, annoyed because they were teaching the people and proclaiming in Jesus the resurrection from the dead" (4:1-2); "But the high priest rose up and all who were with him, that is, the party of the Sadducees, and filled with jealousy they arrested the apostles and put them in the common prison." (5:17-18) Their appellation has at its root the name of the biblical high priest Zadok. It stands to reason then that their stand against the resurrection would have to do with the fact that the priests gave importance to progeny which would secure their priestly lineage

---

[16] In vv. 17 and 19, the word *kēnson* refers to tax money, because in 17:25 it is both paralleled to *telē* (tax money in Rom 13:7) and is explained as money that is sent to the temple.

[17] See comments on Mt 17: 24-27

and thus the continuance of priesthood "for ever." But the kingdom revolves around and is sustained by the "marriage" of the messiah, God's son (Mt 22:2, 8-10), and not that of human beings (vv.25, 30). Human progeny is bound to come to an end (*eteleutēsen*, v.25) in spite of all human efforts (v.26); therefore, the only progeny that will ultimately be important is the spiritual progeny of Abraham (v.32), whose lineage was a gift of God and not the fruit of human sexuality. Indeed, the messiah is ultimately "the son of Abraham" (1:1); furthermore "God is able from these stones to raise up children to Abraham" (3:9).[18]

The Great Commandment (22:34-40)

The third party is that of the Pharisees, who considered themselves the keepers of the Law and the authoritative interpreters of scripture. The commandments of the Law are all, as Paul emphatically taught, summed up in the love for the neighbor (Mt 22:39-40; Gal 5:14; Rom 13:9-10) and it is on this basis that one faces judgment in Matthew, a point which will become evident later in the scene of the final judgment (Mt 25:31-46). Yet even in this passage the matter is subtly addressed by Matthew's use of the special verb *kremannymi* in order to make his point: "On these two commandments depend (*krematai*, hang) all the law and the prophets." (22:40). The only other time this verb occurs in this Gospel is at 18:6: "but whoever causes one of these little ones who believe in me to sin, it would be better for him to have a great millstone fastened (*kremasthē*, hung) round his neck and to be drowned in the depth of the sea." The unique use of this verb makes Matthew's larger point clear: violation of the law of love for the neighbor

---

[18] This statement is actually addressed to the Sadducees who are mentioned there for the first time in the Gospel (3:7).

will lead inexorably to an unfavorable judgment. Most probably
Matthew borrowed this imagery from Paul himself who founds
his injunction of love on the example of Jesus:

> I have been *crucified* with Christ; it is no longer I who live, but
> Christ who lives in me; and the life I now live *in the flesh* I live by
> *faith* in the Son of God, *who loved me* and gave himself for me.
> (Gal 2:20)

> For through the Spirit, by *faith*, we wait for the hope of
> righteousness. For in Christ Jesus neither circumcision nor
> uncircumcision is of any avail, but *faith working through love*. (5:5-
> 6)

> For you were called to freedom, brethren; only do not use your
> freedom as an opportunity for the flesh, but through love be
> servants of one another. For the whole law is fulfilled in one word,
> "You shall love your neighbor as yourself." But if you bite and
> devour one another take heed that you are not consumed by one
> another. But I say, walk by the Spirit, and do not gratify the
> desires of the flesh … But the fruit of the Spirit is *love*, joy, peace,
> patience, kindness, goodness, faithfulness, gentleness, self-control;
> against such there is no law. And *those who belong to Christ Jesus
> have crucified the flesh* with its passions and desires. (5:13-16, 22-
> 24)

However, in this same epistle, Paul describes Christ's love on the
cross, with which he redeemed us, in the following terms:

> Christ redeemed us from the curse of the law, having become a
> curse for us—for it is written, "Cursed be every one who hangs
> (*kremamenos*)[19] on a tree"—that in Christ Jesus the blessing of

---

[19] This is the only instance of the verb in the Pauline literature. In the rest of the New
Testament, the verb *kremannymi* occurs only in Luke-Acts (Lk 23:39; Acts 5:30;
10:39; 28:4).

Abraham might come upon the Gentiles, that we might receive the promise of the *Spirit* through *faith*. (3:13-14; italics mine)

The conclusion seems to be that, since Paul is quoting LXX here, Matthew extrapolated on Paul's use with an unrelated LXX image. Matthew was thus able to mold a term that is negative in this context and reinterpret it *both* as a positive image of how to obey the law, but also, interestingly, into a negative image of what happens to one who doesn't obey the law of love –that person will actually end up like the cursed one in the law who hangs on the tree.

The Messiah as David's Son (22:41-46)

The first challenge having ended with Jesus' giving the correct interpretation of "*all* the Law and the Prophets" (Mt 22:40), the discussion with the Pharisees moves into the Writings, the third part of scripture, of which the Psalms are the prototype.[20] Jesus' riddle offered to the Pharisees is the last invitation to them to acknowledge that the lordship of the messiah lies ultimately not in his being son of David, but rather the Son of man upon whom will be bestowed divine authority at his resurrection from the dead *after* his suffering and death on the cross. Indeed, with this pericope ends Matthew's references to the "son of David"; from this point the phrase "Son of man" takes over (24:27, 30, 37, 39, 44; 25:31; 26:2, 24, 45, 64). It is the Son of man who will be seated to judge all as the king, and thus as messiah, son of God:

---

[20] See "These are my words which I spoke to you, while I was still with you, that everything written about me in the law of Moses and the prophets and the psalms must be fulfilled" (Lk 24:44).

When the *Son of man* comes *in his glory*, and all the angels with him, then he will sit on his glorious throne. Before him will be gathered all the nations, and he will separate them one from another as a shepherd separates the sheep from the goats, and he will place the sheep at his right hand, but the goats at the left. Then the *King* will say to those at his right hand, "Come, O blessed of *my Father*, inherit the kingdom prepared for you from the foundation of the world" … When Jesus had finished all these sayings, he said to his disciples, "You know that after two days the Passover is coming, and *the Son of man will be delivered up to be crucified.*" (25:31-34; 26:1-2; italics mine)

Woe to the Scribes and Pharisees (23:1-36)

Chapter 23 begins a cycle of teaching lasting through the end of chapter 25 that constitutes the final word of warning to the leadership of the Gentile church, which is threatening to repeat the mistakes of the Jerusalem church. Since the church's members are grafted onto the trunk whose root is Abraham through Paul (Rom 11), Israel's scripture is intended for the edification of the Gentile believers.

The passage begins with an expanded rendition of a Markan invective (Mk 12:38-40). However, Matthew transformed it in a carefully structured passage. The invective here is linked with a few other texts which are the only instances in Matthew of "*the* scribes and Pharisees" (Mt 5:20, 12:38, 15:1, 23:2). In 5:20 the leaders/disciples are compared with scribes and Pharisees as teachers (v.19) and light of the world (v.14). This quality is underscored in Matthew 23 where, in the only instance that the scribes and Pharisees are not addressed as hypocrites, they are called "blind guides" (v.15; repeated in v.24). The only other time "blind guides" appears in Matthew it is connected with "hypocrites" (15:7 and 14) in conjunction with scribes and

Pharisees (v.1) where again the leaders/disciples are asked not to follow the example of this group. In a clear indication that the woes are specifically directed to the leadership of the mostly Gentile Matthean church, the address is given "to the crowds and to his disciples" (23:1), just as was the messianic law in Matthew 5:1. Compare with Paul's injunctions to the Gentiles:

> Now I am speaking to you Gentiles. Inasmuch then as I am an apostle to the Gentiles, I magnify my ministry in order to make my fellow Jews jealous, and thus save some of them. For if their rejection means the reconciliation of the world, what will their acceptance mean but life from the dead? If the dough offered as first fruits is holy, so is the whole lump; and if the root is holy, so are the branches. But if some of the branches were broken off, and you, a wild olive shoot, were grafted in their place to share the richness of the olive tree, do not boast over the branches. If you do boast, remember it is not you that support the root, but the root that supports you. (Rom 11:13-18)

> I want you to know, brethren, that our fathers were all under the cloud, and all passed through the sea, and all were baptized into Moses in the cloud and in the sea, and all ate the same supernatural food and all drank the same supernatural drink. For they drank from the supernatural Rock which followed them, and the Rock was Christ. Nevertheless with most of them God was not pleased; for they were overthrown in the wilderness. Now these things are warnings for us, not to desire evil as they did ... Now these things happened to them as a warning, but they were written down for our instruction, upon whom the end of the ages has come. (1 Cor 11:1-6, 11)

The repeated accusations of hypocrisy (Mt 23: 13, 15, 23, 25, 27, 29) recall the charges leveled by Paul against Peter (Gal

2:13),[21] who is the church leader par excellence in Matthew, as well as linking the Pharisees of the church to those of Israel, who had just been labeled as "hypocrites' (Mt 22:18). The number of woes is also indicative of the divine fullness of the judgment; just as there were seven parables of the kingdom of heaven, so there are seven woes.[22] The number seven also reflects the universalism of the message: it applies to all the churches.[23]

Notice how the church leaders can fall in the same trap as the Jewish leaders. Matthew claims that the scribes and Pharisees "*bind* [*desmeuousin*][24] *heavy* [*barea*] *burdens* [*phortia*], hard to bear, and lay them on men's shoulders; but they themselves will not move them with their finger" (23:4), thus acting like the Jewish leaders and not like Jesus who said:

> Come to me, all who labor and are *heavy laden* (*pephortismenoi*), and I will give you rest. Take my *yoke* upon you, and learn from me; for I am gentle and lowly in heart, and you will find rest for

---

[21] See my comments *NTI₁* 177-8 regarding this matter.

[22] Mt 23:14 is considered as an addition since it is omitted in the important manuscripts א, B, D. The manuscripts which do bear this verse copy it verbatim from Mk 12:40. It may have been prompted to bring up to seven the number of the address "hypocrites" in ch.23. I believe the number six is the original since it links the woes to what was said earlier to the Pharisees: "Why put me to the test, you hypocrites?" (22:18)

[23] The same is found in Rev 2-3 where each of the seven messages is actually addressed to all seven churches: "He who has an ear, let him hear what the Spirit says to the churches." (2:7, 11, 17, 29: 3:6, 13, 22)

[24] This verb points to the way the Law is "binding" as a yoke. It occurs only once more in the New Testament, in Acts 22:4, to speak of Paul's earlier activity aimed against those Jews who were following the "way" of Christ, and thus were not following the Law: "I persecuted this Way to the death, *binding* and delivering to prison both men and women." The noun "prison" is the translation of the Greek *phylakas* that is from the same root as the verb *phylassō* (keep), which is usually used in conjunction with the Law.

your souls. For my *yoke* is easy, and my *burden* (*phortion*) is *light.*
(11:28-30)

The centrality of this matter can be seen in that it is the subject
of the central woe:

> Woe to you, scribes and Pharisees, hypocrites! for you tithe mint
> and dill and cumin, and have neglected *the weightier matters* (*ta
> barytera*)[25] *of the law*, justice and *mercy* and faith; these you ought
> to have done, without neglecting the others. You blind guides,
> straining out a gnat and swallowing a camel! (23:23-24)

This basic rule of mercy is based on the fact that, ultimately,
the leaders are the brethren of the members of their flock (v.8),
all children of the one Father (v.9) and all disciples of the one
teacher, Christ (v.10). That is why, as it was underscored before,
"whoever exalts himself will be humbled, and whoever humbles
himself will be exalted" (v.12; see 18:14) and "He who is greatest
among you shall be your servant" (23:11; see 20:26-27) the
example being Christ *as the Son of man*: "the Son of man came
not to be served but to serve, and to give his life as a ransom for
many." (v.28) Any church leader who does not heed this rule of
mercy is no better than the Jewish Pharisees: "So you also
outwardly appear righteous (*dikaioi*) to men, but within you are
full of hypocrisy and iniquity (*anomias*; lawlessness)." (23:28)
Such is indeed full and complete lawlessness since its perpetrators
do not heed the messianic law of love for the neighbor and thus
are the progeny of those who were lawless throughout the
scripture of "the Law and the Prophets," from the murder of
Abel in the book of Genesis to the book of Zechariah, the last in
the "Prophets":

---

[25] Compare with the adjective *barea* of Mt 11:28. These are the only instances of the
adjective *barys* (heavy) in Matthew.

Therefore I send you prophets and wise men and scribes, some of
whom you will kill and crucify, and some you will scourge in your
synagogues and persecute from town to town, that upon you may
come all the righteous blood shed on earth, from the blood of
innocent Abel to the blood of Zechariah the son of Barachiah,
whom you murdered between the sanctuary and the altar. (23:34-
35)[26]

Lament over Jerusalem (23:37-39)

Galatians seems to be the ultimate background of this Matthean
instruction based on the rule of love:

Brethren, if a man is overtaken in any trespass, you who are
spiritual should restore him in a spirit of gentleness. Look to
yourself, lest you too be tempted. Bear (*bastazete*) one another's
burdens (*ta barē*), and so fulfil the law of Christ. For if any one
thinks he is something, when he is nothing, he deceives himself.
But let each one test his own work, and then his reason to boast
will be in himself alone and not in his neighbor. For each man will
have to bear (*bastasei*) his own load (*phortion*). (6:1-5)[27]

The reason for this request, as is clear from the last verse of this
passage and the following verses 7-10 (Do not be deceived; God
is not mocked, for whatever a man sows, that he will also reap.
For he who sows to his own flesh will from the flesh reap
corruption; but he who sows to the Spirit will from the Spirit
reap eternal life. And let us not grow weary in well-doing, for in
due season we shall reap, if we do not lose heart) is that all
church members, with the leaders at their front, will undergo

---

[26] There is some conflation in Matthew between the prophet Zechariah, who is the son
of Barachiah, and the murdered prophet Zechariah son of Jehoiada from 2 Chr
24:20ff, who is murdered by servants of King Joash.

[27] I showed in *Gal* 309-314 that this passage is addressed to the church leaders.

judgment. That is why Matthew ends his woes with the lament over Jerusalem:

> O Jerusalem, Jerusalem, killing the prophets and stoning those who are sent to you! How often would I have gathered your children together as a hen gathers her brood under her wings, and you would not! Behold, your house is forsaken and desolate. For I tell you, you will not see me again, until you say, "Blessed is he who comes in the name of the Lord." (Mt 23:37-39)

The church members, who were told they were children of the new Jerusalem (Gal 4:26), are not exempt from the divine judgment and will have to accept the same message which the old Jerusalem refused—that Jesus is the messiah—and intone the same "Blessed is he who comes in the name of the Lord" that was asked to be endorsed by the old Jerusalem (21:9). All will have to face the messiah Jesus as the Son of man coming to judge all (24:27, 30, 37, 39, 44; 25:31). Notice how earlier the church leaders were addressed with the same vocabulary that had been used toward the Jewish leaders: "You serpents, you brood of vipers, how are you to escape being sentenced to hell?" (23:33) The same judgment applies to both:

> But when he saw many of the Pharisees and Sadducees coming for baptism, he said to them, "You brood of vipers! Who warned you to flee from the wrath to come? Bear fruit that befits repentance, and do not presume to say to yourselves, 'We have Abraham as our father'; for I tell you, God is able from these stones to raise up children to Abraham." (3:6-8)

> Therefore I tell you, every sin and blasphemy will be forgiven men, but the blasphemy against the Spirit will not be forgiven. And whoever says a word against the Son of man will be forgiven; but whoever speaks against the Holy Spirit will not be forgiven, either in this age or in the age to come. Either make the tree good,

and its fruit good; or make the tree bad, and its fruit bad; for the tree is known by its fruit. You brood of vipers! how can you speak good, when you are evil? For out of the abundance of the heart the mouth speaks. (12:32-34)[28]

The Beginning of Woes (24:1-14)

Matthew uses the term *epideiknymi* ("show") three times as a way to introduce critical teachings about the kingdom of heaven. In the first instance (Mt 16:1), the Pharisees and Sadducees ask Jesus to show them a sign from heaven, which he uses as a way to attack them for their short-sightedness in interpreting the events unfolding before them. In the second (Mt 22:19), Jesus himself is the one who asks for an object (a coin) to be shown to him, in order to use it to make distinctions between the kingdom of God and the kingdom of Caesar.[29] In the present instance (24:1), it is the disciples themselves who undertake, unprompted, to direct Jesus' attention to the structures of the Temple complex. Jesus uses this as an opportunity to introduce the lessons on the signs of the final times.

When one compares Matthew 24:1-3 with the Markan original (Mk 13:1-4),[30] one cannot help but notice the following changes:

---

[28] These three account for the only instances of the phrase "brood of vipers" in Matthew.

[29] In a related instance, Satan "shows" (*deiknymi*) Jesus all of the world's kingdoms as a means of testing him. (Mt 4:8)

[30] "And as he came out of the temple, *one of his disciples* said to him, 'Look, Teacher, what wonderful stones and what wonderful buildings!" And Jesus said to him, "Do you see these great buildings? There will not be left here one stone upon another, that will not be thrown down.' And as he sat on the Mount of Olives opposite the

1. Instead of the one disciple asking the question in the name of the others, we have in Matthew "his disciples," meaning all of them.

2. Instead of the four pillars being addressed, it is "the disciples." Thus we have an intended generalization of the teaching to all "the" disciples, reflecting a time when the original leaders are no more.

3. This is confirmed in that, instead of the question being specifically about the destruction of the temple (as in Mark), it shifts to Jesus' coming (*parousia*) together with "the close of the age." The latter is a specifically Matthean expression (5 times in Matthew and only once in Heb 9:26) indicating that, for Matthew, the following "step" is the final end. Besides its use here and at the end of the Gospel, it is found 3 times in the specifically Matthean parable where we have a differentiation between the kingdom of God and that of the Son, which is the time of the "church" in the world

---

temple, *Peter and James and John and Andrew* asked him privately, 'Tell us, when will this be, and what will be the sign when *these things are all to be accomplished?*'" (Mk 13:1-4; italics mine); "Jesus left the temple and was going away, when *his disciples* came to point out to him the buildings of the temple. But he answered them, 'You see all these, do you not? Truly, I say to you, there will not be left here one stone upon another, that will not be thrown down.' As he sat on the Mount of Olives, *the disciples* came to him privately, saying, 'Tell us, when will this be, and what will be *the sign of your coming and of the close of the age?*'" (Mt 24:1-3) (compare with Matthew 23 and 28, where "the disciples" are addressed). Consequently, in Matthew it is the post-apostolic church that is addressed instead of the first Jewish War generation. If one places the composition of Matthew in the second century, then the background could well be the period prior to the Bar Kochba revolt of 132-135. (Notice Matthew's interest in the "star"/*kokab* in ch.2)

No one is exempt from the test since the entire church membership has to face the same hurdles as the apostles regarding their testimony for the gospel of the kingdom before the end comes:

> Then they will deliver you up to tribulation, and put you to death; and you will be hated by all nations for my name's sake. And then many will fall away, and betray one another, and hate one another. And many false prophets will arise and lead many astray. And because wickedness is multiplied, most men's love will grow cold. But he who endures to the end will be saved. And this gospel of the kingdom will be preached throughout the whole world, as a testimony to all nations; and then the end will come. (24:9-14)

The specific phrase "*this* gospel" is a reference to the gospel book of Matthew. Matthew skillfully connects "the close of the age" here and the episode in Matthew 28 where the disciples are to repeat to the nations all the words of Jesus until "the close of the age."

The Great Tribulation (24:15-22)

Matthew's interest in underlining the challenges facing the mainly Gentile church is further evidenced in his reworking of

Mark's text about the final tribulation. Already in Mark the real danger is not the threat of the destruction of the city (Mk 13:14-20), but rather being led away from the faith by false Christs and prophets (vv.21-24). This is in accord with the consistent scriptural message that the real source of pressure against God's community comes from the leaders of the people themselves. (One of the most compelling instances of this theme is found in Jeremiah, where the false preaching of Hananiah, directed against God's true prophet Jeremiah, is of dramatically more concern than the invading Babylonians.) The tribulation pericope generally mirrors Matthew's shift from Jerusalem to the Roman setting of the church: what the Jewish apostles had to undergo in Israel (Mt 10:5-6), the Gentile disciples now face in the Roman empire after the destruction of Jerusalem. False Christs and prophets are to be found in that Roman empire at large: "in the wilderness (of the Gentiles)" and "in the inner rooms (*tameiois*)" (Mt:24:26) which are the disciples' places of prayer.[31] These false Christs and prophets can well be the church leaders themselves just as we were warned in Matthew 23. If the earlier believers were asked not to put their hope in the city of Jerusalem, which was unsuccessful in facing the threat of Rome, much less are the latter believers to rest in the security of the victorious Roman empire, since the ultimate threat—the final judgment—is in the hands of the Son of man: "For as the lightning comes from the east and shines as far as the west, so will be the coming of the Son of man." (24:27) Rome lay in the west, while threats against it came from the east (particularly from the Persian empire, which had threatened the empires of

---

[31] Cf. Mt 6:6: "But when you pray, go into your room (*tameion*) and shut the door and pray to your Father who is in secret; and your Father who sees in secret will reward you." This and Mt 24:26 are the only instances of this noun in Matthew.

the Mediterranean region since the fall of the neo-Babylonian empire in 539 B.C.). At the end, the lightning—destroying light—of the Son of man will come from the east to strike *as far as the west.*

The Coming of the Son of Man (24:29-31)

The superiority of the suffering of God's Christ over the Roman power is the main message of the Book of Revelation. The closeness between Revelation and Matthew in this matter is evidenced in the way the Evangelist handles the earlier tradition describing the coming of the Son of man:

> But in those days, after that tribulation, the sun will be darkened, and the moon will not give its light, and the stars will be falling from heaven, and the powers in the heavens will be shaken. And then they will see the Son of man coming in clouds with great power and glory. And then he will send out the angels, and gather his elect from the four winds, from the ends of the earth to the ends of heaven. (Mk 13:24-27)

> Immediately after the tribulation of those days the sun will be darkened, and the moon will not give its light, and the stars will fall from heaven, and the powers of the heavens will be shaken; then will appear the sign of the Son of man in heaven, and then all the tribes of the earth will mourn, and they will see the Son of man coming on the clouds of heaven with power and great glory; and he will send out his angels with a loud trumpet call, and they will gather his elect from the four winds, from one end of heaven to the other. (Mt 24:29-31)

The reference to the appearance of the Son of man as a "sign" is specifically Matthean.[32] For Matthew, the sign of which the disciples inquired (Mt 24:3) is none other than that of the Son

---

[32] The appearance of the Son of man is not Matthean, but calling it a sign is.

of man, which is addressed to "all the tribes of the earth." Consequently, the lesson of the fig tree (24:32-35), a parable concerning Israel, applies now to all nations.

Earlier, Matthew (12:40) adds to the Lukan passage of the sign of Jonah the concept of death and resurrection (in Luke it refers to the preaching and the penitence). This addition heightens Matthew's general message that Jesus will be coming again *to judge*. Here, the sign of the Son of man points to his glorification after death by crucifixion. The addition of "all the tribes of the earth will mourn"—a gospel text that is unique to Matthew—is imported from Revelation 1:7. All of the nations are included in Matthew's text. Repentance, earlier addressed to Israel as the sign of Jonah, is now addressed to the universe (see Mt 28:16-20)

Furthermore, in Mark Jesus sends his angels, but here in Matthew the angels are sent at the call of the trumpet, which makes clear that the end is the reference of the passage. (This same feature is also found in Mt 13:41). Matthew systematically advances the thesis of Mark that Jesus wishes to be called Son of Man and not Son of God, as the authority of the Son of man is in his teaching. The critique of the prophets against the king was that he played upon his status as the offspring of the deity to secure his own power instead of to act as the shepherd and teacher of his people. However, here Jesus sends his messengers in his capacity as Son of Man, not as the Son of God.

It is in Matthew that Jesus makes the reference to Peter as "*bar jona*" (Mt 16:17), who under this title is given the keys to tie and to untie. In giving Peter this title, Jesus is identified as "the Christ" in his capacity as Son of man: the one speaking is not Jesus as "Christ" but Jesus as Son of Man. This identification proleptically corrects the subsequent misinterpretation of Peter, who protests in v. 22 against Jesus' predicted suffering and death. Therefore, Peter first stands as the "*bar jona*," but later is identified as *Satanas*. However, it is the word of the gospel that permits its recipients time to correctly assess Jesus as the Son of man, as indicated by the gap between the proclamation of the gospel in 24:14 and the coming of the end in v.31. The vacillating figure of Peter will therefore have some space to come to an ultimately correct apprehension of Jesus' message.

The Unknown Day and Hour (24:36-44)

Matthew's interest in the universalization of divine judgment, already expressed in his special parable of the weeds among the wheat (13:24-30, 36-43), is shown by his conclusion of Jesus' teaching on the end with two texts on the necessity of watchfulness (24:37-44) borrowed from Luke and rephrased to fit the new context. In the first he likens "the coming of the Son of man"[33] to that of God in Noah's times, stressing thus the idea of judgment. The hearer cannot miss this purpose since the point of likeness is repeated:

> As were the days of Noah, so will be the coming of the Son of man. For *as in those days before the flood* they were eating and drinking, marrying and giving in marriage, until the day when Noah entered the ark, and they did not know until the flood came and swept them all away, *so will be the coming of the Son of man.* (vv.37-39; italics mine)

Mark's final invitation to watchfulness (Watch therefore for you do not know when the master of the house will come, in the evening, or at midnight, or at cockcrow, or in the morning; Mk

---

[33] Just as the sign of Jesus' coming is that of the Son of man (24:3, 30), so also the coming itself of Jesus is that of the Son of man (24:3, 37).

13:35) is plainly put in conjunction with the coming of the Son of man (Watch therefore, for you do not know on what day your Lord is coming ... Therefore you also must be ready; for the Son of man is coming at an hour you do not expect; Mt 24:42, 44) and is bolstered with two sayings borrowed from Luke: "Then two men will be in the field; one is taken and one is left. Two women will be grinding at the mill; one is taken and one is left" (vv.40-41);[34] "But know this, that if the householder had known in what part of the night the thief was coming, he would have watched and would not have let his house be broken into." (v.43)[35]

The Faithful and the Unfaithful Servant (24:45-51)

Although his chapter 24 is addressed to all the disciples instead of only the leaders (as in Mark 13:3), Matthew includes a forceful caveat to the church leaders (Mt 23).[36] His interest in the higher responsibility of the leaders surfaces again in his use of a parable borrowed from Luke 12:41-46. However, here Matthew borrows with an eye toward his special concern: the church in the setting of the Roman empire and the special responsibility of the leadership.

He changes Luke's *therapeias* ("household" in RSV), which means "(a place of) healing,"[37] into *oiketias* (also "household" in

---

[34] Compare with Lk 34-35 that occur in the same context in which the Lukan material about the days of Noah (17:26-36).

[35] Compare with Luke 12:39 (But know this, that if the householder had known at what hour the thief was coming, he would not have left his house to be broken into) that introduces: "You also must be ready; for the Son of man is coming at an unexpected hour." (v.40)

[36] Cf. chapter 18.

[37] I explained its use according to Luke's interest in the gospel as being addressed to the Gentiles who are healed by its teaching; see *NTI₂* 108.

RSV), which means the household of slaves. This term fits perfectly the setting of the Roman empire where the household was based on the authority of the *paterfamilias* who controlled a "household" composed mainly of slaves. Notice how, in Matthew, the co-servants of whom the assigned servant is in charge are referred to as *syndoulous* (co-slaves, 24:49) instead of *paidas kai paidiskas* (menservants and maidservants, Lk 12:45). Moreover, the place of punishment where the former head slave is consigned is again described as where "men will weep and gnash their teeth" (compare Mt 8:12; 13, 42, 50; 22:11-13). As for Matthew's interest in the church leadership, it is demonstrated by the affiliation of the unfaithful servants-in-charge with "the hypocrites,"[38] an epithet with which both the leaders of the church and the scribes and Pharisees are consistently addressed.

The Parable of the Ten Maidens (25:1-13)

What was said to the leaders applies also to all the disciples: they are accountable to the Lord. The reference to the general church can be ascertained from Matthew's use of the virgins as the subject of the parable and by his employment of the number ten: the latter symbolizes the entirety of a body while the former is in concord with the classic image of the church as the bride of Christ (Jn 3:29; 2 Cor 11:2; Rev 21:2, 9; 22:7). The good virgins are said to be "wise" (Mt 25:2, 4, 8, 9), just as the faithful servant (24:45), while the other virgins are called "foolish" (25: 2, 3, 8), like the hypocrite leaders (23:17). The basis of the virgins' judgment is their possession of a sufficient quantity of

---

[38] Luke has "with the unfaithful" (12:46)

elaion (oil; 25:3, 4, 8), a homonym of *eleos* (mercy).[39] Oil is used as a healing agent for the sick (Mk 6:13), and is itself an expression of the apostolic preaching (vv.7-13). The finality of the judgment here can be deduced from the vocabulary: the bridegroom is the Son of God, i.e., the messiah, whose eschatological wedding it is (Mt 22:1-14);[40] upon his arrival the virgins "rose" (*ēgerthēsan*, 25:7) to "meet him" (*hypantēsin*, v.6);[41] the wise virgins are said to be "ready" (v.10) and thus have heeded the call to "watch therefore, for you know neither the day nor the hour" (v.13).[42]

The Parable of the Talents (25:14-30)

The importance, if not priority, given by Matthew to the threat of divine judgment over the church, can be seen in that the message of the preceding two parables (24:45-51; 25:1-13) is taken up, and thus underscored, in the following two: the first deals with the leaders (25:14-30) while the second addresses the entire church membership (vv.31-46). That which was required of the exemplary leader is now asked of all leaders to whom the

---

[39] See *NTT₂* 129n. See also Theone Stateson's M.Div. thesis, *Parable of the ten virgins: an analysis*, St. Vladimir's Orthodox Theological Seminary: Crestwood, NY, 1998, for the Patristic understanding of oil in this parable as referring to the acts of mercy or the good deeds.

[40] See also Mt 9:15/Mk 2:19-20/Lk 5:34-35; Jn 3:28-29; Rev 18:23.

[41] Compare with 1 Thess 4:16-17: "For the Lord himself will descend from heaven with a cry of command, with the archangel's call, and with the sound of the trumpet of God. And the dead in Christ will *rise* (*anastēsontai*) first; then we who are alive, who are left, shall be caught up together with them in the clouds to *meet* (*hypantēsin*) the Lord in the air; and so we shall always be with the Lord."

[42] Compare with Jesus' earlier admonition "Watch therefore, for you do not know on what day your Lord is coming ... Therefore you also must be *ready*; for the Son of man is coming at an hour you do not expect" (Mt 24:42, 44).

master "entrusted (*paredōken*) his property (*ta hyparkhonta autou*)" (25:14).[43]

Matthew's focus on the rising Gentile leadership in the church is betrayed throughout the parable, the rephrasing of the Lukan original not being the least indication. While Luke speaks of ten servants receiving each the same amount, one talent, here we are told of three servants receiving decreasing amounts. The last, in spite of his lesser gift, has no excuse not to produce comparatively as much as each of the other two servants, double the amount granted to him. The Lord reaps not only in his own field, but throughout the world, since he is not the God of Jews only, but also of the Gentiles (Rom 3:9) and he "makes known the riches of his glory for the vessels of mercy, which he has prepared beforehand for glory, even us whom he has called, not from the Jews only but also from the Gentiles" (9:23-24). But if the mercy is equal, then so is the accountability.

I believe there is a subtle reference to the Gentiles reflected by the wicked servant's mishandling of God's trust in him, a reference having to do with a matter that is central to the Pauline gospel. In Luke already, the servant is indicted in these terms: "Why then did you not put my money into the bank (*epi trapezan*), and at my coming I should have collected it with interest?" (Lk 19:23) The noun *trapeza* means basically "table"[44] and occurs in the New Testament mainly in conjunction with table fellowship between Jews and Gentiles, i.e., the Eucharistic gathering (Mt 15:27/Mk 7:28; Lk 16:21; 22:21, 30; Acts 6:2;

---

[43] All the other instances of the verb *paradidōmi* (give, deliver, hand) in conjunction with Jesus have the meaning of "betray, give over, hand over."

[44] The money handlers use tables, hence the secondary meaning of "bank" associated with this word in Greek.

16:34; 1 Cor 10:21). This intention is made clear in Matthew, which changes the Lukan *trapezan* into *trapezitais* (bankers) which could also mean "commensals, table-fellows" so that the master's saying may be rendered as "you ought to have invested my money with the [your] table-fellows" (Mt 25:27).

The Judgment of All the Nations (25:31-46)

This is Matthew's key text, since at the end of it we are told "When Jesus had finished *all* these sayings" (26:1a; italics mine).[45] The basis for the judgment is strikingly clear: Every (son of) man is to do no less than what Jesus, the Son of man, did in accordance with Isaiah:

> That evening they brought to him many who were possessed with demons; and he cast out the spirits with a word, and healed all who were sick. This was to fulfill what was spoken by the prophet Isaiah, "He took our infirmities and bore our diseases." (Mt 8:16-17)

In so doing, he proved to be God's suffering servant who implements fully God's will:

> And many followed him, and he healed them all, and ordered them not to make him known. This was to fulfill what was spoken by the prophet Isaiah: "Behold, my servant whom I have chosen, my beloved with whom my soul is well pleased. I will put my Spirit upon him, and he shall proclaim justice to the Gentiles. He will not wrangle or cry aloud, nor will any one hear his voice in the streets; he will not break a bruised reed or quench a smoldering wick, till he brings justice to victory; and in his name will the Gentiles hope." (12:15b-21)

---

[45] Contrast with the previous endings of Jesus' first four discourses in Mt 7:28; 11:1; 13:53; 19:1.

As seen just above, the concept of mercy is directly linked to the suffering servant. Here Jesus demonstrates the critical qualities of mercy that are necessary for his followers, but also his kingly function of judgment. It is only those who meet the criterion of mercy through their actions that will be judged as the suffering servant and, hence, be eligible for membership in the kingdom.

It is Jesus, as Son of man, who is given the authority to judge as a king (and, therefore, as God himself), and exercises the power of inviting the righteous into his Father's kingdom for having *done* God's will and expelling from it those whom he has cursed for *not* having *done* God's will, which is expressed in the love for the needy neighbor. Indeed, the messianic law of Matthew 5-7 concludes with the statement:

> Not every one who says to me, "Lord, Lord," shall enter the kingdom of heaven, but he who *does* the will of my Father who is in heaven. On that day many will say to me, "Lord, Lord, did we not prophesy in your name, and cast out demons in your name, and do many mighty works in your name?" And then will I declare to them, "I never knew you; depart from me, you evildoers."[46] (7:21-23)

Further Reading

Agourides, S. "'Little ones' in Matthew." *Bible Translator* 35 (1984): 329-334.

Cortés-Fuentes, D. "The Least of These My Brothers: Matthew 25:31-46." *Apuntes* 23 (2003): 100-109.

Grassi. "Matthew as a Second Testament Deuteronomy." *Biblical Theology Bulletin* 19 (1989): 23-29.

---

[46] Compare with Mt 25: 41 (Depart from me, you cursed).

Heil, J. P. "The Double Meaning of the Narrative of Universal Judgment in Matthew 25.31-46." *Journal for the Study of the New Testament* 69 (1998): 3-14.

Meyer, B. F. "Many (= All) are Called, but Few (= Not All) are chosen." *New Testament Studies* 36 (1990): 89-97.

Ostmeyer, K.-H. "Jesu Annahme der Kinder in Matthäus 19:13-15." *Novum Testamentum* 46 (2004): 1-11.

Saldarini, A. J. "Understanding Matthew's Vitriol." *Bible Review* 13 (1997): 32-39, 45.

Wenham, G. J. "Matthew and Divorce: An Old Crux Revisited." *Journal for the Study of the New Testament* 22 (1999): 95-107.

Ware, B. A. "Is the Church in View in Matthew 24-25?" *Bibliotheca Sacra* 138 (1981): 158-172.

The False Judgment of the Messiah and His Vindication by God

The Plot to Kill Jesus (26:1-5)

Matthew's expansion of the short Markan (and Lukan) introduction to Jesus' passion and death aims at putting them within God's overall plan. They take place, we are told, after "Jesus had finished *all* these sayings" (Mt 26:1a), i.e., after he delivered *all* the new Torah of the kingdom that will be necessary for the salvation of all nations: "Go therefore and make disciples of all nations, baptizing them in the name of the Father and of the Son and of the Holy Spirit, teaching them to observe *all* that I have commanded you; and lo, I am with you always, to the close of the age." (28:19-20) As for Jesus' passion and death, they take place according to his prediction:

> He said to his disciples, "You know that after two days the Passover is coming, and the Son of man will be delivered up to be crucified." *Then* the chief priests and the elders of the people gathered in the palace of the high priest, who was called Caiaphas, and took counsel (*synebouleusanto*) together in order to arrest Jesus by stealth and kill him. (26:1b-4)[1]

Matthew's intent is actually reflected in his handling of this matter. In Mark the conspiratorial aspects of the Jewish leaders'

---

[1] Compare with "It was now two days before the Passover and the feast of Unleavened Bread. And the chief priests and the scribes were seeking how to arrest him by stealth, and kill him" (Mk 14:1).

plan are introduced at the beginning of the Gospel and renewed
at the end, *after* their trial of Jesus: "The Pharisees went out, and
immediately held counsel (*symboulion*) with the Herodians
against him, how to destroy him" (Mk 3:6); "And as soon as it
was morning the chief priests, with the elders and scribes, and
the whole council held a consultation (*symboulion*); and they
bound Jesus and led him away and delivered him to Pilate."
(15:1)[2] On the other hand, after having followed Mark at the
beginning (Mt 12:14),[3] Matthew not only makes reference to the
leaders' "counsel" (*symboulion*) at the end of the parable of the
wedding (Mt 22:15), but, more importantly, continues to make
reference to it throughout Jesus' trial (27:1, 7; 28:12), thus
underscoring that their plan was devised according to Jesus'
prediction, and therefore under God's control at every stage of
its implementation.[4]

Actually, Matthew is only underscoring that which was present
already in Mark: the Jews' "plan" could not undo God's "plan,"
since Jesus' passion is according to God's will ("Father ... yet not
what I will, but what thou wilt"; Mk 14:38) which is kept
verbatim by Matthew (26:39).[5] This is precisely what Paul
taught in Romans 9-11. Indeed, outside the Gospels, where the
root *symboul-* is consistently used in reference to the Jewish

---

[2] These are the only two verses in Mark to utilize the root *symboul-*.

[3] Which parallels Mk 3:6; the statement is made after Jesus has healed the man with
the withered hand in the synagogue on the sabbath.

[4] Notice that it is also a leitmotiv in Matthew since, compared to Mark who uses once
the verb *edidoun* (in 3:6) and the other time *poiēsantes* (15.1) with *symboulion*,
Matthew has the stereotyped phrase *symboulion labein* throughout.

[5] In Luke we have "Father ... nevertheless not my will, but thine, be done."

leaders' "counsel" to kill Jesus,[6] it occurs in Acts, where Luke uses it in conjunction with the Jews' plan to put Paul to death (Acts 9:23; 25:12),[7] and in Revelation (3:18) and Romans.

At the end of his discussion in Romans 9-11, Paul gives glory to God with a quotation from Isaiah: "For who has known the mind of the Lord, or who has been his counselor (*symboulos*)?" (11:34) In spite of the Jews making their own plan to counteract the plan of God, this is counteracted by giving the message to all the nations, which is then offered to the Jews to accept it, an event that builds specifically on Romans 11:34. In Romans, Paul uses the *symboulion* of God as an *inclusio* for 9-11. God's will is linked to the kingdom in spite of events in the *ekklēsia* (cf. Mt 23). The message is to someone who relies on his richness and yet is blind, and thus actually needs to be healed of his blindness through repentance, which sounds very much like the blind Jewish leader in the Gospels.

The Anointing at Bethany (26:6-13)

That Matthew had in mind Paul's gospel rejected by the Jews in their "counsel" is corroborated in the pericope of the unction at Bethany. In his rephrasing of the Markan original he puts his seal on that Gospel which is the only final word of God and is preserved in the Gentile church to whose membership, and especially leadership, his Gospel book is addressed. Speaking of

---

[6] Besides the occurrences in Mark and Matthew, it is found in Jn 18:14: "It was Caiaphas who had given counsel to the Jews that it was expedient that one man should die for the people."

[7] Again, at the beginning and the end of Paul's activity, similarly to the Markan usage concerning the plot to eliminate Jesus.

the messianic "myrrh" (*myrou*)[8] he compacts Mark's "ointment of pure nard, very costly" into "very expensive (*barytimou*) ointment." This term, unique in the New Testament, sounds like the equally unique *Bartimaios*, which I showed to be a suggestive to Timothy,[9] the official heir of Paul as leader of the Gentile church—represented here by the woman who poured the ointment on Jesus[10]— and thus the official bearer of Paul's gospel after him.[11] It is this Pauline gospel whose torchbearer Timothy was and which was refused by Israel, that becomes *the* gospel *as contained in Matthew's book*: indeed, Mark's original "the gospel" becomes "this gospel" in Matthew (26:9), which is quite unexpected since neither is it warranted by the context nor is it the Matthean usual "the gospel of the kingdom" (4:23; 9:35; 24:14). Matthew here is making his Gospel *the* gospel of the kingdom by constructing an edifice on top of Mark's work, which many of his readers would already have identified as an authoritative word of the kingdom.

Judas Agrees to Betray Jesus (26:14-16)

Whereas in Mark the chief priests promise to give Judas a certain amount of money (*argyrion*) for his betrayal of Jesus (Mk 14:11), in Matthew it is Judas himself who asks for it and they readily hand him thirty pieces of silver (*triakonta argyria*). The intention is to make clear that Judas' betrayal amounted to the refusal of

---

[8] RSV translates this word into "ointment." See *NTI1* 215-6 and *NTI2* 66 where I show that it refers to the myrrh poured upon the king, and thus is an indication of Jesus' messiahship.

[9] See *NTI₁* 202.

[10] See *NTI₁* 215-6 and *NTI₂* 66.

[11] It is interesting to point out here that the expression *kopous parekhete* to speak of "troubling" the woman corresponds to Paul's request at the end of Galatians, the epistle most directly expressive of his gospel, that he not be troubled anymore: "let no man trouble me (*kopous moi mēdeis parekhetō*)."

God's gospel of grace for all nations preached by Paul. Indeed, the source of the statement "And they paid him thirty pieces of silver" (Mt 24:15) is the following passage from Zechariah:

> And I took my staff Grace, and I broke it, annulling the covenant which I had made with all the peoples. So it was annulled on that day, and the traffickers in the sheep, who were watching me, knew that it was the word of the Lord. Then I said to them, "If it seems right to you, give me my wages; but if not, keep them." And they weighed[12] out as my wages thirty shekels of silver. Then the Lord said to me, "Cast it into the treasury"— the lordly price at which I was paid off by them. So I took the thirty shekels of silver and cast them into the treasury in the house of the Lord. (11:10-13)

Matthew uses this passage to show how Judas desires money to block the message of the gospel; the use of the name Judas makes it clear that Matthew is referring to Judah interfering with the transmission of the gospel to the nations (cf. Rom 9-11; 1 Thess 2:14-16). He continues here to emphasize his main point: matters happen to Jesus according to God's will expressed in scripture.

Preparation for the Passover with the Disciples (26:17-19)

The preparation of the Passover parallels Jesus' entry into Jerusalem in the use of the phrase "the disciples did as Jesus had directed them" (Mt 21:6; 26:19).[13] For Matthew, more than in any other Gospel, the messiah is the Son of man bound to suffer and die on his way to the glory reserved to him. Indeed, it is only now while traveling to "keep the passover with his disciples" on

---

[12] Matthew 24:16 uses the same Greek verb *estēsan* found in the Septuagint, which is translated as "paid" by RSV in Matthew.

[13] These are the only two instances in the New Testament.

his way to his Father's kingdom (Mt 26:29), and not at his triumphal entry into the city, that Jesus says "My time is at hand (*ho kairos mou engys estin*)" (26:18). Note also that, in Matthew, the idea of the "(foreordained) time" (*kairos*) being at hand occurs only once more in conjunction with the suffering of God's only son:

> When the season (*ho kairos*) of fruit drew near (*ēngisen*), he sent his servants to the tenants, to get his fruit; and the tenants took his servants and beat one, killed another, and stoned another. Again he sent other servants, more than the first; and they did the same to them. Afterward he sent his son to them, saying, "They will respect my son." But when the tenants saw the son, they said to themselves, "This is the heir; come, let us kill him and have his inheritance." And they took him and cast him out of the vineyard, and killed him (21:34-39).

The Lord's Supper (26:20-35)

Matthew here follows closely the Markan line, making out of it the general Eucharistic practice of the church. His additions are, however, pertinent to the line of thought in his own book. Since for him the messages of the Baptist and Jesus are identical, he omits the phrase "for the forgiveness of sins" from the description of the Baptist's invitation to repentance as found in Mark (1:4) and Luke (3:3), and instead raises it in conjunction with the sacrifice of Christ (for this is my blood of the covenant, which is poured out for many for the forgiveness of sins, Mt 26:28). This literary move allows the Matthean text to follow more closely the Isaianic text of the Suffering Servant:

> Yet it was the will of the Lord to bruise him; he has put him to grief; when he makes himself an offering for sin, he shall see his offspring, he shall prolong his days; the will of the Lord shall

prosper in his hand; he shall see the fruit of the travail of his soul and be satisfied; by his knowledge shall the righteous one, my servant, make many to be accounted righteous; and he shall bear their iniquities. Therefore I will divide him a portion with the great, and he shall divide the spoil with the strong; because he poured out his soul to death, and was numbered with the transgressors; yet he bore the sin of many, and made intercession for the transgressors. (Is 53:10-12)

Just like Isaiah, who links the servant's glorification to his voluntary suffering, Matthew points to Jesus' resurrection by adding "with you" (after "I drink it new") to the Markan statement "I shall not drink again of the fruit of the vine until that day when I drink it new in the kingdom of God" (Mk 14:25; compare with Mt 26:29). This seemingly minor addition links the pre-crucifixion promises to his disciples to the post-resurrectional statement "I am with you always, to the close of the age" (Mt 28:20b). This heightened emphasis on fellowship between Jesus and his disciples is underscored at the outset of the Gospel, in the name Emmanuel, God is with us (1:23), which can thus be considered one of the Matthean leitmotivs.[14]

Gethsemane (26:36-46)

After Peter's denial (26:30-35), this pericope underscores the necessity for the disciples to maintain their fellowship with Jesus by upholding his standards despite the difficulty of doing so. Notice how Matthew twice adds the phrase "with me" to the Markan original: "remain here and watch *with me*" and "could you not watch *with me* one hour?" (Mt 26:38, 40) The rule that most clearly expresses Jesus' standards is the Lord's Prayer (5:9-13). This prayer is echoed in the phraseology employed here:

---

[14] See further in the Gethsemane pericope.

"Watch and pray that you may not enter into temptation" (26:40); "thy will be done" (v.42). One can also add the fact that, in Matthew, Jesus calls God "My Father"[15] (vv.39, 42), which corresponds to his "Our Father" (6:9).[16]

Betrayal and Arrest of Jesus (26:47-56)

Since for Matthew, the entire passion of Jesus as Son of man is under God's control, he refers ironically to Judas' kiss of betrayal as a "sign" (26:48); it works ultimately to ensure that the "sign" of the Son of man be fulfilled. This irony is further confirmed in Jesus' question to Judas, "*hetaire, eph' ho parei*" ("Friend, why are you here?" v.50). On the one hand, the address *hetaire* (friend, companion), special to Matthew, is the same which greeted the worker at the vineyard who was complaining (20:13) and the guest at the wedding feast who was not clad appropriately (22:12).[17] On the other hand, the verb *parei* is from the same root as the noun *parousia* that is used to speak of the Lord's— and, in Matthew, of the Son of man's (24:27, 37, 39)—coming. Thus, what Jesus was telling Judas is that his betrayal was foreseen in God's plan: throughout the scriptural story Israel and Judah keep betraying the Lord who, nevertheless, works out his salvation both for them and the nations. As for the disciples, they are not to use the sword even if their oppressors do: their only weapon is the gospel "word" that reaches the opponent through the medium of the ear. Consequently, the disciple is to "stretch out his hand" (26:51) not for destruction, but for healing and salvation, as Jesus does (8:3; 9:18; 14:31). In the following two

---

[15] Notice how the first invitation "remain here and watch *with me*" is immediately followed by Jesus' "My Father."

[16] Luke has simply "Father" in both instances (11:2; 22:42).

[17] Since its use is always ironical, its choice may have been prompted by the fact it is a homonym of *heteros*, which means "other, different."

pericopes of the trial of Jesus and the betrayal by Peter, Matthew follows Mark closely: true blasphemy, committed by both the Sanhedrin and Peter, is that directed against the true temple, Jesus himself, who cannot be destroyed as the earthly temple of Jerusalem was at the hands of the Romans.

Jesus Given over to Pilate (27:1-2)

Here, Matthew repeats what he said at the beginning of ch.26:

> Then the chief priests and the elders of the people gathered in the palace of the high priest, who was called Caiaphas, and took counsel together in order to arrest Jesus by stealth and kill him. (Mt 26:3-4)

> When morning came, all the chief priests and the elders of the people took counsel against Jesus to put him to death; and they bound him and led him away and delivered him to Pilate the governor. (27:1-2)

So the death of Jesus took place at the hand of the Roman authority to whom he was delivered. This is already evident in Luke, who, in introducing the Jewish leaders' question about allegiance to Caesar, writes: "So they [the scribes and the chief priests] watched him, and sent spies, who pretended to be sincere, that they might take hold of what he said, so as to deliver him up to the authority and jurisdiction of the governor (*hēgemonos*)." (Lk 20:20) The authority of Pilate stems ultimately from Rome: "In the fifteenth year of the reign (*hēgemonias*) of Tiberius Caesar, Pontius Pilate being governor (*hēgemoneuontos*) of Judea..." (3:1a) That is to say, the Jewish leaders intended to present Jesus as a traitor to Rome and, at the same time, dissociate themselves from him, thus taking away from him the protection of Judaism as *religio licita*.[18] Matthew capitalizes on this theme; alone among the Evangelists, he repeatedly refers to Pilate as "governor" (*hēgemōn*) during the trial (27:2, 11, 14, 15, 21, 27). Since whatever happens to Jesus is in God's hands, it is he, rather than Rome, who is the real "governor". This matter was addressed at the beginning of the gospel, through Matthew's composite quotation from scripture: "And you, O Bethlehem, in the land of Judah, are by no means least among the rulers (*hēgemosin*) of Judah; for from you shall come a ruler (*hēgoumenos*) who will govern my people Israel." (Mt 2:6) Consequently, Matthew's repeated reference to Pilate as "governor" during Jesus' trial is an intended irony: the worldly authority only appears to be holding the reins of power. In fact, Pilate is at the mercy of the Jewish leaders, as is evident from the last instance of "governor" in this gospel:

> While they were going, behold, some of the guard went into the city and told the chief priests all that had taken place. And when they had assembled with the elders and taken counsel, they gave a sum of money to the soldiers and said, "Tell people, 'His disciples came by night and stole him away while we were asleep.' And *if this comes to the governor's ears, we will satisfy*[19] *him* and keep you out of trouble." (28:11-14).

The Death of Judas (27:3-10)

Judas, the disciple who personifies Judah, ends by committing suicide, paralleling the result of the province's armed revolt against Rome. Yet, the story is cast, as usual in the New Testament, in a "scriptural" manner. Since Jeremiah is especially

---

[18] This is precisely what happened to Paul when he was held under Roman custody in Ephesus, as one can gather from the letter to the Philippians.

[19] The Greek has *peisomen*, which means "we will convince."

forceful in his preaching against the false triumphalism of the sinful Jerusalem personified by Hananiah (Jer 27-28), this entire pericope, special to Matthew, is cast in the mold of his teaching. From the outset Judas' sin is said to be a betrayal of "innocent blood," which is a trademark of Jeremiah among the prophetic books (Jer 7:6; 22:3, 17; 26:15).[20] Secondly, Matthew explains his appeal to Jeremiah instead of Zechariah concerning the thirty pieces of silver by having the chief priests say "It is not lawful to put them into the treasury, since they are blood money" (Mt 27:6) after that Judas had thrown the money "in the temple"; the reason is that, in Zechariah, the thirty pieces of silver were cast "into the treasury in the house of the Lord" (11:13). But, in the Matthean story, the house of the Lord is doomed to fall into the hands of the Romans; that is why Matthew appeals to Jeremiah, the prophet of doom and at the same time of hope for God's salvation beyond doom. In order to do so, he refers to a Jeremianic text that also speaks of pieces of silver (Jer 32:1-15).

The "earthenware vessel" allowed Matthew to bring in another important passage in Jeremiah, which happens to parallel the above quoted text regarding God's capability of having the destruction wrought by him be transformed into restoration:

The word that came to Jeremiah from the Lord: "Arise, and go down to the potter's house, and there I will let you hear my words." So I went down to the *potter's* house, and there he was working at his wheel. And *the vessel (angeion) he was making of clay* was spoiled in the *potter's* hand, and he reworked it into another vessel, as it seemed good to the *potter* to do. Then the word of the Lord came to me: "O house of Israel, can I not do with you as this

---

[20] Concern with "innocent blood," particularly those who are murdered, is also prominent in the Deuteronomic law code.

potter has done? says the Lord. Behold, like the clay in the *potter's* hand, so are you in my hand, O house of Israel. If at any time I declare concerning a nation or a kingdom, that I will pluck up and break down and destroy it, and if that nation, concerning which I have spoken, turns from its evil, I will repent of the evil that I intended to do to it. And if at any time I declare concerning a nation or a kingdom that I will build and plant it, and if it does evil in my sight, not listening to my voice, then I will repent of the good which I had intended to do to it. (Jer 18:1-10; italics mine)

These two texts from Jeremiah became the source for Matthew's wording:

So they took counsel, and *bought* with them *the potter's field*, to *bury strangers in*. Therefore that *field* has been called the Field of Blood to this day. Then was fulfilled what had been spoken by the prophet Jeremiah, saying, "And they *took* the thirty pieces of silver, the price of him on whom a price had been set by some of the sons of Israel, and they *gave* (*edōkan*) them for the *potter's field*, as the Lord *directed* (*synetaxen*)[21] me." (Mt 27:7-10; italics mine)

Matthew closely follows Jeremiah's approach in the way that he prepares for God's eschatological intervention. Outside Romans 3:13 where the noun *taphos* (grave) occurs in a quotation from Psalms 5:9, the root *taph*— is found only in Matthew, four times as *taphos* to speak of Christ's sepulchre (Mt 27:61, 64, 66; 28:1) and twice in the plural in reference to the "tombs of the prophets" (23:27, 29). Here, in the text we are discussing, the original Greek for the phrase "to bury strangers in" is *eis taphēn tois xenois*. The only other occurrences of the noun *xenos* (stranger) in this Gospel are found in the pericope of the last judgment where the Son of man, judge of all, likens

---

[21] In the book of Jeremiah, the prophet's charge to Baruch (Jer 32:11-16) came from God himself (vv.6-7).

himself to every needy (son of) man (25:35, 38, 43, 44). Matthew's statement, then, is best understood against Paul's teaching in Romans. Israel's refusal of the gospel leads to the salvation of the Gentiles through the resurrection from the dead:

> We were buried therefore with him by baptism into death, so that as Christ was raised from the dead by the glory of the Father, we too might walk in newness of life. For if we have been united with him in a death like his, we shall certainly be united with him in a resurrection like his. We know that our old self was crucified with him so that the sinful body might be destroyed, and we might no longer be enslaved to sin. For he who has died is freed from sin. But if we have died with Christ, we believe that we shall also live with him. For we know that Christ being raised from the dead will never die again; death no longer has dominion over him. The death he died he died to sin, once for all, but the life he lives he lives to God. So you also must consider yourselves dead to sin and alive to God in Christ Jesus ... But thanks be to God, that you who were once slaves of sin have become obedient from the heart to the standard of teaching to which you were committed, and, having been set free from sin, have become slaves of righteousness. I am speaking in human terms, because of your natural limitations. For just as you once yielded your members to impurity and to greater and greater iniquity, so now yield your members to righteousness for *sanctification* ... But now that you have been set free from sin and have become slaves of God, the return you get is *sanctification* and its end, eternal life. (Rom 6:4-11, 17-19, 22; italics mine)

> So I ask, have they stumbled so as to fall? By no means! But through their trespass salvation has come to the Gentiles, so as to make Israel jealous. (11:11)

> Besides this you know what hour it is, how it is full time now for you to wake from sleep. For salvation is nearer to us now than when we first believed. (13:11)

In this same letter, however, the resurrection from the dead is linked to Abraham, the father of all believers, in the following way:

> That is why it depends on faith, in order that the promise may rest on grace and be guaranteed to all his descendants—not only to the adherents of the law but also to those who share the faith of Abraham, for he is the father of us all, as it is written, "I have made you the father of many nations"—in the presence of the God in whom he believed, who gives life to the dead and calls into existence the things that do not exist. In hope he believed against hope, that he should become the father of many nations; as he had been told, "So shall your descendants be." He did not weaken in faith when he considered his own body, which was as good as dead because he was about a hundred years old, or when he considered the barrenness of Sarah's womb. No distrust made him waver concerning the promise of God, but he grew strong in his faith as he gave glory to God, fully convinced that God was able to do what he had promised. That is why his faith was "reckoned to him as righteousness." But the words, "it was reckoned to him," were written not for his sake alone, but for ours also. It will be reckoned to us who believe in him that raised from the dead Jesus our Lord, who was put to death for our trespasses and raised for our justification. (Rom 4:16-25)

> And Jesus cried again with a loud voice and yielded up his spirit. And behold, the curtain of the temple was torn in two, from top to bottom; and the earth shook, and the rocks were split; the tombs also were opened, and many bodies of the *saints* who had fallen asleep were raised, and coming out of the tombs after his resurrection they went into the holy city and appeared to many. (Mt 27:50-53; italics mine)

The Passion, Death, and Burial of Jesus (27:11-61)

The Jewish leaders earlier did not want to take responsibility for their betrayal of the "innocent blood" of Jesus before Judah, represented by Judas, by telling the latter—who confesses to them "I have sinned in betraying *innocent blood*"—"What is that to us? *See to it yourself*" (v.4). Here Pilate proves to be no less guilty. He tries to justify himself before the "crowd" using the same subterfuge: "I am *innocent* of this man's *blood; see to it yourselves.*" (v.24) Yet, he follows the consummation of Israel's sin ("His blood be on us and on our children!") by releasing Barabbas, the false messiah, which is precisely the Jewish leaders' request. This again is nothing less than the teaching of Romans: "No, not at all; for I have already charged that all men, both Jews and Greeks, are under the power of sin." (3:9)

Matthew, for whom the messiah is essentially the suffering Son of man, has a special feature: the "reed" with which the soldiers "struck his [Jesus'] head" in Mark (15:19) becomes the "reed" that is "put in his right hand" (Mt 27:29); in other words, in Matthew, Jesus is the messiah all along, even and especially in his suffering. Consequently, in Matthew, when Jesus refuses to drink of the "sponge filled with (the) vinegar (of wrath)"[22] (27:48), it is clear that he is actually refusing to be an earthly messiah. The messiah comes to avenge, but not until the end. This is corroborated by how Matthew changes the Markan *exepneusen* (breathed his last) into *aphēken to pneuma* (yielded up the[23] spirit, Mt 27:50). There is a clear wordplay here: the request to *aphes* (wait, let go, let him on his own; v.49) him is answered by Jesus' letting go, i.e., releasing, the Spirit, which is a

---

[22] See Rev 14:8, 10, 19, 20 and 19:15 for wine being a sign of wrath.
[23] RSV has "his."

trademark of the eschatological messiah: "There shall come forth a shoot from the stump of Jesse, and a branch shall grow out of his roots. And the Spirit of the Lord shall rest upon him, the spirit of wisdom and understanding, the spirit of counsel and might, the spirit of knowledge and the fear of the Lord." (Is 11:1-2) Indeed, whereas in Mark it is only the curtain of the temple that is torn (*eskhisthē*) following Jesus' breathing his last, in the special Matthean addition this event is presented as the outcome of Jesus' releasing the Spirit.[24] More importantly though, it is also the rocks that are split (*eskhisthēsan*) as a preamble to the resurrection of the dead (Mt 27:51-53), which recalls Ezekiel's presentation of that event as linked to the direct intervention of the Spirit (Ezek 37:1-14). The importance of the Matthean addition is reflected in that it is functional in his presentation, and not just a codicil: whereas in Mark it is Jesus' breathing his last that is the reason for the centurion's faith, in Matthew it is rather the earthquake and the resurrection of the saints that have this function:

And Jesus uttered a loud cry, and breathed his last. And the curtain of the temple was torn in two, from top to bottom. And when the centurion, who stood facing him, *saw that he thus breathed his last*, he said, "Truly this man was the Son of God!" (Mk 15:37-39; italics mine)

And Jesus cried again with a loud voice and yielded up his spirit. And behold, the curtain of the temple was torn in two, from top to bottom; and the earth shook, and the rocks were split; the tombs also were opened, and many bodies of the saints who had fallen asleep were raised, and coming out of the tombs after his resurrection they went into the holy city and appeared to many. When the centurion and those who were with him, keeping watch

---

[24] Notice the additional *idou* (behold) in Mt 27:51.

over Jesus, *saw the earthquake and what took place*, they were filled with awe, and said, "Truly this was the Son of God!" (Mt 27:50-54)

Moreover, Matthew's rephrasing underscores the fact that Jesus is the Son of God, the messiah, *as Son of man*. The reaction of the centurion and those who were with him, i.e., the Gentiles, is the same as that of the disciples at Jesus' transfiguration: "they were filled with awe"[25] (17:6), which is followed with:

> But Jesus came and touched them, saying, "Rise, and have no fear." And when they lifted up their eyes, they saw no one but Jesus only. And as they were coming down the mountain, Jesus commanded them, *"Tell no one the vision, until the Son of man is raised from the dead."* (vv.7-9; italics mine)

The connection is further corroborated by that Jesus' request to the disciples "have no fear" (*mē phobeisthe*) is not found until it is said after the resurrection to the women (Mt 28:5, 10) who "looked on from afar" at what the centurion and his companions saw (27:55).

During the writing of Mark's Gospel Jerusalem and the temple had not yet been destroyed. Therefore, alongside Mark's two Marys (the Gentile and the Jewish church communities at large), there was Salome, a stand-in for the Jerusalemite community still bound to the temple (Mk 16:1). In Matthew, we find only two women: Mary Magdalene and "Mary the mother of James and Joseph, and the mother of the sons of Zebedee" (27:56). For Matthew there is only one church, which is mainly Gentile but nevertheless includes Jews and which remains open for them so long as they endorse the new Torah, the gospel preached by

---

[25] The Greek behind it, *ephobēsan sphodra*, occurs only in these two instances in the New Testament.

Paul. Therefore, in Matthew it is Mary Magdalene who is the main character (the second is introduced later simply as "the other Mary" [27:61; 28:1]).

The Guard at the Tomb (27:62-66)

This special Matthean pericope is specifically addressed to the Jews who are still bound by the Mosaic Law. They claim that it is Jesus who is the one who leads astray (27:63-64),[26] whereas for Matthew he is the one who goes after the sheep that were led astray (18:12) by the false messiahs represented by the Jewish leaders (22:29; 24:4, 5, 11, 24). The Jewish leaders must make their own decision regarding the tomb where Christ was laid. They cannot hide anymore behind the Roman authorities: Pilate, who earlier told them "see to it yourselves" (27:24), reiterates his challenge: "You have a guard of soldiers; go, make it as secure as you can." (v.65) They have to face the "reason" (aitian)[27] for his crucifixion namely, that he is "the King of the Jews," and either accept it or continue to refuse it.

In order to accept it they will have to realize that Jesus cannot be chained under the custody of their Law, which would bind him to the earthly Jerusalem and its temple made out of stone that is destined ultimately to be destroyed. The reference to the Law can be detected in the repeated noun koustōdia (vv.65, 66) that is the instrument with which the Jewish leaders were invited to keep Jesus under control, a notion reflected in the verb asphalizō (secure, keep under control; vv.65, 66). That noun is the Greek transliteration of the Latin custodia (custody), which

---

[26] RSV translates ho planos (the one who leads astray) into "impostor" and hē planē (the leading astray, the teaching that leads astray) into "fraud."
[27] RSV has "charge."

corresponds to the Greek *paratērēsis*. In turn, this noun is from the same root as the verb *tēreō* that is the usual one used to speak of keeping (abiding by) the Mosaic Law and its commandments.[28] The leaders' only way out is to be rid of their "security" with which they want to "control" God's acting in Jesus, and to follow the path of the Gentile centurion and his companions who also tried to "keep (watch over)" Jesus (*etēroun* in v.36 and *tērountes* in v.54) yet ended by confessing his messiahship. Here again, in his own special way, Matthew is inviting the Jews to follow the example of the Gentiles, as Paul had taught in Romans 9-11.

The Resurrection of Jesus (Mt 28:1-10)

Whereas the Jewish leaders decided to secure under their control the sepulchre (Mt 27:64, 66), the women stood looking at it, trying to decipher what was happening, the verb *theōreō* having the meaning of watching intently. They were now in the same state (*theōrēsai*, 28:1) in which they had been (*theōrousai*, 27:55) at the entombment,[29] when an earthquake took place announcing the resurrection of the dead (vv.51-54). A similar earthquake, this time produced by the intervention of an angel from heaven[30]—which is, I am convinced, a reference to Paul whose gospel underscored the resurrection of Jesus[31]—who foiled the plan of the Jewish leaders by rolling back the stone with which they tried to seal Jesus' sepulchre. Matthew's vocabulary in 28:3 betrays his interest in speaking of Jesus as the suffering and then exalted Son of man. Indeed, the noun "lightning" and

---

[28] See e.g. Mt 19:17; 23:3; Jn 9:16; 14:15; 15:10; Acts 15:5.

[29] These are the only instances of this verb in Matthew.

[30] "And behold, there was a great earthquake; *for* an angel of the Lord descended from heaven" (28:1).

[31] See Gal 4:14 and my comments in *NTI₂* 226-27 on the "angel" in Acts 10:1-33.

the adjective "white" to speak of clothing occur in this gospel only in conjunction with the Son of man: in 24:27 (For as the lightning comes from the east and shines as far as the west, so will be the coming of the Son of man) and in the pericope of the transfiguration (his garments became white as light, 17:2) at the end of which "Jesus commanded them, 'Tell no one the vision, until the Son of man is raised from the dead'" (v.9). That the angel is the producer of the earthquake (*seismos*) is further corroborated in that "for fear of him the guards trembled (quaked; *eseisthēsan*)." The original is actually very compelling. What RSV translates as "the guards" is *hoi tērountes* (those who were keeping watch) which is in clear reference to 27:54: "When the centurion and those who were with him, keeping watch (*tērountes*) over Jesus, saw the earthquake (*seismon*) and what took place, they were filled with awe (*ephobēthēsan*)." As for the churches, represented by the women, they are hailed thus: "(as for) you, do not be afraid (*mē phobeisthe hymeis*)." (28:5) The reason given is that they were looking for the *crucified* Jesus. And as Jesus has repeatedly predicted—"as he said" (v.6)—the crucified Son of man shall rise beyond the rubble of the temple stones and appear as the Lord of all in Galilee, i.e., among all the nations (vv.7, 10). The good news of Jesus' resurrection fills the women with a fear that goes hand in hand with joy (v.7); hence the earlier "do not be afraid," which is confirmed by Jesus himself in v.10. The repetition by Jesus of the angel's words to the women[32] is, I believe, Matthew's way of saying that the Pauline gospel is confirmed by the Lord himself, which recalls

---

[32] "But the angel said to the women, 'Do not be afraid ... go quickly and tell his disciples that he has risen from the dead, and behold, he is going before you to Galilee; there you will see him'" (28:5, 7); "Then Jesus said to them, 'Do not be afraid; go and tell my brethren to go to Galilee, and there they will see me.'" (28:10).

Paul's "I received from the Lord what I also delivered to you" (1 Cor 11:23).[33]

The Report of the Guard (28:11-15)

This pericope takes up the theme introduced in Matthew 27:62-66. The verb *diaphēmizō* occurs earlier in conjunction with news about Jesus spreading the gospel of healing: "But they [the two blind men] went away and spread [the news of] him (*diephēmisan auton*)[34] through all that district." (9:31) In Mark we find a more telling sentence with the only other instance of that verb in the New Testament: "But he went out and began to preach/herald much (*kēryssein polla*),[35] and to spread the word[36] (*diaphēmizein ton logon*), so that Jesus could no longer openly enter a town." (Mk 1:45) The combination of *logos* and the verb *kēryssein*, which Paul uses systematically in conjunction with the preaching/heralding of the gospel, leaves no doubt that the reference is to the gospel message.[37] In spite of the fact that the gospel of the resurrection found acceptance among the Gentiles, the Jewish leaders were able to keep their "teaching"[38] among some of the "custody,"[39] i.e., of those who were still interested in abiding by the Mosaic Law.[40] Their teaching is put in opposition

---

[33] See also "And we also thank God constantly for this, that when you received the word of God which you heard from us, you accepted it not as the word of men but as what it really is, the word of God, which is at work in you believers" (1 Thess 2:13).

[34] RSV has "spread his fame" whereas the Greek has simply "spread it."

[35] RSV has "talk freely about it."

[36] RSV has "the news."

[37] See my comments on the Markan sentence in *NTI₁* 146.

[38] The phrase "were directed" in "they took the money and did as they were directed" is the translation of the Greek *edidakhthēsan* (were taught), from the same root as *didakhē* (teaching) used of Jesus (Mt 7:28; 22:33) as well of the Pharisees (16:12).

[39] RSV has "guard."

[40] See earlier my comments on Mt 27:62-66.

to the gospel teaching as can be seen in Matthew's *diephēmisthē ho logos houtos para Ioudaiois* (this word[41] has been spread among the Jews); "the word" refers usually to the gospel. The source for this story is no doubt Paul's statement in Galatians: "I am astonished that you are so quickly deserting him who called you in the grace of Christ and turning to a different gospel—not that there is another gospel, but there are some who trouble you and want to pervert the gospel of Christ." (1:6-7).

The Commissioning of the Disciples (28:16-20)

Just as the mountain of God where Moses received the Law was outside the land of Judah, so also here Jesus leaves with his disciples the new Torah of the kingdom (teaching [*didaskontes*] them to observe [keep, *tērein*] all that I have commanded [*eneteilamēn*][42] you) on the mountain he had directed them to, in the Galilee of the nations. Jesus is presented here as the exalted Danielic Son of man to whom was granted "all authority in heaven and on earth" (Dan 7:14); in this guise he dispenses his Torah that will be the rule at the final judgment, which will be done by him, as Son of man, at "the close of the age."

Further Reading

Alexandre, J. "'A quoi m'as-tu abandonné?' La lecture de Psaume 22, 2 dans Matthieu 27, 46 et Marc 15, 34." *Etudes Théologiques et Religieuses* 79 (2004): 65-68.

Allison D. C. "Anticipating the Passion: The Literary Reach of Matthew 26:47-27:56." *Catholic Biblical Quarterly* 56 (1994): 701-714.

---

[41] RSV has "this story."

[42] From the same root as *entolē* (commandment).

Brown, S. "The Matthean Community and the Gentile Mission." *Novum Testamentum* 22 (1980): 193-221.

Cargal, T. B. "'His Blood be Upon Us and Upon our Children': A Matthean Double Entendre." *New Testament Studies* 37 (1991): 101-112.

Cheney, E. "The Mother of the Sons of Zebedee (Matthew 27.56)." *Journal for the Study of the New Testament* 68 (1997): 13-21.

Grassi. "Matthew as a Second Testament Deuteronomy." *Biblical Theology Bulletin* 19 (1989): 23-29.

Gurtner, D. M. "The Rending of the Veil (Matt 27:51a *par*): A look Back and Way Forward." *Themelios* 29 (2004): 4-14.

Kasselouris, H. "The narrative on the confession of Peter (Matth. 16, 13-20 par) and on the anointing of Jesus (Matth. 26, 6-13 par). Parallel Messianic Narratives?" *Deltion Biblikon Meleton* 23 (1994): 27-33.

Longstaff, T. R. W. "The Women at the Tomb: Matthew 28:1 Re-examined." *New Testament Studies* 27 (1981): 277-282.

Nortié, L. "Matthew's motive for the composition of the story of Judas' suicide in Matthew 27:3-10." *Neotestamentica* 28 (1994): 41-51.

Reeves, K. H. "They Worshipped Him, and They Doubted: Matthew 28.17" *Bible Translator* 49 (1998): 344-349.

Senior, D. "Matthew's Special Material in the Passion Story: Implications for the Evangelist's Redactional Technique and Theological Perspective." *Ephemerides Theologicae Lovanienses* 63 (1987): 272-294.

Sparks, K. L. "Gospel as Conquest: Mosaic Typology in Matthew 28:16-20." *Catholic Biblical Quarterly* 68 (2006): 651-663.

Sternberger, J.-P. "Le doute selon Mt 28, 17." *Etudes Théologiques et Religieuses* 81 (2006): 429-434.

Wenham, J. W. "When Were the Saints Raised? A Note on the Punctuation of Matthew xxvii 51-3." *Journal of Theological Studies* 32 (1981): 150-152.

Index

2 Peter, 103, 104

2 Thessalonians, 95, 96

Abiud, 111

Abraham, 112, 278

Achaia, 74

Achim, 111

Acts, 99, 100

adultery, 135

affliction, 144

aigialon, 185

akoē, 195

Alexander, 58, 75

Alexandria, 56

almsgiving, 141

Alphaeus, 167

anaplēroutai, 186

and, 90

angel of the Lord, 114

anger, 135

anthistēmi, 140

Antioch, 53, 60, 61, 127

Antioch incident, 49

antitheses, 134

apantēsin, 157

Apocalypse, 99

apokteinō, 170

apollymi, 170

apostasy, 135

apostolic mission, 157

apostolic tradition, 84

apothēkēn, 189

Armageddon, 203

Asia, 75

asphalizō, 282

authority, 209, 235

Babylon, 49

Babylonians, 64, 253

banquet, 238

Baptist, 175, 176, 188, 209, 235, 236

Barabbas, 279

Bar-Jona, 205

barn, 189

Barnabas, 28, 47, 50, 54, 60, 95, 103, 105, 182

Baruch, 91

beach, 185, 186

Benjamin, 52

Bethany, 233, 267

Bethphage, 233

biblion, 102

blind, 164, 181, 182, 228

blind guides, 244

body of Christ, 136

bridegroom, 160

building, 147

Canaanite woman, 201

canon, 90, 102, 103

canon of truth, 43

Capernaum, 125, 176, 211

children, 225

children of Abraham, 156

church, 121, 122, 176, 177, 194, 198, 209, 211, 215, 216, 217, 219, 220, 226, 231, 237, 238, 239, 244, 246, 248, 251, 252, 257, 258, 259, 281

church leaders, 159, 248, 249, 253, 257

church order, 218

circular letter, 46

cleansing, 157

close of the age, 147, 251, 252, 286

Code of Holiness, 98

Colossae, 71, 75, 76

Colossians, 47, 76, 80, 94, 95, 96

colt, 231

commission, 168

common table, 56

compassion, 165

Corinth, 63

Corinthian correspondence, 46, 62, 63

Crete, 83

custody, 282

Dalmanoutha, 202

David, 110, 112

deeds, 184

demoniac, 181

demoniacs, 157

deposit, 83

Deuteronomy, 101, 102

Deutoronomy, 55

diaphēmizō, 285

diaspora, 38, 52, 53, 83, 125, 127, 211, 231

diatassomai, 173

didrachma, 211

disciple, 220

disciples, 37, 216, 226, 227

discipleship, 156

doing, 146

dōrean, 169

dove, 205

dumb, 164, 181, 182

earthly Jerusalem, 65, 117, 160, 179

earthquake, 280, 281, 283

Ecclesiasticus, 85

edifying story, 44

Egypt, 99

eisegesis, 27

ekklēsia, 232

ekklēsia, 102, 218, 231, 238

elaion, 258

Eleazar, 112

Eliakim, 111

Elijah, 175, 207, 208, 209, 235

Eliud, 112

Emmanuel, 115

emporia, 238

Ephesians, 46, 48, 80

Ephesus, 55, 60, 61, 62, 63, 71, 75, 83, 125

epideiknymi, 250

epileptic, 209

epithymia, 136

evangelization, 167

evangelizomenos, 50

exerkhomai, 164

exodus, 100

Exodus, 98, 99, 100

Ezekiel, 38, 41, 42, 45, 48, 50, 96, 98, 170

Ezra, 111

farewell letter, 80

farewell speech, 71, 80

fasting, 141, 142, 160

fear, 208

fig tree, 234, 235, 255

figs, 234

finger, 90

fish, 213

forgiveness of sins, 159

four, 126, 214

fruit, 177, 184

fruits, 145, 183, 237

Galatians, 25, 46, 48, 51, 55, 56, 64, 93, 94, 95, 96, 99, 103, 167, 198, 227, 248

Galatians controversy, 156

Galilee, 38, 56, 64, 94, 116, 119, 123, 157, 216, 229, 233, 284, 286

Galilee of the nations, 125

Gamaliel, 52

gate, 145

genealogy, 110

Genesis, 102

Gentiles, 38, 59, 234

gentleness, 177

gift of the land, 131

gospel, 28, 29, 30, 34, 50, 78, 105, 106, 121, 124, 136, 174

Gospel, 57, 105

gospel as scripture, 159

Gospel of John, 102

Gospel of Mark, 29, 51, 55, 93, 94, 95, 96, 105

Gospel of Matthew, 102

gospel of peace, 166

gospel of the kingdom, 30, 268

Gospel of Thomas, 29

gospel to the Gentiles, 166

gospel word, 158

Gospels, 39, 91, 100

governor, 274

grace, 226

Hades, 145

Hananiah, 253

hand, 180

harvest, 165, 188, 226

heart, 135

heavenly Jerusalem, 99, 110, 126, 129, 160

heavenly temple, 98

Hebrew canon, 85

Hebrews, 81, 82

Herod, 116, 195

hetaire, 272

household, 258

humility, 217

hypantēsin, 259

hypocrisy, 245

hypocrites, 244, 258

hypocrites', 246

hypozygion, 232

imprisonment, 174

iniquity, 146

innocent blood, 275, 279

Isaac, 112

Isaiah, 41, 55, 91, 174, 234

Israel, 112, 121, 122, 167, 226

Jacob, 112

Jairus, 162

James, 25, 28, 47, 103, 105, 163, 168, 228

Jechoniah, 111

Jeremiah, 41, 91, 204, 232, 233, 234, 235, 253, 274, 276

Jericho, 228

Jerusalem, 61, 64, 96, 129, 143

Jerusalem above, 64, 179, 221, 228

Jerusalem meeting, 167, 168, 178, 180

Jewish War, 96

Johannine epistles, 104

Johannine literature, 101

John, 25, 47, 51, 55, 56, 57, 102, 105, 163, 228

John Mark, 15, 16, 94, 96, 104, 105, 236

John the Baptist, 15, 93, 105, 121, 123, 173, 195, 207, 236

Joseph, 99, 112, 113, 114, 116, 117

Joshua, 123

joy, 132

jubilee year, 109

Judah, 112

Judas Iscariot, 167

Jude, 104

judgment, 256, 259, 261

kalyptesthai, 157

kanōn, 42, 96

kat 'idian, 210

katapontizomai, 197

kēnson, 240

kērygma, 35

kēryssein, 35, 285

Ketubim, 85

kingdom, 169, 209, 216, 228, 232, 237, 239, 262

klēronomia, 131

kremannymi, 241

laleō, 164

Latter Prophets, 64, 85, 89

Law, 45, 55, 78, 89, 90, 92, 101, 163, 232

law of Christ, 103, 236

law of the messiah, 215

least, 53

leaven, 204

leprosy, 151

Leviticus, 98, 99

life eternal, 226

light, 133

light to the nations, 59, 60

little faith, 208, 209, 210

littlest, 53

logic-al, 66, 67

logikēn latreian, 68

logos, 33, 65, 102, 285

Loukas, 60

love for the neighbor, 127, 134, 139, 215, 216, 221, 226, 241, 247, 262 lowliness, 178

Luke, 51, 57, 58, 59, 60, 70, 99, 105

Luke-Acts, 99, 100

Macedonia, 58, 74, 95, 96

Magadan, 202

magi, 116

Makkabaios, 57

makrothymeō, 220

Malachi, 55

maqqaby, 57

Marcion, 103

marcus, 56

Mark, 30, 31, 46, 51, 54, 55, 57, 58, 60, 91, 95, 96, 101, 105

Mark's longer ending, 31

Mark's shorter ending, 32

marriage feast, 238

Mary, 113, 114

Mary Magdalene, 15

mašal, 44, 45

mattan, 159

Matthan, 110, 112

Matthean genealogy, 110

Matthew, 51, 57, 102, 105, 106, 112, 159, 168

mebasser, 50

mercy, 132, 144, 160, 165, 171, 179, 183, 184, 185, 203, 220, 229, 247, 258, 261

messiah, 279

messianic community, 147, 176, 197, 225

messianic law, 151, 221, 247

metabainō, 158

metanoō, 217

mission, 166

mission to the Gentiles, 197, 205, 211

Mosaic Law, 174, 175

Mosaic Torah, 98

Moses, 208

Mount of Olives, 158, 207, 229, 233, 250

myrrh, 268

nations, 231

Nazareth, 125

new covenant, 118, 129

new David, 109

new Israel, 131

new Jerusalem, 64, 89, 123, 215, 249

new Law, 137

New Testament, 102

new Torah, 134, 136, 170, 216, 217, 281, 286

New Torah, 98

Numbers, 98, 99, 100, 194

numeral five, 90

numeral four, 90, 126, 214

numeral three, 110

oaths, 137

oil, 258

Old Testament, 103, 104, 106

one gospel, 32, 96, 103, 127, 167, 215

paradosis, 83

paraklēsis, 131

paralytic, 153, 159

parathēkē, 83

parei, 272

parousia, 158, 251

Passover, 269

Pastorals, 101

patience, 220

Paul, 51, 114

Pauline corpus, 46

Pauline gospel, 174

paulus, 51

peace, 132

Pentateuch, 98

perfect, 140

Peter, 16, 25, 28, 35, 47, 54, 56, 70, 91, 94, 103, 105, 145, 163, 167, 168, 197, 198, 199, 200, 205, 206, 208, 211, 213, 214, 215, 217, 219, 220, 245, 255, 273

Pharisees, 111, 241

Philippi, 71, 74, 75

Philippians, 47

Pilate, 274

pit, 199

porneia, 136, 223

prayer, 141, 142, 225

Prior Prophets, 45, 64, 85, 89

progeny, 241

Prophets, 39, 45, 55, 78, 85, 89, 96, 232

proseukhē, 225

prōton, 161

Pseudonymity, 69

publican, 167, 168

Q, 29

Rachel, 118

reconciliation, 135

reed, 279

repentance, 177, 203, 236

resurrection, 34, 115, 116, 157, 207, 240, 243, 277, 278

retaliation, 138

Revelation, 99, 100, 254

rhēma, 184

righteousness, 111, 122, 130, 141, 143, 144, 209

rock, 147

Roman sea, 155, 156, 196, 197

Romans, 46, 48, 76, 77, 79, 82

Rome, 56, 76, 124, 129, 143, 273

rule, 42, 55, 65, 96, 103, 219, 286

rule of faith, 43

Ruth, 109

sabbath, 158, 178, 179

Sadducees, 111, 203, 240

salt, 132, 133

salvation, 160

Samaria, 64, 96

Saul, 51

scribes and Pharisees, 244, 246

scriptural canon, 43

scripture, 46, 65, 90, 91, 92, 103, 121, 133, 174

Second-Isaiah, 49

seed, 36, 188

seismos, 157

Servant of the Lord, 59

service, 171, 228

seven, 109, 246

Shealtiel, 111

sheep, 179, 181, 201, 218

shekel, 213, 214

sign, 254, 272

sign of Jonah, 185, 203, 255

Silas, 96

Silvanus, 95

Simon, 35, 205, 212

Simon the Cananaean, 167

Sirach, 89

skandalon, 197, 206

Sodom, 177

Solomon, 112

son of Abraham, 109, 241

son of David, 109, 114, 243

son of Jonah, 205

son of man, 37, 38

Son of man, 206, 227, 228, 243, 247, 249, 253, 254, 255, 257, 261, 262, 279, 281, 283, 284, 286

splankhnizomai, 220

stadion, 196

stadium, 196

star, 117, 252

Stephen, 72, 81

šub, 217

suffering servant, 180, 261

Suffering Servant, 36, 37, 38, 168, 270

swine, 157

sword, 272

symboulion, 266, 267

sympherei, 136

sympheron, 136

Syria, 127

table fellowship, 25, 104, 159, 176, 260

table of the kingdom, 237

taphos, 276

Tarsus, 53, 54

taxes, 213, 240

tē emē kheiri, 50

teacher, 35, 160, 208, 209

teaching, 27, 34, 39, 42, 45, 207, 208, 227

teleō, 211

telos, 211

temple, 234, 251

temple of Jerusalem, 215

ten, 258

tēreō, 283

Thaddaeus, 167

theōreō, 283

three, 109

Timothy, 15, 59, 60, 63, 80, 95, 182, 268

Titus, 179, 180, 181

toledot, 112, 113

Torah, 39, 45, 85

Torah of the kingdom, 185, 265

tradition, 83

trapeza, 260

trapezitais, 260

treasury, 142

tree, 183

tribulation, 253

Troas, 71

truth of the gospel, 101, 145

twelve, 167

unction, 267

Uriah, 110

vineyard, 236, 237

virgins, 258, 259

watchfulness, 256

way, 144, 145, 228

weeds, 188, 200

Wisdom of Sirach, 85

word, 65, 136, 272

word of God, 43, 65

workers, 226, 228

wrath, 135

Writings, 39, 85, 89, 243

xenos, 276

yoke, 174, 177, 187, 217, 230, 231, 232, 233

Zadok, 110, 111, 240

zealots, 239

Zechariah, 275

Zerubbabel, 111